THE DEAD TRAVEL FAST

Also by Eric Nuzum

Parental Advisory: Music Censorship in America

THE DEAD TRAVEL FAST

STALKING VAMPIRES FROM NOSFERATU TO COUNT CHOCULA

Eric Nuzum

THOMAS DUNNE BOOKS
ST. MARTIN'S PRESS ❦ NEW YORK

For bonus materials, photos, and miscellany that wouldn't fit in this book, visit thedeadtravelfast.com. For near-daily doses of nonsense, visit ericnuzum.com.

THOMAS DUNNE BOOKS.
An imprint of St. Martin's Press.

www.thomasdunnebooks.com
www.stmartins.com

Library of Congress Cataloging-in-Publication Data

Nuzum, Eric.
    The dead travel fast : stalking vampires from Nosferatu to Count Chocula / Eric Nuzum.—1st ed.
        p. cm.
    "Thomas Dunne Books."
    ISBN-13: 978-0-312-37111-1
    ISBN-10: 0-312-37111-X
    1. Vampires—United States. 2. Popular culture—United States. I. Title.
BF1556.N89 2007
133.4'23—dc22

                                                                2007021035

First Edition: September 2007

10   9   8   7   6   5   4   3   2   1

For PLP

Ridiculously Unnecessary Author's Note

ALL THE CONTEMPORARY events in this book are true and all the characters are real. However, I have changed some names, altered certain details, and created some composite scenes—none in a way that changes the basic facts. This is not a James Frey thing. I do not claim to have spent time in jail, saved drowning kittens, prevented a revolution, or whatever.

It is what it is.

Contents

V

FROM WAMPYR TO WHITBY

In which the author travels to England to find exploding graves, great bargains at Top Shop, coffin-shaped candy, and gay men spilling into the streets.

VI

GOD IS DEAD AND NO ONE CARES

In which the author meets many vampires and two rats, then refuses to dress like a gay pirate.

VII

I MAY BE DEAD, BUT I'M STILL PRETTY

In which the author sits through 144 episodes of Buffy the Vampire Slayer, *sits in the dark with 1,000 people, and cringes a lot.*

VIII

WELCOME TO DARKWING MANOR

In which the author concludes his journey celebrating Halloween in Oregon, choking on PoliGrip, and trying not to contract salmonella.

Acknowledgments

In which the author shouts out to his peeps, yo.

Trickle drops! my blue veins leaving!
O drops of me! trickle, slow drops,
Candid from me falling, drip, bleeding drops,
From wounds made to free you whence you were prison'd,
From my face, from my forehead and lips,
From my breast, from within where I was conceal'd, press forth red
   drops, confession drops,
Stain every page, stain every song I sing, every word I say, bloody drops,
Let me know your scarlet heart, let them glisten,
Saturate them with yourself all ashamed and wet,
Glow upon all I have written or shall write, bleeding drops,
Let it all be seen in your light, blushing drops.

—Walt Whitman, *Leaves of Grass*

THE DEAD TRAVEL FAST

I

MONSTERS WANTED

In which the author defines his vampire quest, dresses in a stinky mummy costume, watches too many movies, and then throws up.

WATCHING MY OWN blood drip down the bathroom mirror, there's only one thought running through my head: In a lifetime of questionable decision making, this is not one of my finer moments.

Like many things in life, it started off with the best of intentions. It was an experiment—a quest, actually. When I set out to write about the history of vampires, I decided to pursue three specific tasks. It seemed to make sense—in order to truly understand vampires and what they mean, I'd not only have to do the usual research and reading, but I'd have to find ways to *experience* vampires as well.

The gore sprayed all over my bathroom was the result of the last of these undertakings: to drink blood. The whole blood-drinking thing, as you can imagine, posed several problems.

Most of these difficulties were rooted in the particulars. In my book, to drink something means to take a mouthful of something and to swallow it—"tasting" or "sipping" wouldn't be acceptable. This, of course, requires a sufficient quantity of blood.

Even though blood fetishists don't advertise their gatherings in the Sunday paper, they aren't particularly hard to find. However, anyone willing to let me drink their blood probably isn't someone whose blood I should be drinking.

Then I got an idea: I could drink my *own* blood.

I imagine you are full of questions.

It's pretty simple, actually.

If you look at every culture, throughout history, they've all had some variation on the vampire. Very few have been called *vampires,* but every culture has some type of a supernatural creature that comes back from the dead and draws its power by preying on the living. Are there such things as actual vampires in the world? I've never seen one—nor has anyone I've ever known or met. Yet you can go to just about anyone, anywhere in the world, mention the word *vampire,* or show them a picture of some ashen-faced bad guy with fangs and a long cape,* and they'd know what you were talking about.

Vampires are a lot like Santa Claus—each culture morphs the lore to fit its own needs and values. England has Saint Nicholas, Greece has St. Basil, Holland's Sinterklaas arrives on a ship, French children wait for Père Noël, Italy has the good witch La Befana, and in China, Dun Che Lao Ren brings presents to children every winter. That said, St. Nick doesn't have a fondness for sucking blood out of the necks of virgins. Well, if he does, he's done a good job of keeping it on the down low.

This all started one morning during breakfast. I was pleasantly munching on a longtime favorite, Count Chocula, while CNN played on the TV. A story came on about energy costs and President Bush was offering a solution: destroy all vampires. Energy vampires, that is. The president was blasting cell-phone and computer manufacturers who used power chargers that drew electricity regardless of whether the device was actually using or storing it. These were commonly known as "energy vampires" and the president was urging Americans to solve the world's power crisis by unplugging their cell phones once they were finished charging.

---

* Non sequitur trivia for you: Bela Lugosi never wore fangs while playing his defining role in *Dracula*—or any other vampire movie he appeared in. He had a thing about prosthetic makeup, which is also the reason he turned down playing the monster in *Frankenstein.*

Looking away from the screen and down toward a magazine I was pretending to read, I turned the page and saw a vodka ad featuring a woman with a cape and long fangs. The ad encouraged potential vodka purchasers to "drink in the night."

Even in my early-morning sleepiness, I stopped to consider this for a moment: Within a five-minute period, I'd encountered three references to vampires, of all things. This might make sense around Halloween, but it was early July.

Why vampires?

As I pondered this over the following days, I began to realize that I saw direct or indirect mentions of vampires everywhere—in an interview in *Rolling Stone,* during an episode of *Seinfeld,* a song lyric, a conversation on a plane. Vampires are invoked as metaphors all the time. It's hard to go through a single day without seeing some reference to vampires.

So if the vampire is that ubiquitous . . . how did this happen? Why did it happen? I wanted insight.

There are two basic ways to experience history.

Basic Way #1: Sit in a dark library and read old, smelly books that put you to sleep. I am not an advocate of this Basic Way; it isn't very fun. Plus, this is definitely not one of those books.

Basic Way #2: History isn't static. Most history reverberates through time, making things different than they'd otherwise be. Therefore, it's important to understand it as it survives and resonates today. According to this Basic Way, to experience living history one needs to . . . live it.

So to truly undertake my quest to understand vampires, I'd have to go out in the world and encounter them firsthand. This required a little prep, which led me to these tasks.

Which led me to drinking my own blood.

Which led me to vomiting all over my bathroom.

Which led me to the first thing I've learned in this quest: *I am a total fucking idiot.*

People are afraid of the dark.

It isn't the absence of light that messes with your head, it's the possibility contained in darkness. In the shadows you can find anything. You could step right up to a grizzly bear, evil marauder, or four-hundred-foot cliff and never know it's there. *Not* knowing is what makes your heart beat faster.

That's where monsters come in. There is no evidence that monsters exist—vampires or otherwise. Yet despite this, we all cringe in scary movies. Clearly, there is nothing hiding in the closet, but we still make sure the door is closed before going to bed.

Monsters always start off in darkness: a strange noise, a feeling of presence. We imagine them at their most horrific. That's why good horror movies never show you the monster during the first act—what we imagine them to be is infinitely scarier than what they actually are.

Eventually, the monster leaves the darkness and comes into full view. And what do we see?

Ourselves.

We create monsters for all kinds of reasons. They're often the result of our own misguided ways. They offer vengeance for our follies. They are metaphors for our worst fears: The Blob represents concerns about pollution and the spread of Communism, the Swamp Thing symbolizes the cultural separations between the North and South, Frankenstein stands in for our fear over the clash between medical innovation, ethics, and religion. King Kong embodies the fear and helplessness of the Great Depression. Godzilla signifies concerns over the danger of nuclear technology. The most ubiquitous monster of all isn't the one who fills the darkness around us, but the darkness within ourselves: the vampire.

The vampire is the only monster that people actually *want* to be. You won't find much desire to be a mummy or zombie. You'll never experience envy at the powers of the Frankenstein monster. No one ever wants to become a ghost or werewolf. Becoming any other type of monster is a curse, becoming a vampire is a key to power and a way to control what we fear.

When I started on my quest's first task, it wasn't fear I felt, but dread.

This questing nonsense started out as an attempt to discover vampires the way that most people do, through movies. I decided to watch every vampire movie ever made—all six hundred and five of them. It surprises many people that not only is *Dracula* the most adapted story in film history (there have been forty-three sequels, remakes, and adaptations of the story), but Count Dracula recently surpassed Sherlock Holmes as the character portrayed in film more than any other. On top of all those, there are several hundred films and TV movies featuring other vampire characters. All told, six hundred and five—and I planned to watch every one.

I started with the easy choices that everyone knows, *Dracula* and *Nosferatu*, along with some more contemporary fare like *Interview with the Vampire, Near Dark,* and *Blade.* However, only thirty-six movies into my viewing the quality of the movies was becoming a bit thin, including such gems as *The Little Vampire, My Grandfather Is a Vampire,* and *It! The Terror from Beyond Space.* To compound things, as is my usual idiotic style, I announced this task to almost anyone who'd listen. While I may have been able to back out if I'd kept my mouth shut, on this one, I was committed.

Today's selection: the 1936 film *Dracula's Daughter,* which seems appropriate since yesterday's selection was *Son of Dracula* (the 1943 ham fest starring an aging Lon Chaney, Jr., as Count Alucard, the son of the infamous count). *Dracula's Daughter* was the sequel of the 1931 original *Dracula* starring Bela Lugosi, literally picking up where *Dracula* left off. In *Dracula's Daughter,* a mysterious countess, named Marya Zaleska, arrives in London to claim Dracula's now completely dead corpse. When the authorities go to retrieve Dracula's coffin, it comes up missing. At the same time, bloodless bodies are discovered nightly around London. It's the countess—who, once discovered, hotfoots it back to Transylvania in a 1930s version of a high-speed chase with Scotland Yard. The countess eventually takes a wooden arrow through the heart and all are safe once again (though no explanation is ever given for what happened to Dracula's corpse and coffin).

Dracula's Daughter was one of the original horror movie sequels and is on about the same cinematic level as *Halloween 5* or *Bride of Chucky*. On almost any aesthetic scale, *Dracula's Daughter* bears no similarity to the original. Gone are the originality, dark gothic imagery, eerie passages of silence, and subtexts of sexual repression and fear of technology. Replacing it are campy attempts at humor, melodrama, and painfully obvious sexual innuendo. The pacing is slow, with long bouts of over-the-top dialogue. The so-called suspense scenes are anything but, due in large part to the overly schmaltzy soundtrack that gives everything away.

Watching all these films has led to my first major discovery about vampire movies: They suck.

I'm not trying to make some clever use of puns here; by and large vampire films are not good movies when viewed today. Watching almost any vampire movie in a contemporary context, even the 1931 original *Dracula* or the first vampire film, the silent *Nosferatu,* is an exceptionally disappointing experience. There's a reason for this: Vampire films capture the fears, desires, and values of their time in a way that doesn't age well. It's like platform shoes or beehive hairdos—things that seem hip and cutting edge at one time, end up looking ridiculous in hindsight. What once was horrifying, now seems overblown, melodramatic, and kitschy.

Vampire films, books, and the undead's appearances in contemporary culture are the same way. Most vampire lore suggests that vampires don't cast reflections in mirrors. Yet, vampires are reflections. Vampires reflect our desires, dark ambitions, fears, longings, and despair. Vampires equally represent what represses us and what sets us free. The blood-drinking undead provide a stark example of what makes societies and cultures unique and different. They are the perfect metaphor. As vampire scholar Nina Auerbach wrote, "Every age embraces the vampire it needs." However, none of these deep thoughts are making *Rape of the Vampire* any easier to watch.

Rape of the Vampire, along with films such as the 1952 Bela Lugosi stinker, *My Son, the Vampire,* leave viewers puzzled as to how the movie they've just viewed has any connection with its title. In *My Son, the Vampire,* Lugosi plays an evil vampire scientist building a killer robot to take over the world.* While there was a character named Mother Riley, there appears to be no son in *My Son, the Vampire.* Likewise, in *Rape of the Vampire*—there is no rape.

I'm not sure what *Rape of the Vampire* is supposed to tell me about life, culture, or the filmmaker's view of the world. That is, besides that he must have had a thing for breasts. From what I was able to follow, the film apparently tells the story of a group of beautiful vampire women. These vampires, who feed only from other women, can't seem to manage a bite on the neck unless everyone involved is naked from the waist up first. One of the vampires falls in love with a mortal man who wants to become a vampire himself. Then it seems everyone is desperately trying to find a cure for vampirism. All this nonsense apparently upsets the head vampire woman, who looks and dresses more like an aborigine than a vampire. The characters run around screaming and crying for a while, and then everyone dies.

It's a 1960s French film, which should explain everything.

My second prevampire-hunting task was to understand what it means to be a vampire. I wanted to walk in his shoes, wear his cape, sleep in his coffin—whatever.

This quest was easy to accomplish, because I'd already done it. I was a vampire, once. Well, for a weekend, more or less.

---

* Though Lugosi's vampire seems to have no interest in blood, is not bothered by being out in daylight, and eventually succumbs to gunshots at the end of the film. Oops, sorry, I guess I just ruined it for you.

I was thumbing through the car ads in the paper one late summer morning and a classified caught my eye. It featured a poorly drawn Grim Reaper over the bold-faced headline MONSTERS WANTED. It was an ad for the House of Terror, a haunted house located in an unused school building. The want ad promised "fun, excitement, and $$$" for "responsible actors" interested in portraying characters in its facility.

After reading the ad, I went on with my day, but I kept thinking about it. As a kid, I loved going to haunted houses and had always thought it would be awesome to actually work in one. Whenever I'd catch a glimpse of the people working in haunted houses, they always wore chain wallets, Aerosmith or Led Zeppelin T-shirts, and looked pretty mean and frightening even without the masks and props. The coolest of the cool were the kids who played vampires. They got to scare the hell out of visitors by jumping out of a closed coffin, grabbing a hot-looking girl (another haunted house employee), and biting her neck. They were scary and cool, and I fantasized about being one of them. Specifically, I wanted to be the girl-grabbing, neck-biting vampire. Now, more than twenty years later, here was my big chance.

After dinner that night, I fished the paper out of the recycle bin and called the number listed. The recorded message indicated that interested applicants should show up at the House of Terror at exactly 8:00 A.M. on the Saturday of Labor Day weekend with proper ID and a social security card. It informed callers that the process would take the better part of the morning. The message warned that no one would be admitted before eight and anyone showing up late would be turned away. Without discussing it with anyone, I just scooted out of the house that morning and headed over.

I figured that since it was a holiday weekend, turnout would be light. I further assumed that the "responsible actors" would be other fun-loving haunted house enthusiasts like me looking for something interesting to do as well as a part-time paycheck. As soon as I was within sight of the House of Terror, I began to realize how mistaken I was. It wasn't even 7:30 A.M. and there were at least two hundred people lined up outside the building. To someone driving by, they might sum up the assembled crowd as people you'd expect to respond to a "free tattoo" or "free mullet trimming" offer rather than an employment ad. They didn't look like vampires, were-wolves, and ghouls—they looked like carnival ride operators.

At a few minutes after eight o'clock, a guy emerged, identified himself as Tom, and led us into the old school's cafeteria to fill out our applications. Before we started, Tom told us we were to stay in our seats while we filled out our applications. We were not to get up and move around, not even to go to the bathroom. Once we were finished with the applications, we'd be taken out—one table at a time—to the interview area, where we'd be individually inter-viewed by one of the house's managers. Another manager, named Sue, told us that anyone who turned in an incomplete application, left the room, got up to talk to others around the room, fell asleep, smoked, drank, or ate, would be immediately rejected and sent home. Sue also gave a rundown of what was expected. Most of the rules would be covered at orientation, she said, but going over the basics might save us all some hassle. The houses would be open 8:00 P.M. to midnight on Thursday through Sunday and every "ac-tor" would be required to work both Friday and Saturday nights plus one other night. Each actor would have to show up one hour before work and stay one hour afterward. Pay was sixty dollars a week, paid only if the actor completed all their assigned shifts. Lastly, actors wouldn't be employees, but independent contractors.

"And another thing," Sue said. "You can pick the role you play, but forget about being a chain saw guy—those roles fill up with re-turning actors."

I wanted to ask about the demand for vampires, but I was too caught up on the sixty dollars. Three nights a week, six hours a shift—that's barely three dollars an hour. So much for the prom-ised "$$$," which was apparently as subjective as the "fun and ex-citement" and the definition of "actor."

There were eight guys sitting at my table. I had completed my application in about five minutes and was the first one finished by at least ten more minutes. The task seemed very difficult and taxing for my tablemates. To be honest, it looked like almost any task would be taxing for my tablemates. It seemed that the act of getting out of bed and being here at 8:00 A.M. had sucked all the energy out of them. Three of them had violated the "no sleeping" rule within the first twenty minutes.

Our table was in the back corner, and since people were being interviewed table by table (starting at the other end of the room), we knew we'd be there for quite some time—well more than an hour at the rate things were going. After my tablemates had struggled through recalling their names, addresses, and meager employment histories, we started to chat among ourselves. Our applications finished, a conversational hierarchy soon emerged at our table. Our moderator was a guy named Steve, who decided what we'd discuss, for how long, and passed judgment on who was "full of shit."

Steve raised his hand and was reluctantly acknowledged by Tom.

"Say, how do you want me to list my service—by assignment or branch, or the time I was in the army?" he asked.

"It doesn't matter, just write it down," replied Tom.

Steve turned back to us and interrupted the conversation to tell his third military story in the past ten minutes.

"I was over in Iraq for the Gulf War, you know."

Yes, we did know. He had told us this at the beginning of every story.

"The whole time I was over there, all I could think about was eating fried chicken," he said.

"I kept thinking that the thing I really missed about home was fried chicken and I kept asking the mess guys if they would ever make fried chicken. They never did. Then, right before we headed home, the cooks made some shitty fried chicken. I figured, 'What the fuck,' and got a huge plate full of fried chicken.

"I was so happy to have fried chicken and told all my buddies to chill while I ate some. My one buddy thought he'd be real funny and moon me while I was eating. So he walks right up to me, right, and drops his pants and spreads his butt cheeks—right there in front of me. And I said, 'Man, what the fuck, all I want to do is eat my fried chicken.' He just laughs and wiggles his butt in my face.

"I was so mad, 'cause I had been looking forward to eating fried chicken for weeks. So I picked up a chicken bone and stuck it up his ass. Right up there. Man, was he mad."

We were all laughing when Tom came over to settle us down. He warned Steve that using profanity could get him ejected and he should consider that his warning. He told us to just sit down, shut up, and wait.

Around the room were several photocollages of actors from past seasons in their costumes. Basically, all the characters were a collection of weapons, torn clothing, stage blood, and various foreboding props. In each group there would be one or two people who stood out—white skin, slick hair, black clothes, and fangs. The vampires.

VAMPIRES ARE SO easy to pick out because there isn't any other horror archetype that's so immediately recognizable. Not simply by look, but actions as well.

The vampire we think of today came from the undead legends of Slavic nations such as Serbia, Hungary, and the infamous Transylvania. Most people assume our contemporary vampire originated there, but that isn't entirely true.

Our modern understanding of vampires did flourish in Eastern Europe, but got its start in Greece.

Following a long Christian tradition of coopting pagan and folk traditions, the Greek Orthodox Church took the country's various legends of blood-sucking undead and used them to reinforce Church doctrine. As a result, for many centuries there was scarcely a Greek village that didn't have some sort of local vampire story.

In the eighth century, the Greek Church declared that the bodies of those excommunicated by the Church would not decompose until they had been granted absolution. While former members were in this state, they were doomed to wander through the world, feeding off the blood of the living. Very frequently, the graves of suspected vampires were opened and the bodies were found with ruddy complexions and veins distended with blood. When lanced, large quantities of blood would pour out of the body, blood presumably drawn from the bodies of young, fresh human beings.

The belief became so popular in Greece that the Church expanded the declaration to murders, suicides, those guilty of heinous sins, practitioners of the magic arts, and anyone cursed by their parents. Whenever something bad happened or an unexplained illness or death fell upon a friend or neighbor, people would immediately cast about looking for a recently deceased local black sheep to blame. Their only course of action would be to campaign for the Church to grant absolution or dig up the offender, drive a stake through his or her heart, and burn the corpse. Until recently, the Catholic liturgy for excommunication still included the sentence, "After death, let not thy body have power to dissolve."

Fueled by the endorsement of the Church, vampire lore began to spread throughout Europe. Most of the early tales weren't created through folklore, but by bragging priests and bishops. Many Church officials of the time wrote of their experiences encountering and dispensing with vampires who were once excommunicated pirates, thieves, murderers, harlots, and other undesirables.

Logical assumptions started to emerge in the lore. If the vampire's fate was controlled by the Church, the belief surfaced that vampires would cower when confronted by crosses or other religious symbols.

As the belief in vampires spread throughout Europe, the lore became more sophisticated. The blood-sucking undead became the scapegoats for all types of misfortune, including stillborn children, unexpected death, bad weather, disease outbreaks, and even impotence. Maladies such as severe nightmares, migraine headaches, and wasting disease were all blamed on vampire attacks. As the beliefs and abilities of vampires grew, so did the methods that could turn someone into a vampire. In addition to excommunication, evil deeds, and untimely death, it was commonly thought that vampirism could be spread like a disease. Once one person in a community rose from death, it was thought that his curse could be spread through his attacks, especially his bite. Some stories stated that the curse could be spread by consuming meat from cows fed upon by vampires. Some thought that vampirism was hereditary—after one member of a family turned, others in the same family would meet a similar fate after death.

Once otherwise unexplainable happenings were blamed on a vampire, oftentimes a village or city would fall into a vampire hysteria, attempting to link almost any unusual happening to their undead interloper. For example, in the spring of 1727 in the Serbian city of Meduegna (near modern-day Belgrade), a young man named Arnod Paole, about to be married, died shortly after falling from a horse. Within a few weeks of his death, several young women in the town died. The locals were convinced that Arnod had come back from the grave as a vampire, due to his untimely and unfortunate death, and was spreading his grief among his neighbors by feeding off their blood. Fearing the worst, the villagers dug up Arnod's body and found that his body looked pink and lifelike, and his hair and nails had grown longer. There were also traces of blood around his mouth. Local authorities quickly staked and burned Arnod's body and returned it to his grave. Just for good measure, they also staked four other recently deceased townspeople, fearing that they may have been Arnod's victims and might soon come back to wreak havoc as well. Over the next five years, the villagers logged more than a dozen incidents that they attributed to Arnod's brief tenure as their local undead. Two women dying of what is now known as tuberculosis claimed to have drunk Arnod's blood and were eventually staked and burned after their deaths. Family members of a deceased eight-year-old child dug him up after a few months and drove a stake through his heart after finding an unusually healthy-looking corpse. Three other men were found with large quantities of blood in their corpses after death and were staked for good measure. Things got so out of hand in Meduegna that almost all of the deceased locals were dug up, staked, turned facedown in their graves, or had their mouths stuffed with herbs and garlic to prevent them from spreading their evil among the living.

The residents of a nearby village became so freaked out that vampirism might spread to their town that they were forced to gather together in two or three houses every evening, burning candles and taking turns watching over the others. In order to make sure everyone kept to their anti-vampire routines, some of the village leaders would cast their shadows against the buildings, howl and shriek in the night, and leave spatters of blood and cow dung in abandoned houses.

WE SAT AROUND the House of Terror cafeteria for about another twenty minutes before our table was called. Once we reached the front of the interviewing line, we saw four tables, with two managers on one side and an interviewee on the other. The interviewee would take a seat, then some questions and polite conversation would go back and forth. At the end of each interview, the interviewee would scream, thank the interviewers, and leave.

When my turn came, I answered the standard questions,* but my mind was on the scream. What was it for? Would I have to scream? Would I be asked to scream, or was it just something that one person did to impress the managers, then others started to follow suit?

Then, one of the managers told me that being an actor in a haunted house was tough, thankless work. I'd have to perform for hundreds, if not thousands of people a night, and I'd have to give

---

* Such as "Why do you want to work in a haunted house?" "Do you have any experience?" and "Is the section on your criminal record complete and would you like to explain it?"

as good a performance to the last person as I had to the first. As a sign of my acting skills, she asked for my best scream.

"Now?" I asked.

"Yes," she responded, looking confused, as if she wondered how I had missed the seventy other screams that morning.

"Okay, what am I screaming at?" I asked.

"I'm sorry, like . . ."

"I mean, what is my motivation?"

"For screaming?"

"Yeah."

"Because I told you to."

Fair enough. With that, I let out my best scream. Well, it was a shriek, actually. The kind of high-pitched shrill yelp you'd expect from a teenaged girl when Jason or Freddy Krueger jumps out from behind the sofa.

My two interviewers looked at each other, then back at me.

"Do you want to try that again?" one asked.

"Was that bad?" I responded.

"Well," said the other. "We're kind of looking for scary, not scared."

"But I want to play a vampire," I said.

"That's fine, but vampires scream, too."

"Why?"

"I'm sorry . . ."

"Why would a vampire scream?"

"Because we told him to."

I tried again. Slightly better, though still hoping anyone I know didn't hear me.

"Very nice, you can expect a call next week."

"So, I'm in?" I asked.

"We'll call you if we need you," she replied, extending her hand in an obvious gesture that meant our time together was over.

A week went by with no call. Then another week went by—nothing. They said that there would be only seventy-five hires, but I figured that even with my girly scream, I could at least make the top quartile. After waiting a few more days, I called Tom. He found my application, paused while he read over the notes, and told me that they were all full and didn't need me.

"You can try again next year," he offered.

"Will you have any openings later on this season?" I asked.

"Sure," he responded. "Just give us a call later on." He paused and stuttered, obviously trying to backpedal. "But, you know, we had lots of qualified applicants, you may be pretty far down on the waiting list."

Qualified applicants? I am a college graduate and a published author. I have been steadily employed since I was sixteen. I wondered how seventy-five Ph.D. Mensa members had snuck through the application process that day without me noticing.

I followed Tom's advice and checked back the next week, and every week thereafter, until the middle of October. Finally Tom, probably more annoyed with my constant phone calls than anything else, told me to come to training on Thursday night.

When I arrived, I found the other actors starting to get into their costumes, I found Tom and asked what I was supposed to do.

"We need a mummy. Why don't you put on that stuff," he replied.

"Do you need any vampires, instead?" I asked.

"No, only have a few, but they're taken care of. Do the mummy and we'll see what we can do for you next time."

The mummy getup involved applying tan pancake on my face, then slipping into a set of thermal underwear with rags sewn on it. The ripe odor coming off the costume indicated it had been used several times by others since its last cleaning. That is, assuming there had been a previous cleaning.

I had just finished applying the makeup and dreading the thought of slipping into my stinky mummy gear when Tom came up to me.

"Seems you're in luck," he said. "One of the vampires didn't show up tonight, so you can take his place if you like."

Because of my interest in being a vampire and lack of interest in wearing that thermal underwear, I enthusiastically accepted.

"You can just put on this suit and meet me on the third floor. Make it quick."

"What about my face?" I asked.

"There are fangs in the costume supply box," he replied.

"But my face is brown," I replied.

"So?"

"Who has ever heard of a tan vampire? Vampires can't be in the sun to tan."

"No one will care, just get in the suit and meet me upstairs."

I took a look at the suit. It was a gray tuxedo, a wrinkled white dress shirt—and a dickey. Worse yet, a white dickey with red-tipped fringe.

"Ah, Tom . . . I'm supposed to wear this?"

"Yeah, what's wrong with it?"

What's wrong? No self-respecting vampire would be caught in anything but a crisp black tailcoat. Wearing this, I wouldn't look like a vampire; I'd look like a prom king from 1978, a well-bronzed one at that.

"This is all wrong," I said. "No one's going to think I look like a vampire in this."

"Listen, fella," Tom said, pretending to care. "It's the fangs that make it, plus the coffin."

"But there's no cape."

"You don't need a cape, just put it on and come upstairs."

"OKAY," TOM SAID once I'd arrived in my tuxedo and plastic fangs. "When they leave the Hall of Mirrors, you'll hear their footsteps. If you look through this hole in the side of the coffin, you'll see them comin' in to your room. That's your cue to sit up in your coffin and scream. Then you lie back down."

"No biting anyone?" I asked.

"No," Tom replied, not understanding where I was going. "Just jump up and swing this stake at them."

Tom handed me a wooden stake lying next to the coffin.

"*I* threaten *them* with the stake?"

"Yeah, just throw open the lid, scream, and point this stake at them."

"But the stake is supposed to kill the vampire, not his victims."

"Do you want people driving stakes through your heart?"

"No."

"Then you hold on to that stake and swing it at them."

About fifteen minutes later, the house opened and I could hear people working their way through the House of Terror. I grabbed my stake, positioned myself inside the coffin, shut the lid, and waited.

I hunkered down and looked out the coffin's peephole until I could see the outlines of bodies. I threw open the lid, sat up, screamed, and waved my stake at them.

They screamed. I laid back down.

At this point, I should share some sort of contextual anecdote about what it means to jump out of a coffin and scare someone. That's supposed to be the whole point of this adventure. However, there really wasn't anything deep about it at all. I screamed, they screamed. It was fun. In fact, it was really fun. I was a vampire, and I couldn't wait for the next group to show up so I could do it again.

My joy slowly dissipated as the evening wore on. Since I was lying down in the coffin and then bolting up to a sitting position, I was basically doing a sit-up. Just like doing regular sit-ups, the first few were no problem. But after the first dozen groups, I realized that this was going to be a workout.

After the second dozen, my screams of "Aaaaargh!!" switched to "Agh." After a few more, my "Agh" became more like an "Ugh." By 11:00 P.M., I was opening the lid, propping myself up with my arm, lazily waving my stake, and lying back down.

The repetition was numbing. I'd get up, make some kind of

noise, wave the stake, and they'd scream. As the evening dragged on, the screams were getting less frequent, occasionally replaced with looks of pity and sympathy.

After one late group right before closing, I was back inside the coffin when I heard a noise. Just as I was about to look out the peephole, I heard a large thud on the top of the coffin. I tried to open the lid to see what was going on, but I couldn't open it. I tried pushing, hitting, kicking—nothing. I was stuck.

I started to scream—for real. The coffin was pretty large—two people could have fit inside of it. But lying there, trapped inside, it started to feel smaller and smaller. I felt as if I couldn't breathe and fell into a complete panic.

What I was experiencing, or just the idea of experiencing being trapped inside a coffin, is an important component of vampire lore. Being trapped inside a coffin, struggling to get out, explains why different cultures and societies created vampires instead of de-monic groundhogs or evil magic broomsticks. It fit the fear.

Modern medicine and diagnostics can blind us to the fact that in the past, declarations of death were commonly less than certain. To the unsophisticated observer, someone in a coma or the end stages of terminal illness may appear to be dead, but may still be very much alive. If someone taken for dead, but only in a comatose state, was brought back to consciousness (often by grave robbers or the commotion during a wake), the witnesses were sure to think that the person was returning from the dead. As late as the 1920s, it was reported that on average one premature burial occurred in the United States *every week*. And those were the reported ones.

Throughout history, especially before embalming practices be-came common, those who had cause to unearth the dead often surmised that there had been some struggle to escape from the cas-ket. The corpses sometimes had distorted features and were found in twisted positions. Given the evidence—along with the refusal to believe that someone could be misdiagnosed as dead—the logi-cal conclusion was that the deceased had come back from the dead and were attempting to leave the grave to attack the living.

Further, many corpses were found to have rosy complexions and were slightly bloated. Many also appeared to have new hair growth, longer nails, and blood around the nostrils, mouth, and ears.*

The conclusion? They were vampires—freshly filled with blood from hunting the living and grown gruesome from their evil activities. What to do? Drive a stake through their heart.

In Eastern Europe, staking became a common practice not only for the undead, but for any recently deceased neighbor or relative. Initially, driving stakes through bodies and into the bottoms of wooden caskets was considered a preemptive measure. Not only would the deceased not become vampires, but if they did, they'd be pinned to their caskets and unable to get out. Staking was also considered a good way to ensure that the deceased were actually dead. At a funeral, a stake would be driven through a loved one's chest. If they weren't already dead, they would be after that. The practice spread throughout Europe. In the nineteenth century, it was common for wills to include a proviso that the deceased couldn't be buried until their heart was pierced. It also became common to equip new coffins with interior release switches or methods to signal that the people buried inside were, in fact, very alive.

My coffin at the House of Terror contained no such method, except for my screams and kicking. After beating the coffin lid for what seemed like an hour, the lid suddenly popped open. A few other actors stood around laughing. It was part of some hazing that went on among the house's actors—pranks on the new guy. They had all been victim of it and now it was my turn.

---

* Before embalming, what one would find inside a deceased's exhumed casket was a guessing game. Left on its own to decompose, a corpse goes through two simultaneous biological processes—one drying out the body while the other liquefies it. The results were always rather nasty, yet unpredictable—varying according to the condition of the body at burial, quality of the casket, temperature and humidity levels, and time of year. Sometimes bodies would look relatively undisturbed, other times they would be horribly disfigured and unevenly decomposed. What appeared to be hair and nail growth was actually the result of drying (and thus, receding) skin. What was thought to be blood around the mouth and nose (as well as the source of healthy-looking skin) wasn't blood at all, but the ooze from liquefied internal organs.

We heard some bumping coming through the Hall of Mirrors and all of them hightailed it out through the back way. More customers, more sit-ups, and more "Ughs."

The next morning I got a call from Tom, stammering his way through telling me that the regular vampire had come back to work and I wasn't needed anymore.

In so many words, my career as a vampire was over.

ABOUT FOUR WEEKS into my vampire movie watching, I realized that, while not even one-tenth of the way through the list, I was scraping bottom. Over seven days, I had viewed such cinematic wonders as *Jesus Christ Vampire Hunter,** *Blacula,* *Samurai Vampire Bikers from Hell,* and *Rockabilly Vampire* (a low-budget tragedy in which the vampire is an Elvis impersonator), bringing my total movies viewed up to forty-eight.

As is often the case with vampire movies, just when you think you can't take it any longer, something hits you that is ultimately revealing about the filmmakers, their intended audience, and the moment in time the film captures.

Take *Blacula,* the 1972 film that brings the Dracula bloodline to South Central. It tells the story of an African prince, named Manuwalde, who visits Dracula in 1780 and is turned into a vampire himself. However, Manuwalde is locked in a coffin soon after and lies dormant for almost two hundred years. In the 1970s, two gay antique dealers buy up the remnants of Dracula's castle and transport them to Los Angeles, hoping to turn big profits. Once they get everything back to the States, they open Manuwalde's

---

* A kung fu action movie focusing on Jesus' Second Coming where he battles a vampire cult for control of the earth. Featuring the taglines: "The first testament says 'an eye for an eye.'—The second testament says 'love thy neighbour.'—The third testament . . . Kicks Ass!!!" and "The Power of Christ Impales You." When Jesus gets into trouble with the vampire, none other than masked Mexican wrestling legend El Santo shows up to cover his back. And by the way, it's a musical.

coffin and out pops Blacula. He immediately feeds on the antique dealers and heads out in search of the reincarnation of his African lover, named Luva, who died waiting for him to return from Transylvania (and now is conveniently reincarnated as a black woman in South Central—since the princess's bloodline was brought to the States via the slave trade). While he searches, the police figure out something is fishy and try to track down Blacula. At the moment he hooks up with Tina, his recycled sweetie, the cops show up and try to shoot Blacula, hitting Tina instead. Blacula swoops up Tina, carries her back to his coffin, and attempts to turn her into a vampire before she dies from the gunshot wound. Once the cops catch up, they find Luva-Tina in the coffin, and drive a stake through her heart, killing her. Blacula, despondent at losing Luva twice, throws himself into the daylight and is incinerated.

While the plot is simple and trite, it speaks volumes about cultural life in 1972 Los Angeles. In that sense, it's classic blaxploitation. The movie's racial undertones are obvious and easy. But there are several more subtle themes, such as the metaphors for slavery. Manuwalde was turned to vampirism by a European aristocrat and then imprisoned for more than two centuries. When he finally gains his freedom, nothing makes sense—he is an outsider in a society where people look and act similarly (most of the time), but he can never be their equal. Also Luva, dead as an African woman, is able to be "reawakened" through reincarnation as an African-American, once she is reunited with her African prince.

Another disturbing metaphor is captured in the humor and intolerance found in the characters' attitudes toward the gay antique dealers. Soon after the cops discover the dead couple, the black antique dealer's corpse disappears. When the police are informed, they respond by saying, "Who'd the hell want a dead faggot?"

Shortly after watching *Blacula* I took a look at the next title in my pile, *Killer Barbies vs. Dracula*. It was time for a break. That's when I decided to pursue my final task—drinking blood. Specifically, my own.

Blood is the essence of vampirism. It's the universal symbol of horror, death, and life that gives the vampire his power. The belief that blood is connected to the soul or life source of humans originated with the Egyptians as early as 2500 B.C. Throughout Eastern and Western cultures over the following 4,000 years, it was commonly believed that blood was the seat of the soul, connecting the spirit to flesh. In early societies, spectators would drink the blood of fallen warriors and gladiators with the hope of transferring some of their strength to the recipient.

Despite an almost total lack of scientific understanding of what blood was or how it functioned, the ancients were more right than wrong. Blood, though it seems like a relatively straightforward substance, is amazingly complex. It is the biological glue that holds us together and keeps us alive. The average adult carries about 1.3 gallons of blood in his body, which has about a four-month life span. Though blood seems like a whole substance, it is actually made up of a bunch of different components, each with a unique purpose.

The Greeks believed that blood was one of four essential bodily fluids, along with phlegm, black bile, and yellow bile (a.k.a. the four humors). The Greeks also pioneered the practice of bloodletting as a form of healing. At the time, they believed that there was only one disease, kind of like a generic illness. The way to combat this illness was to restore a proper balance of all four basic fluids. The easiest to control was blood, so the Greeks initiated the practice of draining blood to heal sickness.

In Western societies, the practice went in and out of vogue, but became especially common from the twelfth to nineteenth centuries. Before that, bloodletting was a religious endeavor, undertaken by clergy in an attempt to rid the body of demons. During the twelfth century, the Church decided it wanted out of the bloodletting business and turned it over to barbers.* Strangely,

---

* The iconic red-and-white barber pole originated as a sign that the barber practiced both haircutting and surgery.

physicians at the time did not practice surgery, they considered the practice beneath them. Surgery and bloodletting were thought of as a last resort when other, more sophisticated forms of treatment, failed to produce results.

The most favored method of bloodletting was via venesection (drawn from a vein) with the patient standing. The barber would draw out between sixteen and thirty ounces of blood (about a third of the blood in the patient's body), depending on the ailment. The desired effect was lowered fever, a softer pulse, and faintness (of course, this was also a sign that the patient was dying, but why split hairs—dead patients no longer complain about illness, right?).

By the late 1800s, bloodletting was falling out of fashion—not because it was an ineffective and barbaric practice, but because it went against the grain of scientific thinking of the era. Disease was thought to be the result of depression, something that could be overcome with a brighter attitude or outlook. Bloodletting tended to *cause* depression in patients, so the practice was abandoned. While blood removal is still practiced as a treatment for some blood ailments, its use as a general treatment died out by the beginning of the twentieth century.

In addition to blood's association with life, blood also has a long track record with religion. In addition to Christianity's belief that the Eucharist involves drinking the blood of Jesus to receive spiritual redemption, many religious texts forbid the consumption of blood due to its role as a purifier. Especially Judaism, which uses this as one of the bases of kosher food preparation. The foundation of this originates in Leviticus 17:11: "For the life of the flesh is in the blood, and I have given it to you upon the altar to make atonement for your souls, for it is the blood that makes atonement for the soul." All this only adds to the appeal of blood as part of vampire lore—not only is it the essence of life, it is forbidden fruit. Forbidden fruit that I wanted to sample.

While at the doctor's office for a routine physical, I asked if he wouldn't mind drawing an extra vial of blood for me to take home. He declined, saying he didn't think it was a very good idea. Well, compared to my other options for getting a sufficient quantity of my own blood, I considered it pretty fucking stellar.

I was buttoning my shirt after he left when I realized that the examining room's supply cart was stocked with needles, vials, alcohol swabs, and cotton balls. I simply grabbed one of each and nonchalantly dropped them into my backpack before the nurse showed up.

Back home, drawing the blood was easier than I expected. Of course, I had just witnessed a demonstration at the doctor's office earlier that morning, so I picked a spot about an inch south from his and repeated what he'd done. Almost as soon as the needle pierced my skin, the vial started to fill with blood. No problem.

I figured the tough part was over.

During my reading about blood-fetish practices, I'd often read that blood is much more tasty when chilled. Considering that, I pulled out some dusty barware, grabbed some ice, and poured the contents of my vial into a cocktail shaker.

I though it would be best to drink my blood neat and cleaned out a shot glass, which I then filled with my chilled bodily fluid.

I thought that if I pondered this too long, I'd talk myself out of doing it. So I raised my glass and took it all in one gulp before I had a chance to think about what I was doing.

As soon as the blood passed into my throat, I realized how stupid an idea this was—as I could feel my breakfast coming up to meet it. Having been told to fast for twelve hours before having my blood drawn at the doctor's office, I had stopped on the way home for a hearty breakfast.

I bolted for the bathroom and was just inside the door when a mixture of scrambled egg, Diet Coke, apple, bacon, and ice-cold blood exploded out of me all over the bathroom.

The results were surprisingly gory—worse than you'd think. There was blood and breakfast all over everything, as if Freddy Krueger had just dispensed with three cheerleaders moments ago.

After taking a deep breath, I realized that I was as ready as I was going to get. I had all I needed to find the literal and figurative influence of vampires. Arguably, I'd been ready before I'd even started any of these ridiculous tasks. The world is filled with fear, mistrust, passion, and desire. Today in America, vampires are everywhere—and not just in the movies—from *Sesame Street,* fetish clubs, toy pencil sharpeners, advertisements, kids' cereal boxes, and role-playing games to crossing your fingers as a gesture for someone to back off or go away.

In an age of corporate-accounting scandals, pedophile priests-congressmen-whatever, African warlords, influence-peddling lobbyists, and terrorists—let alone various geeks, freaks, outcasts, and the normal people you pass walking down the street—vampires were everywhere.

I just had to look.

II

BERRIES IN A PAIL

In which the author sets out to find vampires and in the process deconstructs Girls Gone Wild, fights off porn ads, and ponders the evolution of flies.

V AN HELSING PARTY, please."

I couldn't believe I had to say this out loud.

I was told to come to a local Jillian's restaurant (across from the Medieval Times theme restaurant) and ask for the Van Helsing party. That was the only info I was given to find the people I was supposed to meet.

"Van Helsing?" the hostess asked, browsing fruitlessly through the reservation list. "Like the movie?"

"Yes," I replied. "Just like the movie."

"Ummm . . . I'm sorry," she said. "I don't see anything even close to Van Helsing. Do you know any of the names of the people in the party?"

"No, I'm afraid I don't."

She looked up at me for a moment.

Yes, it was true. I was there to meet a group of people—I knew no one's real name—and the group wanted to be identified as the Van Helsing party. I wanted to tell her it was okay. I really wasn't surprised this was a problem. I'd been through this a couple times already. I'd been stood up a few times, led to places that don't exist, and knocked on the doors of empty houses.

Even this early in my pursuit of vampires, I'd picked up this lesson—finding vampires is easy. Meeting vampires is hard. Despite attempts to meet with some self-declared vampires, my number of successful meetings was low. In fact, so far, it was zero.

Judging by most vampire lore—you don't find vampires, vampires find you. But what if you are, say, writing a book, and don't want to wait around for a vampire to come knocking on your door whenever he or she feels like it? How do you go about finding one? The same way you'd find an ultrarare, mint condition Princess Leia action figure or the lyrics to Leo Sayer songs—go online.

If you think the Internet offered an impressive number of conspiracy Web sites, readerless blogs, and porn—try searching for vampires online. Simply Googling the word *vampire* brings up more than seven million results.* I decided I'd zip through the first hundred or so to see what I could find.

However, the difficulty of locating vampires wasn't the first thing I learned from this research. My first lesson was, "Don't surf random vampire Web sites on your lunch break at work." This foray into the cyberworld of vampires resulted in a nasty piece of spyware embedding itself on my work computer, periodically putting ads for porn sites on my screen. They'd pop up while I was working on e-mails, conducting meetings in my office, and in the middle of employee evaluations. I was so terrified that someone else might see them that I'd jump to my mouse whenever one would start to emerge. It became like a cyberporn version of Whack-a-Mole.

The irony was that the vampire Web sites I viewed featured no risqué adult content, they mostly featured bad poetry, tedious short fiction, and message boards. Regardless, when I called our IT guy, I felt like I was requesting penicillin for the clap. He suggested I lay

---

* This is twice the number of results for *zombie* and four times that of *Frankenstein*. That said, it is only half of what *ghost* brings back and a third of the results for *monster*. According to wordcount.org—a site that ranks words on the Internet compared to all other words—*vampire* is the 23,688th most popular word on the Internet, right between *Cheddar* and *briefs*.

off the vampire sites. I happily concurred. Plus, I was sick of combing through hundreds of online pages with black backgrounds and white, purple, or green text.

There's an old story that begins, "There was once a time when vampires were as common as leaves of grass, or berries in a pail, and they never kept still, but wandered around at night among the people." While that may have been true at one time, it certainly isn't true today.

During my Web site hunting, I had sent out dozens and dozens of e-mails, especially to any vampires I found in the D.C.-Virginia-Maryland area.

I thought I'd hit pay dirt with my first contact, Steve. I was so convinced that I was on the right track with him that I ended up sitting alone in a dark park, not completely unconvinced that someone wasn't lurking in the bushes watching me.

While trolling the Internet for vampires, I had seen just about every odd name possible: Garth, Marina, Vigil, Ahab, Death Angel, Bug, Kyrmsin, Lady Rae, dozens of Vlads . . . and Steve. I'd noticed Steve posting on some vampire message boards, sometimes several postings per topic per day. Since he seemed like such a chatty Patty online, I figured he'd be a natural interview subject.

We exchanged many e-mails before he agreed to meet me. In all those e-mails, I'd really only managed to learn two things about Steve: (a.) he considered himself, in fact, a true undead vampire; and (b.) his real name wasn't Steve.

"Steve is an odd pseudonym for a vampire," I wrote. "Honestly, I'd expect something spookier."

"How do you think I've managed to live undetected among you mortals?" he replied. "I'm not just some kid who likes to pretend he craves blood."

This statement, of course, just made me think that he was, in fact, a kid who likes to pretend he craves blood. I figured he was harmless.

Steve agreed to meet me in a park north of Military Road in

D.C., just a few blocks away from my apartment. It wasn't ideal, but it was a public place. Since this was the first time I was meeting an actual vampire, it was also the first chance I'd had to implement the "system." My wife, Katherine, and I came up with the system as a safety measure for whenever I traipsed off to meet potentially dangerous strangers who were convinced that they were undead and needed to drink blood from the living (read: me). Basically, as soon as I met with the vampire person in question, I'd immediately call Katherine under the guise of letting her know when I'd be home. The real motivation behind the phone call was to make sure the interviewee understood that someone knew specifically where I was (and with whom). *However . . .* if I mentioned my buddy David in any context, it was a signal to Katherine that I was in trouble and needed help. As far as systems went, admittedly, it wasn't great. I figured that if I was in serious trouble, I was dead anyway. Why worry the missus?

I didn't think much about meeting in a park at 7:30 at night until the meeting time came and I remembered that during November it is completely and totally dark at 7:30 at night. The park itself was shaped like a big triangle, with a ball diamond in one corner, basketball and tennis courts in another, and benches and kiddie play equipment in the third. The area with the benches is surrounded by a partial wall, trees, and shrubs. The park was completely empty when I arrived, though an occasional person did pass along the sidewalk.

Sitting there waiting in the moonlight for a vampire to show up, you'd think that I'd feel very alone. That was the problem. I didn't feel alone at all. I felt crazily attuned to the surroundings—hearing every branch rustle, twig snap, and leaf tumbling along in the light breeze. But 7:30 came and went. I became increasingly jumpy as I sat on the bench, nervously checking my watch and spinning my head around to make sense of every little noise I'd hear. That's when I thought I saw someone standing between two bushes at the side of the park shelter.

"Hello," I called out weakly.

Nothing. Every time I'd convince myself that the shape I saw wasn't a person, I'd notice something move or adjust and thought I saw a shoulder or arm.

"Steve?"

Nothing. That's when I started to think of questions I should have asked myself, well, before I wandered into a dark park mostly obstructed from view by the street. Like why Steve wanted to meet someplace near *my* house, not his? Why would Steve choose to hide in the bushes instead of waiting on the bench or outside on the sidewalk? Why would I agree to do something like this in the first place? I don't care how much you paid for this book; this shit simply wasn't worth it.

After sitting there for a moment fondling my cell phone, I stood up and took a step toward the bushes.

"I'm sorry, is there someone there? I can't see you."

A car passed along the side street. At first I could see the headlights drift between the bushes. Then something swung between the branches and blocked out the light. Whatever it was—a thick tree branch, a very big squirrel, a vampire, or a nutty kid convinced he was a vampire and moments away from proving it—there was *something* in the bushes other than bushes.

I realized that whatever it was, continuing to walk toward it was . . . hmmm . . . a mistake! Without saying anything else to whatever or whoever it was, I dashed out the gate and was about half a block down the sidewalk—all in about four seconds. As soon as I got home, I tried e-mailing Steve to ask what happened to our meeting.

I never heard from Steve again. Since then, I've never found any of his postings on the message boards, either.

I got a few other responses to this query, most of which went nowhere, including, I thought, my trip to Laurel, Maryland, to meet with a group of self-professed vampires from D.C.

"Could you check again?" I asked the Jillian's hostess.

She looked mildly annoyed, but started through the reservation sheets again. Just as she was about to send me off, another hostess walked up to the desk.

"Let me guess," said Hostess Number Two. "Van Helsing party, right?"

I nodded.

"Come with me."

As I followed her, I alternated between two thoughts. First, I wondered how she knew I was with the Van Helsing party. Second, I wondered what the other members of the Van Helsing party looked like. In my head, I was running through all my expectations—jet-black hair, pale skin, dark clothing, heavy makeup, and various metal things covering their clothes and skin. I expected them to look and act very uncomfortable being here at a massive chain "restaurant and entertainment complex" like Jillian's.

The hostess rounded a corner then extended her arm toward a cluster of tables.

"Here you go," she said. "The Van Helsing party."

"Thank you," I said, turning to face my D.C. vampires. Seeing them made me take a deep breath and try to figure out what to do.

"Are you Eric?" a woman said. "Come, sit down. Join us."

There was a chair directly in front of me so I pulled it out a few inches and slid in. I looked up and down the table, taking all this in. I thought to myself that I at least got the hair right.

Sitting around the table were seven people, all smiling, all fairly normal-looking.

They were all African-Americans.

MY PATH FROM Google to a moonlit park to a bunch of black vampires at a table across from the virtual motocross game in a Jillian's wasn't as random as it might sound. After a few weeks of frustration trying to contact self-declared vampires, I began to notice that quite a few of them mentioned belonging to groups at Meetup .com, an online social networking site for special interest groups.

At Meetup, I found there were 476 active vampire groups, with a total of more than 12,000 members.*

Most of the group's ninety-six members included a photo and brief introduction, which ran the gamut from unironic self-awareness to utter fantasy.

"Hi, I'm Danny," read one entry. "I'm not really sure that I am, or am ever going to be a vampire. Also, I'm underage for blood donation. But I'm really interested in vampires. I play more fantasy RPGs than anyone I know."

"HELLO I'M 23YRS OLD I'VE BEEN THIS WAY SINCE I WAS 6YRS OLD AND I WOULD LUV TO BITE U."

"Greetings to you all. I am Akuma Graev. I consider myself quite exceptional with the makeup tools and also exceptional with conversations. I am an avid costumer also."

Some read like personal ads: "Educated, professional gentleman . . . fascinated by vampires, but no, not one myself!"

One description and photo that caught my eye was CrimSol. Her photo showed her topless, but only visible from the collarbone up. She had her hand drawn up behind her head and a "come hither" look on her face. Her description read, "I am Lady Shara of House of Insurrection under Order of Manipera residing in DC/VA/MD area. Look forward to constantly meeting others." The description also featured an e-mail address. We corresponded a few times, which resulted in an invitation to come to Jillian's and ask for the Van Helsing party.

It was CrimSol who greeted me and asked me to sit and join them.

---

* While this might seem like a lot, I found an almost equal number of groups and members devoted to the rap group Insane Clown Posse, as well as 96 groups devoted to ferrets, 230 groups of Sean Hannity fans, 47 people trying to start a group focused on unicorns, 2 groups composed of mule enthusiasts, and 138 groups on at-home birthing. For fun, I started to search for groups with more deviant devotions. I found little—it may be because of Meetup's policies on explicit and illegal material. I found 31 groups on "medical" marijuana, but no fetish, drug, or sex groups. So while there is no group on felching (look it up), I learned there is a Felch, Michigan—with 15 Meetup members.

As I got comfortable, CrimSol turned to the woman next to her. "Was he the presence you just felt?"

The woman shyly shook her head and pulled her sweater closer around her chest. Her name was Petra. She looked to be in her late teens and was very pregnant. She was avoiding eye contact, choosing instead to bury herself deeper in the arms of her boyfriend, Andy. I'd noticed Petra's profile on the group's message boards because she was very striking. Unlike CrimSol, I would not have guessed she was black. Her features seemed like a mix of ethnicities and the photo she posted was tinted. She just looked like a serious goth. The only difference from her photo was that here she looked like a black, pregnant goth.

I extended my hand to CrimSol and thanked her for the invitation. She looked at my hand, then back up at my face, and then looked across to one of the other group members. She never lifted her hands out of her lap. I went around the group, learning their names and exchanging pleasantries. In addition to CrimSol, Petra, and Andy, there also was Tim, a big, tall guy with light blue eyes and mini-dreadlocks. Next to me was Charlie, a very strong-looking man who told me right away that he was a cop from D.C., and who seemed to be in charge of tonight's meeting. Next to Charlie was Loren, who was quite obviously an effeminate man, but everyone kept referring to "her" using feminine pronouns. Sitting on the other side of CrimSol from Petra was a guy named Dan, who stared intensely at whoever was speaking, but never said anything the entire evening outside of an occasional "yeah" and giving the waitress his order. I extended my hand to the first few, but they, like CrimSol, made no effort to shake my hand. After a while I just dropped it.

After I settled in, the conversation picked up where it seemed to have left off with my arrival—CrimSol's babies. It seemed that CrimSol loved wolves, and was trying to raise a pair of them in her two-bedroom townhouse in D.C., hoping to breed them. To everyone's surprise but me, the D.C. Department of Health had threatened to take away the wolves if she didn't get rid of them. She had moved them to her ex-husband's property.

"I miss my babies so bad," she said. "I get to visit them when I take my son to see his daddy, but I want them *back home*."

"You should've told them they were dogs," said Tim.

"I did! When the Animal Control guys come round, I told 'em they was malamutes. I don't know if they believed me, but they had their answer and just left me alone."

"Malamutes don't look nothing like wolves," Charlie exclaimed.

"Like hell they don't," CrimSol answered. "They don't got the skinny legs, but you could pass a wolf as a malamute, especially when they're young. But then, the head guy at Animal Control come over and said, 'They ain't no malamutes! They got to go or I'm takin' 'em. If those wolves are still here when I come back, you're in a big mess.'"

"You should have told them you kept them for religious purposes," said Charlie.

"Really?" she asked.

"Straight up. If you tell them they're for your religion, they can't touch them. That's separation of church and state—if you say something is for religion, they can't touch it."

"How can that be?" I chime in, trying to join in the conversation. "If I say that snorting cocaine is part of my religion or that stealing cars is part of my religion, that doesn't make it legal for me to do it."

Charlie looked a little annoyed by me shooting down his idea.

"Well, then . . . what about Indians?" Charlie asked. "They worship wolves and bears and all kinds of shit. CrimSol, all you've got to do is tell them that you worship the Indian religion and they have to let you keep 'em."

I wanted to press the point, but the vibe of the black vampires was definitely with Charlie. I decided just to roll with it and try to change the subject.

"So, how often do you folks get together?" I asked.

"We get together all the time. We have barbeques and stuff when the weather's nice. And then we talk all the time."

The others started to giggle softly. I got the impression I was on the outside of an inside joke.

"Just the other night I'm lying in bed and Charlie calls me, 'CrimSol. CrimSol.' And I'm like, 'Huh?'"

The giggling continues.

"And he keeps calling me 'CrimSol. CrimSol' is all he says. I'm like, 'Damn, nigger, leave me alone! I'm tryin' to sleep!'"

The others laugh out loud; I still don't get it.

"Why didn't you just turn off the ringer?" I asked.

"What?" CrimSol replied.

"The phone. Why didn't you just turn it off so that he can't bother you?"

"The phone? Why would I turn off the phone?"

"So he can't keep calling you."

"Phone? No, fool, he wasn't calling me on the phone!"

"I was callin' out to her," Charlie interjected, while pointing from his forehead to hers. "Projecting, not speaking."

"I'm sorry," I said. "Is that considered rude?"

Charlie and CrimSol looked at me as if they were trying to muster some patience. Usually when I'm asking questions in a group of black people, I get looks like this because I'm asking questions only white people ask. This was the only time I got this look because I was asking questions that only non-vampires ask.

"Callin' out?" CrimSol asked.

"Yeah, is it rude to call out to someone when they're sleeping?"

"Well," Charlie said. "I guess if you don't know 'em. I guess it depends on why you're calling out."

This conversation led to another topic. The ethics of psychic powers.

"So let's say this," CrimSol said. "Let's say you have gifts, and don't know you have gifts. Then you think, 'Man, I really wish so-and-so would get sick.' And they do. Should you get blamed?"

Having stuck my foot in my mouth twice in the first twenty minutes with these folks, I decided to keep my mouth shut and just listen. While my black vampires were fairly normal-looking at first glance, as I spent more time with them, I started to notice tiny things about each of them. Charlie had very long, pointed fingernails and a silver medallion around his neck showing a skull with long fangs. At one point Loren pulled the sleeve of her sweater back while crossing her arms, revealing about twenty one-inch-long scars—obvious legacies of neat, meticulously placed razor cuts—up, down, and across the inside of her forearm. As Petra listened to others while gently rubbing her extended belly, she'd squint and stare at people around the restaurant with the intensity of a hungry animal stalking prey. She could stare a hole in a concrete block. During our ethics conversation, Andy asked about his rights whenever Petra got the "urge to suck the life out of me." He then pulled his sleeve back to reveal about ten fresh slash marks in his arm. Petra turned toward him, ran her tongue along his exposed arm. They all laughed. I didn't.

As the ethics discussion went on, it became very heated and animated. Tim was the last to weigh in on the ethics of psychic power (except for Dan, who just sleepily stared at whomever was speaking, not reacting at all to anything that was said). Tim asked a rhetorical question about sin as a basis for right and wrong.

"Sin?!" Charlie said. "I'll tell you about sin. You know the Bible? You know what that is? Words on paper. You can live your life according to what King James says, but I don't."

Everyone fell silent.

"Our people didn't have the Bible. It was *given* to them. Some master said, 'Here, negro, learn this. . . . Now go pick some cotton!'"

At this point, Charlie was practically shouting and his face was getting flushed. Angry cops always disturb me. It isn't the fact that cops can get worked up or even that some have quick tempers, it's the fact that they do so while most likely carrying a concealed firearm.

Thankfully, our waitress came by to take our food order. Regardless of bloodlust, these vampires were hungry, and ordered up an arsenal of rare burgers, chicken wings, and nachos.

I started making a vampire checklist in my head. When we first arrived it was still light out, so no checkmark near "death by daylight." They all said how hungry they were, so they didn't rely on blood for sustenance. More than half of them were wearing gothic jewelry with crucifixes, so no check there. I could see their reflections in the brass fixtures behind us. One was pregnant and Crim-Sol's kid was running around playing games, so that blew the whole "undead" thing. These people said they were vampires, but so far I hadn't seen too much that fit the basic template. It made me wonder just what exactly they saw in themselves that made them think they were undead?

Throughout the evening I kept picking up references to psy—especially when we were discussing "calling out" or the ethics of secret mind control powers. I'd seen this term thrown around before—it's shorthand for psychic vampires. Psychic vampires believe they possess all the powers and abilities of a traditional vampire, but instead of sucking blood out of the living, they feed on energy, chi, life force, or whatever you choose to call it. Some psy vampires don't even consider themselves undead or nonhuman, just that they have special powers and abilities that correlate with being a vampire, minus most of the bloody vampire stuff. It makes you wonder then what *is* and *isn't* a vampire.

The origins of the word *vampire* are as sticky and unclear as almost every facet of its definition. The word seems to have come from everywhere and nowhere and means many different things. Because our concept of the vampire originated in Greece, Hungary, Turkey, and other Slavic countries, many assume the term *vampire* came from there as well. It didn't.

The earliest recorded appearances of the word *vampire* occurred in English, French, and German in the late seventeenth century chronicling vampires in Russia, Poland, Serbia, and Macedonia. Most early users of the word claim to have picked it up from somewhere else, yet there is nothing documenting any earlier use, nor does the word *vampire*—or anything close—appear in any other language. The word just seems to have appeared.

Despite the Oxford English Dictionary's contention that the word's first English use occurred in 1810, Charles Forman used the term in his *Observations on the Revolution in 1688,* written that year but not published until 1741. Forman wrote about a group of unethical trade exporters, calling them "the Vampires of the Publick, and the Riflers of the Kingdom." Yes, the first known use of the word *vampire* in the English language was as a metaphor. Using a word metaphorically would suggest that it had been around for a while, simply for a reader to get the comparison. Trouble is— try to find it. Earlier English references don't seem to exist.

The word popped up in other languages around that same time. The word *vampyr* showed up in a 1748 German poem by August Ossenfelder. In 1746, Don Calmet popularized the word in French through his work *Dissertations sur les apparitions et sur revenants et les vampires.*

Many of the top vampire scholars argue that *vampire* comes from the Hungarian word *vampir.* Problem is, the emergence of this word in Hungary came after *vampire* popped up in Western Europe. Others have claimed the word comes from Slavic words such as *upior, uper,* and *upyr*—all derivatives of the Turkish word *uber,* which means witch.

Eastern European languages each had many words to describe the blood-drinking undead. In Romania, Russia, and Greece alone, vampires are known as *varcolaci, moroii, strigoi, siscoi, pricolici, oper,* and *vrykolaka.* Each has a slightly different meaning and describes a monster with different traits and ways of taunting the living.

Though no one will be able to offer a definitive explanation, the word *vampire* probably started out as a misunderstanding of one of these words (or several of them). The bastardization most likely looped back east from Western Europe.

It's often thought that vampires originated in Eastern Europe. Not true. You can find vampires throughout recorded history.

According to the Jewish Talmud, the world's first man was haunted by the world's first vampire. In the Talmud's story of creation, Eve was Adam's second wife. His first wife, Lilith, was trouble from the get-go. When Adam wanted to have sex with Lilith, he always wanted to be on top. Lilith, who considered herself Adam's equal, insisted that they switch off. Adam interpreted her behavior as a rebellion and banished her to the Red Sea. Lilith later returned as a demon with vampirelike powers and attacked Adam, Eve, and their children.

Greek mythology has Lamia, a woman who had several children with the god Zeus; the children were later confiscated by Zeus's wife. Lamia went insane with grief and fled, eventually transforming herself into a creature that attacked other mothers' children, drinking their blood. In India, the vampire goddess Kali dates back to the sixth century. She had multiple arms, a necklace made of human skulls, and a mouthful of fangs stained with the blood she drank from the living. Malaysians believed in a vampire that visited the cribs of babies, draining their blood with its long, snakelike tongue. Rivers and lakes in ancient Japan were rumored to contain Kabba, a vampirelike demon that would feed on the blood of passersby. In China, the Shange Te could change into wolves, ripping the heads off their victims and drinking their blood. Legends from ancient Persia (modern-day Iraq and Iran) are filled with tales of unholy demons and creatures who appeared human, but hunt the living at night to feast on their blood. Most of these stories bear the mark of historical hindsight (like the moniker *vampire* itself)—they are all stories that involve supernatural creatures who feed on the life of the living, yet rarely were they called vampires.

Outside of the whole blood-drinking, undead thing—there is one other common element that unites all this lore and connects it with our modern vampire stories—motive.

A vampire without a cognitive reason to hunt is simply a leech—an animal no different than almost any other parasite that feeds off the life of another. Placing a sense of ethics or morality on such creatures is a mistake; being a predator by nature is different than being a predator or parasite by choice.

A great illustration of this is the ichneumon fly, a tiny bug that has periodically found itself at the center of debates concerning the possible morality of animals. Charles Darwin himself wrote extensively about the ichneumon fly. At the time his evolutionary theories were published, most theologians and scientists felt that carnivorous animals were, through God's creation of them, acting benevolently—that by quickly and almost painlessly killing its prey, it was controlling for overpopulation, disease, and lingering degeneration from old age. Creatures like the ichneumon made it difficult for Darwin to make his theories jell well with these prevailing philosophies.

The ichneumon is an especially vicious parasite. The adult female ichneumon seeks out caterpillars, spiders, and aphids to "host" its larvae young. The mother ichneumon injects her eggs inside the host. The larva grows inside the host, eventually eating it from the inside while it grows—kind of like in the movie *Alien*.

While this kind of parasite infestation is common, the ichneumon is exceptionally efficient at the task. When the mother injects its eggs, it also injects a toxin that paralyzes the host, yet keeps it alive (since a dead, rotting host would not provide a good food source). Further, the larva chomps through its host in a manner similar to the old English punishment of being drawn and quartered: dispensing first with the organs that are least necessary for survival. It starts with the host's body fat, entrails, and digestive organs, saving the essential organs for last. When the young flies emerge, they leave behind only a shell of their host. Were the host spider or caterpillar conscious, this would be an almost unimaginably slow and torturous death. However, that's the point. They are caterpillars, they aren't cognizant. They don't have an "oh shit" moment once the parasite enters their body or they realize that they have become paralyzed. The ichneumon mothers or larvae aren't thinking too much about the process, either. They are all simple animals without thoughts, feelings, or emotions. The ichneumon mother doesn't make a choice or lack benevolence toward the host caterpillar—that is simply how it is evolutionarily programmed to reproduce and survive. It isn't evil or mean or lacking in compassion—it is just doing the same thing that humans do when they flinch at a loud noise—an instinctual reaction.

Vampires—be they from India, Greece, Japan, or Transylvania— are different. They have reason and motive for their actions—and that's what makes them so frightening. They use their prey to empower their supernatural supremacy and then use their powers to settle scores with the living. One might argue that vampires don't necessarily have a choice—as many vampire stories illustrate how victims are turned against their will or, in some cases, unknowingly. Even though they didn't make a deliberate decision in becoming a vampire, they still decide to remain a vampire. The drive may be overwhelming, but the decision to attack, feed, and remain a vampire is still optional. It may be more similar to an addiction than a conscious choice—but like any other addict, they can stop if they really want to. But with most vampires, they have no interest in stopping.

What makes vampires so equally terrifying and alluring is the fact that they are both man and animal—they borrow from both to form a creature that mixes an animal's strength and senses with the appearance and intelligence of a human. Vampirism is a return to our primal state. Vampires don't depend on spirits or demons as a source for their power, but simply a return to animal instincts. Vampires give up all that is modern, civilized, and evolved to return to a state of nonmorality while retaining the more desirable elements of being human.

Like eating chicken wings and cheese-covered nachos.

After the waitress brought our food, a few of the vampires took turns heading off to the bathroom and CrimSol whipped out a bottle of hand sanitizer, offering it to those who remained. She poured huge dollops into her son's hands, my hands, and her own. She worked the gel into every crevice and fold of her hands in a way that made you wonder if she was about to perform surgery.

When each of the others returned, CrimSol quizzed them about the conditions of the bathrooms, their use of soap, and how they had dried their hands.

After being properly sanitized and inspected, we all shared in a bounty of fried food and melted cheese. The conversation turned to movies, or more specifically, to the litany of horror films that Loren and Tim had seen since they were last together two weeks ago. Collectively, they'd seen *Deathwatch, Seed of Chucky, Saw,* the new *Texas Chainsaw Massacre, The Eye,* and the remake of *Dawn of the Dead.* Each title they shared was declared more "off the hook" than the previous ones.

"Hey, man," Tim asked me in an attempt to include me in the conversation. "Do you like horror movies?"

"Oh, sure," I replied. "Just last night I watched *Captain Kronos— Vampire Hunter.*"*

"Captain Kronos? What the fuck is that?" Tim asked.

"Well, this guy, named Captain Kronos, goes after a bunch of vampires that killed his wife and child."

"Is he like a space commander or something?"

"No," I replied. "It takes place in old England. Captain Kronos is some kind of solider or knight and has a hunchback sidekick. The vampires attack every hot chick in England, and their victims turn into old women, and then die."

"Well, was it any good?"

"No, actually, it was terrible."

"So, why'd you watch it?"

"I'm on a quest. Part of it is trying to watch every vampire movie ever made."

"Quest?" CrimSol said. "You know, only white people go on quests. Black folk don't have time for nonsense like that. It's like white folks chasing tornadoes. A tornado comes down and white

---

* Fun fact: *Captain Kronos* was actually created as a television pilot about a team of vampire hunters. When it flopped miserably it was retooled as a feature film and . . . flopped.

people decide to go on a 'quest.' Then they get in a van and chase the damn thing. When black people see a tornado, we run."

"Well, I tried to stop watching them, but I can't," I replied. "I watch a few and think they all can't be this bad—but they are. So I swear I won't watch any more, but then I think the next few might be better, and I watch them, and I'm wrong, and, well, I guess it's like a cycle or something."

I threw out the names of a couple other vampire films I'd seen recently, but none of the Jillian's crew had seen any of them. Then I threw out the names of the most popular films, they hadn't seen them either. It was pretty obvious that this group of vampires wasn't very interested in vampire movies. I think, for most of them, it wasn't even a matter of interest—they had never even seen most of the most basic vampire repertoire: Bela Lugosi, Tom Cruise in *Interview with the Vampire*, Wesley Snipes's *Blade*—they were all strangers to them.

Loren and Andy wanted to jump outside for a cigarette and I decided to tag along. For something to talk about, Loren and I were lamenting the recent death of Washington's only alternative radio station. It had been unceremoniously replaced by a Spanish pop music station called El Sol. After taking a beating in the press, Infinity Broadcasting, the radio glutton that owned WHFS/El Sol, announced the station was returning—or at least the format was returning, during the evenings and weekend schedule on one of its Baltimore stations. There was another guy smoking outside who came up to us and spontaneously joined in our conversation. He said his name was Kyle, his neck had no less than eight fresh hickeys on it, and he was really, really, really excited to have WHFS back on the radio.

Kyle couldn't stop talking about how radio sucks, except for WHFS, and he was hoping that they would sponsor more local events, like the Girls Gone Wild night he recently attended at a local bar.

"You shoulda seen it," Kyle exclaimed. "Girls would be comin' in and takin' their tops off. But 'cause they can't show their naked tit-ties, they'd rub paint all over themselves."

Kyle was getting very animated, rubbing his hands over his imaginary breasts as he pretended to wiggle as he walked. I guess it was supposed to look alluring.

"And these girls come out with their painted titties and the cops swoop 'em up, gives 'em a fifty-dollar fine, and throws 'em out in the street," Kyle said. "Now why would you want to go paint up your boobies just to get a fifty-dollar fine and tossed out?"

"Probably because you got paid two hundred dollars to do it," I replied.

"Huh?" Kyle said, looking at me with a slightly drunk, slightly confused look.

"They probably got paid two hundred dollars to do it, took a hit for the fifty-dollar fine, and go home with one hundred and fifty," I said.

"Well, it still sucks," said Kyle, somehow needing to turn this conversation into a mild win for his argument. "'Cause you have to pay to get in, and it's packed full, and then all you see is a bit of painted tit and then—boom—they're gone," Kyle added.

"Why didn't you just stand outside?" I asked.

"Huh?" Same look.

"If you have to pay to get in . . . but the women are only in the bar for a moment . . . and you can't see them before they're thrown outside . . . why not just save the cover charge and stand outside," I said.

"Why?"

"Because when the women are thrown out of the bar, they'll be standing there right in front of you . . . for more than a few sec-onds . . . for free."

Kyle needed to think about this one for a minute. Clearly, I had just blown his mind.

"Ah, cut it out, man," he said. "You're just fuckin' with me."

I assured Kyle that I, indeed, was certainly not fucking with him.

"Well, besides. You know. I can understand why a restaurant wouldn't want naked titties all over—'cause it ain't sanitary and all," Kyle reasoned.

Loren and I looked at each other, trying to understand how breasts are any less sanitary than, say, elbows.

"But a bar, man, people just go there to have fun."

Loren puckered his lips and shook his head, seeming to agree that no one in a bar would really care if there were dirty, unsanitary titties flopping about.

Kyle's friends came out of the restaurant and we took this as our cue to head back to our group. When we returned, Charlie was holding court on his latest business venture. Charlie was making money hand over fist by assuming mortgages. Since we were all friends, he said, he had decided to let us in on how it worked.

Charlie would get wind of someone who had fallen behind on their house payments and he'd come in and offer to get them back on their feet. The homeowners would basically sign over their mortgages to Charlie for the remaining balance, forgoing any equity in exchange for the bailout. The now-former owner could rent the house from Charlie until he sold it, keeping any proceeds for himself. The homeowner avoided what seemed like an inevitable foreclosure and implosion of their credit rating. While Charlie talked this idea up as a guaranteed moneymaker while helping out your fellow man, it struck me as exploitive. Sure, some people get in over their heads, but there had to be alternatives. People could be signing over many thousands of dollars in equity for help with a handful of house payments.

Charlie considered this a service to his clients. However, he still bragged that he'd make almost twice as much this year from taking over mortgages than he did from his cop salary. He continued to regale us on his mortgage-salvaging exploits.

Just then an announcement came on notifying us that in fifteen minutes Jillian's would switch to "twenty-one and over" only. Petra, Andy, and Loren were all underage, let alone CrimSol's son. We took this as our cue to leave.

As everyone got up, CrimSol invited me to come over and hang out with them at her house in a few weeks. I thanked her and extended my hand to her.

"Remember, I just sanitized," I said.

She looked at my hand, gave a small smile, and raised hers to shake mine. After we shook hands, the others gladly extended theirs to shake my hand good-bye.

As I walked out of the restaurant toward my car, I realized that outside of my movie list, the word *vampire* had never once been uttered by anyone the entire evening. Even with that, the only one who'd mentioned the word was me.

COUNTESS MINA WAS giggling and it was kinda freaking me out. Well, it wasn't really a giggle, but a breathy staccato laugh. The kind of laugh you make at a friend's joke that isn't really funny. She did this a lot—as in every time she made eye contact with someone. The laugh wasn't what bothered me. It was the ghost stories. The giggling vampire just made them worse. To compound things, people were starting to stare at us. I couldn't really blame them. I think it would be quite natural to wonder why four guys and a vampire were standing outside a bar on Nob Hill. In the wind. And rain. And freezing cold. For a long time. While the vampire talks. And talks. And talks.

"The Nob Hill Café's only been here for about fifteen years, but the reason I bring people here is because of the history of what happened here," Mina said. "This is the site of the most brutal battle between mortals and vampires in U.S. history."

Countess Mina went on to tell us how this bar was once an infamous vampire hangout, big-time. Local vampires used to "feed" off customers that went into the bathroom alone. According to Countess Mina, despite a gentlemen's agreement with the local authorities things eventually blew up with the cops, resulting in an all-out war.

The vampires lost. The four of us, along with a family that was eavesdropping on this segment of the tour, were all very sad.

Countess Mina offers a vampire-themed tour of San Francisco's Nob Hill neighborhood every Friday and Saturday evening and has done so every weekend since 2001. She's become a big draw, usually attracting about two dozen curious tourists to plop down twenty dollars for a stroll through Nob Hill to hear tales of the vampires that, according to Mina, have lived underneath the city streets for more than a hundred years.

On that particular evening, I arrived at Huntington Park to find about sixteen others waiting in the dark for Countess Mina's arrival. Even in an eclectic place like San Francisco, it wasn't difficult to identify her. She was the only person walking down the street in head-to-toe black Victorian finery, white makeup, bloodred lips, and holding a battery-powered candelabrum with five flickering bulbs.

The Countess started off by explaining that she was Mina Harker from the novel *Dracula*. She was turned into a vampire and then sent to San Francisco by Count Dracula himself. Mina had lived underground with the other area vampires for most of the time, but came up periodically to meet groups of humans like ourselves. She pointed our attention to a stunning gothic church across the street.

"When I finally got the nerve to come aboveground and explore the city on my own, Grace Cathedral was the first place I felt welcome," she said. "One of the main purposes of tonight's tour is to dismiss a lot of Hollywood's lies. There's just no other word for it. Hollywood has you guys so snowed. They have told you things about us to the point of making us look utterly ridiculous, and I'm going to clear a lot of that up tonight, and the first thing is that a vampire *can* enter a church."

She continued on about Grace Cathedral and all the San Franciscans associated with the church who were either (a.) in league with the local vampires or (b.) vampires themselves. The story goes on for almost fifteen minutes.

"Okay, are there any questions?" Countess Mina asked, followed by a giggle.

"Yeah," said one guy. "Are we going to stop at any bars?"

"Why, yes," Mina answered. "Our next stop is a bar on the other side of the hill. But we won't go inside."

"So no beer on this tour?" he asks.

"No," Mina answered, followed by another giggle. "But we do stop in a bar for drinks at the end of the tour."

"When will that be?" the guy asks.

"Oh, about two more hours, give or take," Mina responds.

"Hey, where are your fangs," said another tour customer, correctly pointing out that despite her makeup and costume, she had no pointy and/or long teeth.

"They only come out when I feed. You don't want to see them," she replied, turning to lead the group across the park toward the Nob Hill Café. As we walked, Mina started in on the ghost stories. It seems that almost every building we pass has some creepy story about ghosts that thrills Mina.

I should offer a bit of explanation here. I am scared of ghosts. I mean, I am really scared of ghosts. To be even clearer, I have a completely irrational fear of ghosts that leads me to avoid ghost stories, ghost-themed movies, and any place rumored to contain ghosts. Beyond that, the macabre doesn't really bother me much. I can eat spaghetti during slasher films. I can get a good night's rest after hearing stories about child-eating cults that live in basements. But start talking about ghosts and I turn into a sniveling little pussy. Game over.

I can't even watch *Casper the Friendly Ghost* without thinking that Casper is actually the ghost of a dead child. The last ghost movie I watched (as part of my occasional well-intentioned-but-ridiculously-stupid attempts to confront my fear) was *The Sixth Sense*. I was so freaked out afterward that I slept with the lights on and showered with the curtain open for *two weeks*.

So there I was, walking around San Francisco in the freezing cold, rain, and wind with a group of beer-obsessed strangers and a woman who claims to be a hundred-year-old vampire who lives under the city—and she starts talking about *fucking ghosts*. I started looking in every window, expecting some droopy-faced poltergeist to stare back at me. While Mina was talking, I was not paying attention to anything except the creepy ghost parts.

All I heard was, "Blah blah blah dead girl. Blah blah haunted basement. Blah blah blah seen in the window by many people. Blah Blah cue balls rolling across pool tables on their own." And so on.

When we arrive at the Nob Hill Café, we look around and notice that most of the group has left. Our vampire tour is down to just Mina, three meticulously groomed guys in tight T-shirts, and me. Countess Mina plugs ahead nonetheless.

As Mina is quick to tell you, 85 percent of the tour is fact; the rest she's just made up—stories of vampires in churches, running the city government, owning bars, living in hotels. For example, Emperor Norton was a real person who did a lot of wacky things like print his own money (which several local businesses accepted) and proclaiming himself Emperor of the United States and Protector of Mexico. Mina just added the fact that he was a vampire who faked his own death to serve Count Dracula.

After wrapping up at the Nob Hill Café, we continued on to Pacific-Union Club (packed full of ghosts), the Fairmont Hotel (the seventh floor is haunted), and the Mark Hopkins Hotel (former owner still roams the hallways). Countess Mina's bits of area history and vampire embellishments are amusing, plus the architecture and decoration of the buildings is fun to look at, but the only thing that's sticking with me is the lady in red who periodically spooks the maintenance workers at the Fairmont.

By the time we reached the end of the tour, I was the only one left. Just before arriving at our last stop, another man in a tight T-shirt pulled up and called out to my tour companions, "Come on honeys, we need to motor!"

They all said their good-byes and hopped into the warmth of the waiting car. As they pulled away, Mina asked if I'd like to go get a drink at the Marines' Memorial Club. I quickly agreed.

"The Marines' Memorial Club doesn't have any vampire history to it," said Mina. "I just picked it to end the tour because they're a restaurant and let in people under twenty-one who want to get sodas. Plus, they have a drink named after me—the Bloody Mina!" Followed by the giggle.

As we sat and talked over our cocktails, I learned her real name is Kitty Burns, she works in theater and other day jobs, but hopes to create vampire tour franchises in other cities. She's already created a New York tour, but has plans to expand nationwide, turning it into a full-time gig. Outside of the tours, she isn't that into vampirism.

"I get some of them on the tour every once in a while, or they will be walking by when I'm giving a tour and say something to me. 'Lifestylers,' they call them," Mina/Kitty offers. "They can be pretty frightening people. I mean, I do this for fun. They seem to take things very seriously."

"How seriously?" I ask.

"Well, every few years some homeless guy will show up dead under a bridge and all his blood will be drained."

"That's pretty serious."

"Yeah," Kitty said, with a smile, but no giggle. "Every once in a while I'll meet someone who is looking for vampires. Most times they want to become a vampire themselves and want to find someone to bite them."

While Kitty continues on, I think of an article I'd recently come across in *Rolling Stone* with similar connections to San Francisco—about bug-chasers. Bug-chasers are young men who seek out HIV-positive men for unprotected sex in a deliberate attempt to contract AIDS. The article chronicles several young bug-chasers, some of whom had traveled to San Francisco in search of "gift-givers"—HIV-positive men willing to have unprotected sex with them. Despite the sometime denial of health-care professionals and advocates, as well as a lot of controversy generated by the original article, visits to Web sites like ultimatebareback.com show that the practice is quite real. The article quotes one bug-chaser as saying receiving HIV will be "the most erotic thing I can imagine. I think it turns on the other guy to know I'm negative and that they're bringing me into the brotherhood. That gets me off, too." A lot of these guys reflect this attitude, thinking that "being seeded" brings them into a special group of people who live dangerously. It's as if bug-chasing becomes the ultimate erotic taboo. To these guys, AIDS is nothing more than a manageable disease, like diabetes, and they theorize that once they have HIV, they can have all the unprotected sex they like. "What can happen to us after that?" offers one chaser. "You can fuck whoever you want, fuck as much as you want, and nothing worse can happen to you." As they see it, getting HIV is freedom—much like becoming a vampire.

While bug-chasing is an extreme and niche phenomenon, the connections between AIDS and vampirism are far from simple metaphors. Vampirism has always been connected to disease—be it rabies, bubonic plague, porphyria, and other wasting diseases. In fact, London was suffering from a near epidemic of syphilis during the time that Bram Stoker was writing *Dracula*.

Be it movies, novels, or other forms of entertainment, vampirism's use of blood as a vehicle for transformation, sexual release, eternal life, and death formed a strong parallel with the real world's hopelessness and the lack of control over the spread of HIV-AIDS. During the pinnacle of the AIDS crisis, the number of vampire movies released more than doubled. According to *Videohound's Vampires on Video,* a fairly normal number of vampire films—forty-three to be exact—were released from 1980 to 1985. Between 1985 and 1990, when the magnitude of the AIDS crisis was unfolding, the number of vampire films jumped to eighty-nine. Between 1990 and 1992—during the height of the AIDS awareness and activism—more than two dozen films were put before the public each year.

Frank Rich of *The New York Times* wrote of the vampire/AIDS connection in 1992 when Francis Ford Coppola's *Dracula* was released. "It's a high-pitched, often hysterical acting-out of the subliminal fantasies, both deadly and erotic, of a country that has awakened to the fact that the most insidious post–Cold War enemy is a virus," wrote Rich. "AIDS, after all, actually does to the bloodstream what Communists and other radicals were once only rumored to do to the nation's water supply. Its undiminished threat has made the connection between sex and death, an eternal nexus of high culture, into a pop fixation, finally filtering down to the vocabulary of commercial images."

"You know, if you want to learn more about vampires, I have the perfect idea for you," Kitty offers. "Last year I went on a tour of Transylvania and Romania as part of a group and it was *so amazing*. You'd have such a good time and there are such great people that go on the tour."

She proceeded to tell me about all the places they'd visited and things they saw. This year's tour was just a few months away and Kitty was already set to go back.

"You should come along—it's just a neat experience."

As I half-seriously told her I'd think about it, we went downstairs and bid our good nights. On my flight home from San Francisco the next morning, I was reading the newspaper when I came across an item entitled ROMANIANS SOLVE VAMPIRE TROUBLES. The article told the story of Toma Petre and his relatives in Marotinu De Sus, a town of three hundred in southwest Romania. According to the article, shortly after Toma Petre died, his nephew, daughter-in-law, and grandnephew all fell ill. The conclusion by Petre's family: Toma had come back from the grave as a vampire and was working his way through his relatives. To save the family, Petre's brother-in-law Gheorghe dug him up and killed him a second time by cutting out Petre's heart, burning it, mixing the ashes with water, and drinking the ash cocktail. Despite Gheorghe's assertion that he did so to save his family, and that digging up the dead in rural Romania in order to re-kill them is about as unexceptional and tolerated as smoking pot in the United States, the Romanian State Police were still a little upset by the incident. Gheorghe and his wife (Petre's sister) Flora were brought up on charges, much to the vocal dismay of their friends and neighbors, who said they did the right thing.

Romania is both the literal and figurative birthplace of our modern vampire. In addition to the folklore origins of the contemporary blood-drinking undead, Romania now contains Transylvania, the home of Bram Stoker's Count Dracula. It's a country with a literacy rate *higher* than the United States, yet where being prosecuted for digging up and killing dead relatives makes about as much sense to the locals as being charged with breaking into your own house.

By the time I got home, I was set on following Kitty's advice. My next journey seemed pretty obvious.

III

I DON'T BELIEVE IN GOD; THE CRUCIFIX IS TO KEEP AWAY VAMPIRES

In which the author travels to the land of the vampire and along the way deals with dog attacks, floods, possible amputation, and running out of hand sanitizer.

I'VE RIDDEN IN turbulent airplanes, ferries crossing stormy water, and roller coasters that seem solely designed to separate me from a recently consumed funnel cake, but nothing has quite matched the experience of trying to watch an old black-and-white movie while riding for hours in a tour bus across barely paved mountain roads in Romania.

Nosferatu.

Every time I come across it my first thought is how incredibly tired I am of seeing this movie. On this particular occasion, I couldn't decide which was worse—the movie or the act of watching the movie.

I could have looked out the window, but I was even more tired of looking out the window. All I'd seen that day were winding roads, pine-covered mountains, and tiny country houses with clay roofs.

I went to Romania to tag along with a group of twenty-five vampire enthusiasts on a Dracula-themed tour of Transylvania. It's a collection of people, ranging from the off-puttingly freakish to the shockingly normal, willing to travel halfway around the world to visit the sites of both the historical and literary Dracula, and sometimes a mixture of the two.

To this point, we'd kept to our itinerary, but things hadn't gone smoothly. To complicate matters, things are getting a bit tense on the bus: several people were sick from drinking the water, a few others were plotting how to get rid of one couple, a woman was weeping over a psychic message she received from a stray cat, our "celebrity host," the former child actor Butch Patrick (a.k.a. Eddie Munster of *The Munsters*), has been asleep for hours in the back of the bus, and a twenty-four-hour-old insect bite on my hand is slowly turning from pink to a disturbing shade of black.

The ride wasn't supposed to take this long, but we were forced to reroute our journey through the mountains because of flooding. The day before I arrived, it started to rain and it hadn't stopped since. The floods were big news in Romania, even showing up in the international press. Earlier that day we had stopped at a gas station for snacks and a Romanian man, who guessed that I was an American, confronted me. He was trying to blame me for the floods.

His argument was that the floods were the result of the Gulf War, the Gulf War was Bush's fault, and I, as an American, should feel blame for Bush. Since leaving the gas station, I was alternating between trying to understand his logic and not throwing up.

I had spent most of my time figuring out how a military action 1,500 miles away would cause flooding in the Romanian mountains.* Harder still was understanding my personal responsibility for Bush. To kill time on the longer bus rides, our guide played a variety of Dracula and vampire movies. In the subjective world of vampire movies, even some of these were bottom dwellers: the movie version of the TV soap opera *Dark Shadows*, the pathetic and practically unwatchable Francis Ford Coppola version of *Dracula*, a seventies bio-drama about Vlad Țepeș (entirely in Romanian with bad English subtitles), and this, the silent 1922 orig-

---

* Iraq is southeast of the Romania mountains, at 4,000 feet lower elevation, and in the opposite direction of the weather pattern. There was also the nagging question in my mind as to whether this guy really meant the *Gulf* War or the more recent *Iraq* War.

inal *Nosferatu*. Whenever my mind drifts away from my personal responsibility for washed-out bridges or my churning innards, my eyes wander to the screen and take in *Nosferatu*. Again.

This version of the film is a particularly bad one. During the 1960s, someone decided that *Nosferatu* would be more marketable if they retooled it to be more in-line with *Dracula*. The movie's been reedited and shortened (dispelling the story tangents far from Stoker's tale), the title cards have been replaced with contemporary English, all the characters have been renamed to match their *Dracula* counterparts, and some of the close-ups of signs and books have been reedited with new footage featuring English instead of the film's original German.

In *Nosferatu*, Hutter (the Harker character) is sent to Transylvania to sell property to a mysterious nobleman named Graf Orlock (the Dracula character). Hutter eventually makes it to Orlock's castle and meets Orlock, a bizarre man with a constant stare (Orlock never blinks during the entire film) and gaunt features. The next day, Hutter stumbles across Orlock resting in a rotting coffin and flees just as Orlock packs up and heads to Bremen.

Hutter makes it back to Bremen before Orlock and shares a book of vampire legends with Ellen. She reads that the only way to kill a vampire is for a woman to allow the vampire to feed on her until morning, when the daylight would destroy the nosferatu. Orlock, who'd been watching Ellen from his new digs across the street, gladly enters her bedroom when she deliberately leaves her window open. Orlock feeds throughout the night, and then is reduced to a puff of smoke when sunlight enters the room at dawn (even though death or burning by sunlight has become a part of our vampire lore today, *Nosferatu* was the first time this idea was introduced—previously, vampires were only active at night, but exposure to daylight didn't harm them).

The word *nosferatu* is only mentioned once in the novel *Dracula*, by Professor Van Helsing, as a generic term for vampires, implying that the word originated in Romania. Bram Stoker probably picked this up from one of his primary sources, Emily Gerard's

1888 collection of Transylvanian travel essays called *The Land Beyond the Forest*, which claims *nosferatu* is a folk term for vampires. Problem is, there is no such word in the Romanian language— referring to vampires or otherwise—nor does the word exist in Hungarian or any other Eastern European language. Scholars think that Gerard (who didn't speak Romanian) misread the adjective *nesferit* (meaning "troublesome") as *nosferatu*.

When *Nosferatu* was released, it was widely heralded by critics, who wrote reviews attempting to reveal the heavy metaphors they viewed in the film about World War I, Communism, and all sorts of assorted nonsense. That inclination has continued in the decades since, though the perceived metaphors seem to change with time. Many later critics and film historians have commented that *Nosferatu* is filled with not-to-subtle references to homosexuality (the film's director, F. W. Murnau, was openly gay). However, I don't see it. While most vampire films are laden with sexual imagery and metaphor, *Nosferatu* is the least sexy vampire film of all time. The film's core vampire metaphor seems to be disease rather than sex (homosexual or otherwise). Also, little of anything in *Nosferatu* could be considered subtle.

There was one element missing from Murnau's vampire film: permission.

Back in the early twentieth century, film rights and copyright were in a kind of "Wild West" period. It was very unclear how stage and literary rights applied to the new medium, let alone the twists and turns of international copyrights, so many producers, including *Nosferatu*'s, just winged it. While its opening credits acknowledged that the film was a loose adaptation of Stoker's novel, no one bothered to figure out if it would be a problem to do this.

Nosferatu was the production of a flaky art collective based in Germany called Prana-Films. Prana was founded by artist Albin Grau (who became *Nosferatu*'s production designer). Grau had no experience in filmmaking at all, but felt he could spot a good spooky story when he saw it. Grau was a hard-core spiritualist and member of the Ordo Templi Orientis, a secret offshoot of a group led by renowned Satanist Aleister Crowley.

Permission wasn't the only thing they lacked—they also were pretty short on money, a distribution system, a business plan, or many other elements of a professional film company. Despite plans for several other macabre films, *Nosferatu* was the only film the company ever completed.

Nosferatu had its debut in March 1922, at the Marble Hall of the Berlin Zoological Gardens. Within a month, all hell had broken loose. The company's creditors started demanding payment and Florence Stoker, widow of *Dracula* author Bram Stoker, announced she would sue Prana for violating her copyright. By June, Prana-Films had closed up shop and was in receivership.

After Bram Stoker died in 1912, Florence Stoker, with *Dracula* royalty checks as her only means of support, was pretty tight with the rights. Florence had an odd relationship with *Dracula*. It's obvious from her correspondence that she didn't really care about the artistic or thematic elements of the book. Whenever someone came forward with an offer to adapt, translate, or otherwise exploit the book, Florence's sole concern was the size of the check, rather than maintaining the novel's integrity or story line. Since the time of her husband's death, Stoker had been playing cat and mouse with different stage and film rights schemes and, to her, *Nosferatu* couldn't have shown up at a worse time or been more of a pain in the ass.

Apparently Florence was either unconcerned or unaware that there was *another* unauthorized film adaptation making the rounds in 1921, a Hungarian film with the nerve to actually title itself *Drakula*. While the film (now lost except for some still images) borrowed the title and some plot elements from the book, its characters are more concerned with cutting out people's eyes than with drinking their blood, so it isn't even clear if Mrs. Stoker would've had much of a case. *Nosferatu* was a straight-up rip off, coming at the same time she was negotiating the U.K. and American film rights.

Realizing that a huge (and expensive) legal fight lay in front of her, Florence spent one British pound for a membership in the British Incorporated Society of Authors because one of its services to members was legal representation to defend literary rights infringement. Before the ink was dry on her membership card (seriously, the very next day), Florence contacted the society and asked for their help in suing Prana-Films over *Nosferatu*.

Initially, the Society of Authors was happy to represent Mrs. Stoker, as the film rights issue was affecting many of its members and they saw the *Dracula/Nosferatu* case as a way to score a simple and needed victory. However, mostly due to Stoker's insistence, the case dragged on for years.

After just a few months of championing the case, the society was growing tired of defending the rights of its newest member and incurring hundreds of pounds in legal expenses to keep the case going. Yet every time the society made noise about dropping or settling the case, poor widow Stoker somehow convinced them that this was important, and they soldiered on. At several points during the process, Prana's receivers attempted to settle with Stoker and the society, even offering a portion of the film's proceeds in exchange for allowing them to attach the *Dracula* name to the film in England and America. Florence would have nothing to do with it.

Finally, in 1925, Stoker won her case. However, instead of collecting cash damages, Florence wanted *Nosferatu* destroyed, including all negatives and prints of the film. Like the characters in the film itself trying to lure Count Orlock into the sunlight, Mrs. Stoker literally wanted the film to disappear in a puff of smoke. *Nosferatu* would continue to haunt her for more than a decade. Contraband copies of the film surfaced in England, America, and Germany, shown under the guise of the film's historical and artistic importance (despite its odd origins, the film was widely seen as a key work of expressionist cinema). Each time, Stoker fought it, wanting the copy of the film destroyed. A few months after a battle ended, another copy of the film would surface elsewhere.

After Florence died in 1937, the film popped up more frequently, but there was little interest in it. In the 1960s, a condensed version showed up on television—the version I was viewing on the tour bus. Soon after, *Nosferatu* was rereleased in its full form under a few different titles—*Nosferatu the Vampire, Terror of Dracula,* and even under the *Dracula* moniker itself. Despite a fifteen-year battle over the film, Florence Stoker never once did what my traveling vampire fans and I were doing on that bus: watch it.

While the bumpy bus ride was bad enough, the real stomach churner was the fifteen-hour-old pizza sitting on the seat in front of me. Eating it wasn't making me sick; looking at it was making me sick. The pizza's owner was Elaina, one of the gothiest among my fellow vampire-lovin' travelers. Elaina was a twenty-four-year-old devout vegetarian PETA member who, coincidentally, didn't like mushrooms or tomatoes. As a result, her diet appeared to consist of plain Pizza Hut pizzas, Doritos, chocolate, and French fries. While Pizza Hut isn't uncommon in Bucharest, hot water and electricity were hard to find out in the mountains—let alone a Cheese Lovers stuffed crust. After two days of eating nothing but cucumbers, she bribed the manager of our hotel to go out at 2:00 A.M. and get her an "American-style" pizza. What he brought back was this thing in front of me. Among the toppings: corn, fried eggs, venison sausage, whole olives (complete with pits), red chili peppers, chicken strips, sliced potatoes, and goat cheese.

Elaina had thrown up twice since we started out this morning and judging by her skin's gray hue, we were quickly heading toward round three. Despite feeling like an alien was about to burst through her stomach, Elaina and her boyfriend, Brad, had brought the remnants of this unrefrigerated pizza to share with the group. As others piled on to the bus, several would exclaim, "Pizza!" then whip a slice out of the box and into their mouths without much concern over what was on it or what state of biological decay it was in.

The pizza, coupled with shots of flaming brandy and a case of wine consumed at dinner last night, had resulted in three pukers already this morning, not counting Elaina. I was determined not to join their ranks.

Radu, our tour guide, walked up to Elaina and Brad's seat.

"Dr. McAllen, he want you to have this," he said, presenting a small blister pack. It was an antinausea pill.

Until this point, few on the tour knew Dr. McAllen was a doctor. In fact, at that point no one could quite figure out what he and his wife were doing on this tour. Dr. McAllen had come on the tour with his wife and two adult children. Notwithstanding the Scottish surname, they were from Mexico. He and his wife were just a sweet older couple who didn't seem to have any connection to vampire stuff at all. They were here because of their daughter, Sam, who was heavily into all things goth. Sam had just finished college and instead of a big party and presents, she asked to go on this tour. Once her family heard about it, they decided they'd all go together. You'd think that having your parents along would make a young Mexican goth girl cringe, but Sam seemed to enjoy having them there. While the McAllens didn't know much about the undead, they certainly seemed up for a good time.

"We are hoping to see many bampires, eh?" Dr. McAllen told me when we met at the airport.

Both Radu and Brad tried to convince Elaina to take the medicine, but she wouldn't touch it.

"He's a *Mexican* doctor. I don't want it," she said.

Despite the puking, we were slowly making our way to Sighişoara, birthplace of Vlad Ţepeş, a.k.a. Vlad the Impaler, a.k.a. Vlad Dracula, a.k.a. the historical Dracula.

Now, before we get any further into the story, there are a few things we need to get straight. The following are facts—indisputable truths:

- Bram Stoker never visited Transylvania and knew practically nothing about the country or Vlad Dracula, his novel's namesake.
- Vlad Dracula was not a vampire.
- Vlad Dracula did not drink blood, eat flesh, et cetera.

- Vlad Dracula did not worship the devil or pagan gods; nor was he a witch or an evil mystic.
- There never was anyone named Count Dracula.

Those statements seem pretty easy to comprehend, rather cut and dry—yet the other travelers on this trip, the organizers of this tour, and the entire tourist industry of Romania conveniently ignore everything I have just shared. Fact is freely mixed with fiction. Even details of literature are slightly altered to fit the convenience of the tourist trade. I guess it just makes for a better story to play with history a bit.

Lots of things have been pinned to Vlad Dracula over the past 550 years, most (as illustrated in the list above) are not true. However, Vlad was hardly a saint. It's the most heinous stories about him that are usually true; the stuff that makes being a vampire pale by comparison.

Sighişoara provides some clues about the origin of Vlad's famous surname. Many people have pointed to Vlad Dracula's name as evidence that he was evil. *Dracula* can be literally translated from Romanian to mean "son of the devil." A convenient definition, but the context is all wrong. The Romanian word for *devil* and *dragon* are the same. Thus, *Dracula* also means "son of the dragon." Not a major improvement, you'd think, unless you knew about his father, Vlad Dracul.* Papa Vlad was knighted into the Order of the Dragon, a group of nobles who pledged their allegiance to defend the Christian church against all enemies (which, most of the time, was the Ottoman Empire). Afterward, Vlad

---

* If you're confused so far, it gets worse. There were several other Vlads as well, starting with Dracula's grandfather, who was better known as Mircea the Old or Mircea the Great. While the three main Vlads were known as Vlad I, Vlad II, and Vlad III—kind of like the *Blade* trilogy—it's much easier to refer to them as Mircea, Dracul, and Dracula. In total, there were seven guys named Vlad in five generations of the family, including a half brother of Dracula named Vlad the Monk. As you can imagine, history has gotten a lot of them confused.

took the surname "Dracul" to indicate he was a member of the order. His son decided to take on the "son of" variation on his father's surname, Vlad Dracula, to note his continuance of the family's allegiance with the church.

Sighişoara is a small town smack in the middle of Romania. To get there, you have to cross the Transylvanian Alps. Transylvania (Latin for "land beyond the forest") hasn't been an autonomous country for almost a hundred years and beforehand had its own ruler or periodically was controlled by one of the countries surrounding it. Today, it's just an informal designation for the parts of Romania that sit north and east of the Alps and the Carpathian Mountains.

Romania is definitely a country of extremes. Bucharest, the capital city, is a pit, literally the ass end of Europe. While Romania itself was viewed as the European frontier for hundreds of years, the city of Bucharest is Eastern Europe at its worst. In 1977, a massive earthquake (not uncommon in Romania) leveled most of Bucharest, forcing a quick rebuilding of the city simply so that thousands of people would have a place to live. Combine Communist construction standards with the corner-cutting that comes with being in a hurry and you have an explanation as to why the city looks like it's literally falling apart thirty years later.

For the most part, the rest of the country is arrestingly beautiful—pine-covered mountains, quaint small cities and villages, and millions of acres of untouched nature. However, outside of a few cities, the country is pretty rural.

Through tales from acquaintances who'd been to Romania before, I'd learned all this before arriving, but it was still a little difficult to know what to expect. The night before I left, Katherine was sitting at her computer when she stopped typing and looked over at me.

"I want you to pack hand sanitizer for your trip," she said.

"Sure," I replied. "Why do you want me to take hand sanitizer?"

"In case you have to poop in the woods," she said, returning her attention to her screen.

"Poop in the woods?"

"Yes, and if you do, you should use hand sanitizer afterward."

I told her that I would be surprised if the residents of a village founded in the fourteenth century hadn't, in the past seven hundred years, found a better alternative than pooping in the woods. Plus, knowing the abundant and thriving legends about ghosts, vampires, and demons in the Romanian backcountry—the villagers probably thought the woods were haunted anyhow. Who'd want to poop there?

"Still," she reasoned, looking very serious, "you never know."

I packed the hand sanitizer.

Once everyone on the tour arrived in Bucharest, we headed north and seemed to be working our way through the life and sites of Vlad Dracula's life, although in no particular order. In fact, our very first stop was where he can be found today—his grave at the Lake Snagov monastery.

Everyone was excited for our first official destination. Since we'd arrived in Bucharest in scattered groups, some people I'd met back in New York and others I hadn't yet had a chance to say hello to. On the bus that morning, I'd met a few of the folks making up the tour. Kitty, a.k.a. Countess Mina, was there, of course, and she had almost immediately bonded with a woman from Los Angeles named Sandy. Sandy was a very beautiful woman somewhere in middle age with striking features, big curly blond hair, dark eye makeup, and a wardrobe consisting entirely of black and purple clothing. She wore large pieces of goth jewelry, including not one but two rings shaped like coffins. You may not immediately figure out that Sandy was a hard-core vampire lover, but one look at her would tell you she definitely was hard-core about *something*.

Two of my early favorites on the tour were Tim and Tina. They were an example of how much looks can be deceiving. Because I'd never seen either of them wearing anything that wasn't jet-black and they seemed a bit somber at first, I thought they might be a little on the creepy side. However, when we first introduced ourselves, Tim stuck out his hand, gave a big warm smile, and said, "Hi, we're

Tim and Tina from Oregon, and we're *really* into Halloween." I immediately thought to myself that this was probably the one time in my life that anyone would ever introduce themselves to me with that phrase.

Tim wasn't kidding. Earlier that morning Tim and Tina were passing around photo albums. When they got to me, I thought they contained pictures of a haunted house that they owned/ran/worked in. It turns out these were pictures of *their house.* Tim and Tina spend an entire month turning their home into an ornate haunted house every Halloween. Then they invite all the area people to come through. Last year, they had 1,400 people visit their decorated home.

As we rode along exchanging stories, most of the participants didn't realize that we'd arrived at our first stop. As its name would imply, the monastery where Dracula is buried is at Lake Snagov, or specifically, on a small island in the middle of Lake Snagov. By the time we had arrived, Radu had prepped us that there were no roads or bridges to the island, so we'd have to take a boat. This didn't seem like a big deal—until we arrived at the boat dock.

The dock was the first example I encountered of what I'll call the "Romanian liberal use of descriptive terminology." The "boat dock" was a loose collection of assorted lumber that started at the end of an unpaved road and slowly descended into the lake itself. The portion of "dock" that was above water seemed to be held together by about a half dozen nails. The only reason it hadn't fallen apart and floated away was that it looked as if no sane person had attempted to use it in ten years.

My shock at the condition of the dock was quickly forgotten once I saw the "boat"—an ancient three-foot by six-foot rowboat that was so filled with water that it had almost disappeared below the waterline. It wasn't clear if this boat was sinking from rainwater or a festering and substantial leak.

As the bus emptied, my vampire tourists quietly gathered at the edge of the "dock" and stared at the "boat."

After a few moments, a fellow traveler finally broke the silence.

"You've got to be fucking kidding me."

"No, no, no," said Radu. "It because of the rains. It a good boat, you see?"

Radu was pointing at some anonymous villager who had stepped into the boat and was gingerly bouncing up and down in it to—I guess—demonstrate its resilience.

A few moments later, three local teenage boys came by and started bailing out the boat with a soda bottle, a small bowl, and their hands. Radu got on his cell phone and nervously spoke with someone in Romanian. During the ten minutes we stood there in the soaking rain while Radu chatted, the boys had managed to remove about three inches of water from the boat.

"Okay," Radu stated, pointing across the lake. "We go to monastery. I need four people to go in first boat now. I call over to monastery; they send bigger boat soon."

No one wanted to get into the boat, which still had about four inches of water in it. Finally, Ralph, a worker's comp lawyer from New Jersey with an encyclopedic knowledge of horror films, stepped into the boat.

"What the hell," he said. "Who knows what the other boat will be like?"

Buying into Ralph's logic, a few others slowly entered the boat, which now tipped perilously close to the waterline. Everyone stood staring at the boat as one of the teenagers started rowing across the lake. Ten minutes later, they were across and we could see them standing on the island's dock, jumping around and high-fiving each other as if they had just won *Family Feud.*

As soon as the teenager and empty boat were back on our side, Radu grabbed my arm and informed me I was going in the next group. Since I was soaked from the rain, sitting on a wet seat with water up past my ankles wasn't nearly as uncomfortable as I expected.

The passage from the mainland to the island was maybe 100 to 150 yards, but in that rowboat, it felt like it was miles away. As soon as we set off, I kept eyeing the distance to the dock and convincing myself I could swim it fully clothed once this thing sunk. The boat was sitting so low in the water that when I held on to the side of the boat, my fingertips touched the water. Sitting next to me was Julian, a filmmaker from London. (He'd won his place on this trip as a prize in an independent horror film festival—his film is called *The Last Horror Movie*. It's available on DVD and is quite good.) We hadn't had much of a chance to talk up until this point, but boy, you couldn't shut us up on that boat trip. Bad jokes, favorite pastimes, digital photography tips—we covered it all. Sitting across from us in the boat was a couple from San Francisco, Jeanette and Huge.

Jeanette and Huge were some of my favorite people on the tour. In many ways, they went against type for vampire enthusiasts: They had great social skills. Plus, they were kind of mischievous. Huge was a television producer and Jeanette seemed to have "done" a lot of things. She was a fount of amazing war stories of ex-husbands and boyfriends, rock stars, traveling the world, and of course—bizarre encounters with the unknown. When we first met, Jeanette informed me she was "very spiritual" and she seemed to believe in just about everything—ghosts, UFOs, government conspiracies, vampires . . . you name it. When we first met at JFK Airport, she told me how excited she was about this pilgrimage to "the Promised Land."

I turned to look over my shoulder at the same time the rower swung his oar around, the boat wobbled back and forth—my side coming about a half inch away from the water. When we were about halfway across, I heard a noise that sounded like a lawn mower. I looked around and saw a bearded Orthodox monk, in full black robe and hat, driving a powder blue dinghy not much bigger than ours, but with a small outboard motor. As he passed our boat, he raised his hand and blessed us. He was making such good time that he got to the boat dock, picked up another group, and then dropped them off at the island before we even got there.

During Dracula's time, the Lake Snagov monastery was practically a fortress. In a pre-Lutheran belief that good works could atone for bad deeds, Dracula gave a lot of money to the monastery to build up the island. Dracula had a wall built around the island and paid to have the monastery and its chapel expanded into a large church. Eventually there were three chapels on the island, along with a small palace, a prison, and some other residences for visiting *boyars* (nobles).

Dracula's motivations weren't completely philanthropic, but strategic as well. The island's position made it extremely safe, with the lake acting like a giant moat. Legend has it that Vlad buried several barrels full of gold and valuables in the lake near the island in case he had to retreat there at some point. Afterward, he had all the workers on the project killed to keep the treasure's location a secret.

After Dracula's death, the island slowly fell into disrepair. Many of the buildings and most of the wall are long gone. Even the chapel had been rebuilt to its original smaller size after the middle section collapsed in an earthquake. By the nineteenth century, the monastery and island were abandoned, though now the monastery was functioning again. Kinda. The chapel is still standing, as is the tower at the old church's entrance, plus a small cottage and an unused caretaker's house. Technically, the monastery was operational, but there was only one monk—now the island's sole resident. However, at the time of our visit, it could be argued that the monastery was abandoned again—because its only monk was currently cruising the lake in his powder blue dinghy ferrying a group of tourists to Dracula's grave site.

Radu had warned us about three things before we reached Lake Snagov. First, the place was run by a crazy monk. Radu didn't explain what qualified him as crazy, or what crazy things he did—but he was very intent on us understanding that the monk was a little odd. Secondly, while viewing Dracula's grave we should make sure to never step on the grave itself—it's considered rude and the monk gets very upset. Radu was very serious about this. Given the number of times he repeated it, I gathered that in Romania stepping on the grave was about as big an insult as pissing on it. And finally, if we had to go to the bathroom, hold it. The monastery la-trine was disgusting and probably full of snakes.

As I got out of the boat and walked toward the monastery, I kept hearing dogs barking. Stray dogs are everywhere in Romania. The country has had a massive stray dog problem since the earth-quake that took down Bucharest. Once people became homeless from the quake and moved into pet-unfriendly apartment build-ings, they simply abandoned their dogs. Since Europeans are so much more refined than us barbaric Americans, they won't eutha-nize unwanted strays. They just spay or neuter them, tag them on the ear to indicate they've already been fixed, and then release them back into the streets. Still, strays are everywhere—even here on this remote island—kind of like the Romanian version of mice or rats.

As we rounded the first corner toward the monastery, Jeanette was walking back toward Huge and me with a little dog in her arms.

"Look guys! I made a little friend!"

The dog looked a bit overwhelmed by the attention, not sure if he should lie back and roll with it or jump down and run away. Jeanette was petting this dirty little fleabag and all I could think about was making sure she didn't handle any food at dinner that night.

About a hundred yards from the monastery, I noticed two other dogs. One was running in between the arriving tourists, barking at everyone and no one. The other, an overgrown poodle mutt with white, dirt-caked hair, was straining at the end of a rope, barking and snarling at anyone who passed by. I noticed Ralph's pant leg was rolled up and he was fishing around in his fanny pack. As I got closer, I noticed blood was running down Ralph's leg.

"The white one bit me," he said, hoping in vain that this expla-nation would end the matter. No such luck.

By this time, about a dozen of us were watching Ralph open moist towelette packets and fight a losing battle to sop up the blood from his calf.

Ralph told us that he was walking toward the monastery when

this dog came out of nowhere and bit into his leg and wouldn't let go. Ralph tried to break free, but the dog wasn't giving in. Eventually, the dog took off and ran in circles behind a bush until the next group came along. Luckily, the dog hadn't torn through Ralph's jeans, but still managed to tear up Ralph's skin pretty badly.

"Maybe we can find some paper towels or get some paper from the outhouse?" one woman suggested.

"No," a few of us said in unison.

"Why not?"

"There are snakes in there," someone said.

"Oh, yeah, right."

The women on our tour deluged Ralph with a pile of tissues, napkins, and assorted paper products. Once the bleeding stopped, it seemed that the dog had only damaged the surface of Ralph's calf and hadn't penetrated any deeper.

Radu showed up and surveyed the situation, then went to talk to the monk.

"All is good," he said, walking back to the group and attempting to herd us away from Ralph and into the chapel. "I spoke with monk. Yes? He say dog no have rabies."

Without questioning the monk's veterinary credentials, we all—including Ralph—seemed willing to accept this and walked into the chapel.

I wasn't prepared for what was inside: It was stunning. Every inch of the chapel's walls and columns, floor-to-ceiling, was covered with frescoes of saints, martyrs, biblical scenes, and benevolent royalty. We were spending so much time looking at the paintings that few noticed the votive candles burning on the floor in the front of the chapel. After giving us a few minutes to dry off, the monk stood behind the votives, which marked the grave of Dracula.

"Once you finish making the pictures . . . the monk . . . he wants to do his show for you, yes?" Radu said. "Come to the altar—but remember, please—"

"Don't step on the grave," Tim added.

"Yes, exactly."

Within a few minutes, we were all assembled in a semicircle around the monk and Radu, who stood next to each other on the opposite side of the grave. The grave itself was just a solid piece of stone in a cobblestone floor, set off by a thin border of white marble. Sitting on the gravestone was a tin relief of Vlad Dracula, the three votives, and a blue vase holding a few withered flowers.

The monk raised his arms and began to speak. Though his face remained expressionless, he spoke loudly and gestured a lot with his arms and hands. Being on this island in this fourteenth-century chapel with a monk dressed in full garb gives you an odd sense of time. It was almost as if we'd stepped back into another era by coming here. After a few sentences, he'd pause and Radu would translate.

Two things were pretty obvious. First, Radu was editing the monk's speeches. The monk would go on and on for a few minutes in Romanian, and then Radu would come back with something simple and short like "Many other members of Dracula family had ties to monastery, too." The second thing was that the monk obviously understood some English, because he'd occasionally interrupt Radu's translation and they'd have a sidebar argument over which version of the story to tell. Since none of us spoke Romanian, we all got Radu's interpretation by default. However, as I'd noticed several times during the trip, Radu's version of Dracula's history, both as a historical figure and as a literary character, was often way off base.

According to Radu (and, I assume, the monk), despite controversies over the years, there is now no doubt that Dracula was buried here at the foot of the church's altar and most of his remains are still there underneath the marker. I say "most" of his remains because, according to every version of this story, his head never made it into a grave.

Dracula was only seven weeks into his final go-round as ruler of

Wallachia and Transylvania* when he was ambushed by a group of his own men and killed a few miles from Snagov. The soldiers cut off Vlad's head to take to the Turkish sultan as proof of his death and then discarded his body, which was later found by some of the monks and brought to the monastery for burial. Coincidentally, regardless of circumstance, this was exactly where Vlad had hoped to be buried. It was common to bury royalty in remote locations to make it more difficult for conquerors, enemies, or vandals to mess with the remains.

The head went all the way to Istanbul, where it was impaled on a stick outside the city gates for six months. The sultan chose this location to display Dracula's head to demonstrate that Vlad was not the fulfillment of an Arabian legend that stated a dark prince would crash through the city gates and destroy the Ottoman Empire. Nobody has a clue what happened to the head after the six-month exhibit. There were some rumors that the sultan sent it back as a gift to some of Vlad's enemies, but it was lost or stolen in transit. It's nice to know that the postal service was about as dependable in the fifteenth century as it is today. Regardless, the head never resurfaced.

Despite Radu's assertions, the location of Dracula's grave is not a settled matter. From the time of Vlad's death in 1476 until the early twentieth century, the slab in front of the crazy monk and Radu was the undisputed location of Dracula's grave. Then, in 1931, the Romanian Commission on Historical Monuments commissioned an archeological investigation of the island, including Dracula's resting place. When the slab was removed, they did find evidence of a grave. However, once they cleared out the grave, all they found was the skeleton of a horse.

Once we got past the death and burial of Dracula and a quick inventory of his heinous crimes and valiant attempts to keep the

---

* Vlad ruled Wallachia on three different occasions during his life.

Turks out of Wallachia and Transylvania, the crazy monk lost interest in the story and let Radu take the lead.

Radu offered a theory about the horse bones that actually makes a lot of sense. It is common Romanian folklore that vampires morph into animals before exiting the grave and attacking their former friends and family. In one of several attacks on the monastery after Dracula's death, Radu hypothesized that Dracula's enemies opened the grave and put the horse bones in there to prove to future excavators that Vlad was evil and destined to be a vampire. Opening graves is pretty common in Romania, so it would have been a safe bet that the bones would have been discovered sooner or later.

Radu's certainty about the grave location was based on his assertion that the archeologists found a button, similar to one Dracula would have worn, buried with the horse bones. Even if this were the case, finding a button would pale in comparison to what the archeologists found along one of the side walls of the chapel.

While examining the foundation of the chapel's walls, they found a worn-down grave marker along the side wall just inside the current front entrance. When they dug it out, they found the rotted remnants of a coffin covered in purple cloth embroidered with gold. Inside was a headless skeleton, clothed in fragments of a yellow-brown silk and silver buttons. There were also several trinkets in the coffin and in the folds of the tattered clothing. All of these things could be loosely linked to Dracula. Short of a "Hello, my name is Vlad Dracula" name tag found among the remains, most historians are certain Vlad is buried along the wall, not in front of the altar. Yet many of the "buried by the altar" crowd just can't seem to accept that he probably isn't there. There are lots of theories about what happened. Most figure around someone moving the coffin to protect it from grave robbers and Vlad's enemies, or that the monks simply rethought burying such a notorious person in front of their altar. Throughout the twenty-minute narration, Radu never mentioned the grave found along the wall—and neither did I. As I did on several occasions during the tour, I just let some of this stuff slide.

As we prepared to leave, the rain started coming down in sheets again. All of us stood by the front door trying to strategize our path out through the rain, avoiding the dogs and snakes, in order to get to the boats, which were more than likely filled with water again. Once we realized there was no clear way to get through this without some sort of peril, we all meandered around the back of the chapel, gawking at frescoes and taking more pictures. I looked around for the other grave marker. It was right there against the wall—a solid slab with a very faint cross etched into the top. It was covered in wet footprints.

"Hey, what's happenin', man!?!" I heard a groggy voice from behind me exclaim.

"Butch!" I said. "Top of the afternoon to you!"

Butch Patrick had forsaken his "celebrity host" duties and slept through the whole monastery visit. When people started climbing back into the bus, Butch woke up, not entirely aware that the rest of us had stopped and gotten off hours before.

Our next stop was about an hour away, Bran Castle.

"Oh, that should be fun, I like castles," he said, as if that was somehow a revealing statement.

By Butch's own admission, his "celebrity host" role was ill-defined. In short, he was comped for the costs of the trip in exchange for using his name to promote the tour. Outside of his professional connection to vampires, Butch didn't seem very interested in Vlad Țepeș, Count Dracula, the sites we were visiting, or Romania for that matter. Butch had one objective for his Romanian vacation—partying. So far, despite a substantial effort, his results were slim.

Compared to other former child actors, Butch has things pretty well together. Despite being in his early fifties and best known for a role he played at age eleven, he seems comfortable with his place in pop history. He doesn't take himself too seriously and isn't a walking tragedy, cliché, or self-parody. He'll be the first to tell you that he starred in a timeless television series, but he also had smaller roles in six other shows, as well as sixteen movie roles, hundreds of commercials, and still works regularly today. He'll also be the first to tell you he loves to go barhopping, listen to music, and meet girls.

To kill time while we headed to the castle, and to keep his mind off his throbbing leg, I started quizzing Ralph about movies. At one point I pulled out my notebooks and shared a list of rare vampire movies that I'd read about but couldn't locate. Not only had Ralph seen almost every one, he could rattle off where I could find them.

"*Mark of the Vampire* . . . yeah, that's a hard one," Ralph said. "It's out on VHS and it shouldn't be tough to find a used copy—it's also on Turner Classic Movies a lot. *Brides of Dracula* . . . that's coming out on DVD in September as part of a box set. *Vampire Lovers* . . . that's the topless film, right? You can find copies of that on DVD as a double feature with *Countess Dracula*—both star Ingrid Pitt. Then there's the sequel, *Lust for a Vampire*, starring Yutte Stensgaard—the hottest vampire of them all, if you ask me. *Japula* . . . you can find that on eBay—same with *Dracula Sucks*. *Spermula*, *Rockula*, and *Gayracula*—what are those?"

"Vampire pornos," I said.

"Oh, I've never seen them but you can probably find dubbed copies online—you can probably find dubbed copies of any of these online. Louis Jourdan's version of *Dracula*, you can find import copies of that on tape . . . but they'll be PAL, not NTSC, you'll have to get them converted."

We piled out of the bus at the foot of Bran Castle, which is one of the most picturesque castles you'll ever see, due largely to the fact it was continuously occupied as a private residence from a renovation in 1622 until after World War II. It sits on top of a tall hill or small mountain, overlooking a tourist trap gypsy bazaar and the city of Bran. Many people mistakenly assume this was Dracula's castle because it has a tenuous connection to Vlad as well as having served as a set for several vampire movies.

As we walked through the castle, Radu pointed out an alcove and said that Vlad was held captive there for seven months following his second reign as ruler of Transylvania and Wallachia. That's a bit of a stretch. Dracula probably spent a few nights here as a captive while en route to a prison in Hungary, as well as some time here and there while he was ruler, but his collective presence is better measured in days rather than months.

The castle itself was different than you'd expect a Transylvanian castle to be. Far from the dark, dank, looming structure filled with cobwebs, rats, and armadillos,* this place is downright quaint. It has small cozy rooms, bright white walls, and breathtaking views.

"Now, Vlad Dracula, he stay here for a while, but his brother, Radu—called Radu the Handsome—he live here once, too," said Radu—our Radu, the tour guide, attempting to explain the apparent non sequitur from Bran Castle to Vlad Dracula to Radu the Handsome. "Now Radu the Handsome and Vlad Dracula both were held captive as children, yes? But Radu, he was corrupted and he sleeps with the men. Now, Bram Stoker, he was of the gays. And Radu the Handsome was of the gays, too. Bram Stoker knew this and was writing a gay book, *Dracula,* okay? Stoker, he wanted to name his book after Radu, but Radu is not a scary name—this I know, right? So Stoker, he reads about Radu's brother Dracula and uses the Dracula name for his gay book."

Everyone nods. Everyone except for Butch, who was leaning against the kitchen hearth and starting to fall asleep.

Of course, Radu's story is total bullshit.

However, I let this slide without saying a word. This might strike you as odd, but sometimes the pursuit of truth can be tire-

---

* I'm not kidding—watch *Dracula.* For some unexplained reason, there are armadillos running around the castle. Probably a low-budget attempt at surrealism.

some. Being a writer who deals with history is chilling work, sometimes leaving you with the impression that almost no fact can be trusted. You can have two people witness the same event, yet come away with completely different recollections of what happened. How do you know which is "true"? As anyone who has written about history can tell you, you spend most of your time sorting through the mistakes, shortcomings, misunderstandings, complete lack of effort, and lies of those who chronicled history before you. Some people were trying to make a point; others made innocent or sloppy mistakes. Try reading everything you can find about almost any given topic and you'll be shocked at how many errors and discrepancies you'll come across.

There is no shortage of debate over Bram Stoker's sexuality, with his biographers split on the issue. In addition to being almost impossible to prove (Stoker had no documented physical relationships with men and was very guarded in writing about himself), it's a nonsense discussion. Despite his orientation or physical relationships, there is no doubt that, at a minimum, Bram Stoker was in love with several men in his life. That doesn't mean that he had sex with them or even wanted to have sex with them. The "Bram as boy toy" theorists make the silly assumption that only a gay man can be in love with another man.

What's almost certain is that Stoker never heard of Radu the Handsome or even knew that Dracula had a brother. In fact, by the time you finish this chapter, you'll know more about Vlad Dracula than Stoker ever did. Stoker's research on Dracula was limited to one six-page German essay written and first printed in 1488. It was a collection of semi-accurate biographical anecdotes, a list of some of the heinous stuff he did, and a final entry about how he was redeemed by baptism and did many good deeds (convenient for the monks, but untrue—he was baptized, but for political reasons). While our Radu can offer all the rationalization he likes, Stoker picked Dracula simply because he liked the name.

After a quick trip through the bazaar and a bus ride to the city of Brasov, we checked into our hotel for the night and set out for dinner. By this time, the group was starting to get to know one an-other and dinners felt more like parties . . . including wine. Lots of wine. And for vegetarian Elaina, cucumbers and tomatoes. Which led to the late-night pizza. All this led to a progression of pukers on the road to Sighișoara.

"Now, you may recognize this place, okay?" said Radu, gesturing across the city square in the center of Brasov. "It in very famous woodcut showing Vlad. He eating his lunch among impaled bodies, yes? This is it, where Vlad would impale hundreds of the bodies."

While it is true that Vlad had a big thing for impaling, it didn't happen here. Vlad's city square full of impaled bodies (depicted in the aforementioned woodcut) happened in Targoviste, on the other side of the Transylvanian Alps, where Vlad had his main castle and spent most of his time. However, Targoviste wasn't on our tour itinerary, Brasov was.

Radu was giving a quick walking tour before we headed to Sighișoara. It was early, so the full effects of the previous night's pizza and wine hadn't kicked in yet.

Despite its lack of a corpse-filled square, Brasov does represent an important facet in understanding why Dracula became such an incredibly violent and ruthless ruler. During Dracula's lifetime, Brasov was one of several independent Saxon city-states inside Transylvania, mainly set up to aid trade from Asia to Europe. While not under the country's rule, these city-states could make or break a candidate for the throne. Get in good with the city-states, and you had the power of Europe and the Catholic Church behind you. On the other extreme were the Turks. Wallachia and Transyl-vania were just one battle away from being swallowed by the Ot-toman Empire. The key to success for any Romanian ruler was to keep both the Europeans and the Ottomans content to leave him alone.

The Europeans weren't interested in ruling Romania, just in

keeping a friend in power. The throne of Wallachia (and Transylvania) didn't follow family lines like most monarchies. Instead, the boyars would get together and elect a prince—like a board of directors electing a chairman. That prince would stay in power until the nobles decided to replace him. As you can imagine, that was quite often. In the three decades before Dracula's rule, the average tenure of a Wallachian prince was just two years.

Dracula's first go-round as prince occurred when he was seventeen, and lasted all of two months. At the time, Dracula was a stranger in his own land. When he was a child, he and his brother Radu* were given as hostages to the Turkish sultan by their father, Vlad Dracul. They were collateral to ensure Dracul's loyalty to the sultan. Less than a year later, knowing it would likely mean the torture and death of his two sons, Dracul allied with the Catholics for the crusades of 1443. The boys weren't tortured or killed. Instead, they remained captives among the Turks under the constant fear of death.

Despite being sold out by his father at age eleven and raised without a family, things got even weirder for Dracula from there. He lived among the Turks for seven years until his father's assassination. Despite their past, Dracula vowed to take revenge for Dracul's death, gathered some Turkish troops, and took the throne of Wallachia. He was quickly deposed by the same Hungarian army he defeated two months earlier, and then he fled to Moldavia. Dracula stayed in hiding for a few years, eventually allied with his father's killer (despite his earlier vow to kill him), and worked his way up through the ranks of power, eventually taking over his father's old position as a member of the Order of the Dragon. Then, in 1456, he was elected as ruler of Wallachia and Transylvania a second time.

In trying to strike a balance between the Turks on one side, and the Saxons, Hungarians, Europeans, and both the Catholic and

---

* A.k.a. Radu the Handsome, a.k.a. the gay one.

Roman Orthodox churches on the other, Dracula came up with a philosophy that would guide him in all decisions, as well as cement his role in history. Vlad made a conscious effort to rule by fear. His tactic: Vlad always wanted to be the craziest motherfucker in the room. He wanted to be perceived as so insane that no rival, inside or outside the country, would dare go up against him. Dracula had one method for dealing with his problems, large and small—death.

Vlad realized early in his tenure that in order to control the country, he had to control the boyar class. Within a few weeks of Dracula taking the throne, one of the most powerful boyars tried to organize a revolt. When Dracula found out about it, he had the boyar impaled, along with all the members of his family. The following spring, Dracula organized a huge feast for all the boyars at his castle in Targoviste. After finishing the meal, he had all his potential rivals and their wives taken outside and impaled. The remaining guests, including women and children, were marched fifty miles away to Poenari, where they became slave laborers on the construction of a new castle. During another attempt to root out a resistance movement in Transylvania, Dracula raided the town of Amlas and had the entire town impaled.

Vlad came to appreciate impalement while growing up among the Turks. Impalement, like many forms of torture, was then considered an art form, and Dracula was obsessed with perfecting it. A proper impalement pierced the body without damaging any of the internal organs, so the impalee would die slowly and painfully, usually from blood loss. Dracula experimented with all kinds of variations, entering and exiting the body at various points, even using multiple stakes or combining impalement with other forms of torture. He was so fascinated by the process that he'd often sit and study the victims while they died, even taking in a meal during the process. Once a servant bringing Dracula's meal complained of the smell. Dracula ordered the servant impaled on a thirty-foot stake so he would be above the stench.

But Dracula didn't limit himself to impaling. To punish the deserving he also decapitated, burned, buried alive, skinned, lynched, strangled, crucified, nailed, roasted, forced cannibalism, and cut off ears, noses, genitals, and limbs.

Most important of all, Dracula wanted nothing about himself to be predictable or expected. Once, in an unusual display of derision, some of Vlad's remaining political rivals complained at the number of poor and sick. After hearing their complaints, Vlad sent out word that he would host a banquet at a large hall for all of the country's sick, lame, poor, and blind. Thousands came, ate heavily, and became very drunk. Once the event was winding down, Vlad had the hall sealed shut and burned to the ground, killing everyone inside. As Vlad saw it—poverty problem solved.

Despite this, Vlad had a decidedly "pro-peasant" stance, mostly due to the fact that 90 percent of the country lived outside the cities. While he tried to control the boyars through intimidation, he often tried to ingratiate himself to the masses by dismantling the feudal system and ridding the country of most crime.

During Dracula's reign, petty crime was practically unheard of. Dracula had a habit of judging criminals himself—with most ending up on top of a stake. All told, estimates by historians of the number of civilians killed by Dracula range wildly from a minimum of 20,000 to an improbable 100,000. While he wasn't in the same league as Pol Pot, Stalin, or Hitler, it's all relative. Even given the most conservative figures, that still means that Dracula killed the equivalent of 4 percent of his country's population during his six-year reign.

When it came to international diplomacy, he wasn't much better.

During one attempt to make nice with Dracula, the sultan sent some diplomats to visit Vlad. When they arrived, Dracula asked why they did not remove their turbans in the presence of royalty. The diplomats answered that it was a religious thing—they were never supposed to remove their turbans. Vlad said he understood. He then ordered his men to nail the turbans to the diplomats' heads and sent them back to Istanbul.

When Dracula had discovered that a group of forty-one Saxon exchange students had been sent to Wallachia to learn the Romanian language, he had them impaled, assuming they were spies. When a Saxon diplomat arrived to try to smooth things over with Dracula, Vlad threatened him with impalement, too. Finally, one of Vlad's rivals, with the support of the Saxons, mounted an unsuccessful offensive against Dracula. Afterward, Dracula forced the rival to dig his own grave and buried him alive.

The Pope and European leaders turned their heads from Vlad's brutality—mainly because it was working. They all knew that if Dracula could keep Wallachia and Transylvania safe and stable, the rest of Europe wouldn't have to worry about Ottoman expansion.

Throughout his reign, Dracula's relationship with the Turks had deteriorated as he positioned Romania as the last bastion of Christianity. After a failed kidnapping plot against him in 1461, Dracula knew it was only a matter of time until the Ottoman armies arrived. With an army a fraction of that of the Turks, Dracula drafted every person he could find, including women and children, and set out to meet the Turks. Dracula attempted a variety of tactics to weaken the Ottomans while drawing them into Wallachia. Dracula made the first use of germ warfare by sending people infected with the plague, leprosy, and syphilis into the Turkish camps. He also led a scorched-earth campaign, destroying crops, livestock, and entire villages, to make it difficult for the Turks to find provisions along their invasion route. Dracula drew them all the way to Targoviste, where he had laid out a surprise for them. As the sultan's troops approached Targoviste, they saw a picket fence of impaled bodies surrounding the entire city—all Turkish troops captured in other battles. The miles of dead soldiers looked like they had been mercilessly tortured and brutalized while dying from their impalements.

There were twenty thousand of them.

In total shock, the sultan's troops refused to fight, and retreated back out of the country.

While this might seem like a home run for Dracula, it was actually the beginning of his undoing. With the Turks sent packing and order and peace restored to Wallachia and Transylvania, Dracula's subjects lost patience with his brutality. Within five months, all his support had been drained away by his brother, Radu the Handsome, who returned to Wallachia for the first time since being sent away as a child hostage at the age of seven.

Dracula was taken prisoner and remained so for more than a dozen years, eventually retaking the throne for his third and final time after Radu the Handsome died of syphilis.

SIGHIȘOARA IS KIND of a letdown as a tourist stop, though the locals are doing their best to deliver. Once you arrive in town, walk to the center section of the city, and look at Dracula's birthplace . . . that's about it. Five minutes, tops.

We burned off some time at a local rinky-dink "torture museum" and then witnessed a reenacted witch trial—entirely in Romanian— before we headed out of town to our overnight stop. The plan was for dinner on our own, but everyone ended up at the same outdoor café.

"Do you have ketchup? Do you have *Heinz* ketchup? Do you use cheese? Like real cheese? You don't use goat cheese, do you?"

The waitress looked understandably confused. We had just found out that she spoke "a little" English, which sent Elaina into an eruption of rapid-fire questions. It was apparent that the waitress's English seemed limited to the pizza toppings and little else.

"Cheese? You . . . want . . . cheese?" the waitress asked.

"Only mozzarella. Not that goat cheese. Regular cheese. Like Pizza Hut. Oh, man! There isn't a Pizza Hut here, is there?" Elaina said, without waiting for an answer before moving on to her next question.

"Elaina, stop it, we'll take care of it," Brad scolded.

"Hello," I said, as slowly and kindly as I could. "I think we'd like two pizzas, one with—"

"What is your bruschetta like? Is it like American bruschetta? How about dessert? *Do you have dessert!?!*"

Elaina was practically screaming at the waitress. We managed to calm her down and point to the pizzas we wanted on the menu.

Elaina was on edge. When she and Brad had come out to dinner tonight, all the tables were full. No one even suggested they pull up chairs. I offered to start a new table with them and we went over to a table on the other side of the room.

"Everyone on this tour hates me," Elaina said as we waited for the waitress to give us menus. "Why is that? We're not the only ones who've been late."

Technically, that is correct—one other time we couldn't find Huge and Jeanette. Another time, we thought we'd lost Butch, but he was asleep in the back of the bus. However, Elaina and Brad had been late every single day.

Elaina seemed like an oversensitive person prone to read the worst in the actions of others. However, this time, her paranoia wasn't that far from the truth. Several members of the group were quietly petitioning Radu to leave them behind. They were slowing down the rest of the group. Having to find their own way to the next city would teach them a lesson. Someone wondered out loud if they'd be better off just going home.

"You know, tomorrow is another day," I said. "We're leaving tomorrow at 10:00 A.M. Just make sure you're the first ones downstairs."

When I came down the next morning, there they were: Smiles on their faces, suitcases in hand, and ready to go fifteen minutes early. We waited around for the others to join us. About five minutes before we left, Elaina looked to Brad and said, "If we are going to be out in the sunshine today, I need to get some sunglasses."

With that, she started to run down the street. Brad chased behind her. The rest of us stood there and watched them disappear around the corner. Not sure what to do, Radu decided we'd take an impromptu walking tour. By the time we got back to the hotel, Elaina and Brad were there waiting.

"Where the hell were you guys?" Elaina exclaimed. "We were just gone for a few minutes. We were the first ones down this morning, you know."

No one even responded to her.

As we headed for the bus, I heard someone calling my name. It was Butch, who'd forgone the walking tour and set up shop in a beer garden with Julian.* Sitting with him were three young women. As I walked up, I could hear Butch talking with them.

"Hey, have you ever seen *The Munsters* on TV before?" he asked.

"Yah," a young Swedish girl replied.

"Well, I'm Eddie Munster."

The young girl sat silently for a few seconds.

"You are not Eddie Munster," she declared.

"No, I am. I am Eddie Munster."

She laughed a bit, then repeated, "No, you are not him. You are not Eddie Munster."

"No, I am," Butch said, looking mildly shocked and annoyed. "I'm the actor who played Eddie Munster. Eric, tell her."

"He's Eddie Munster," I replied.

The girl and her friends kept laughing. It was time to get back, so I started down to the bus. As I walked away, I could still hear the sound of laughing girls and Butch back at the beer garden.

"What's so funny? I am . . . it's me! Eddie Munster!"

※

I FIGURE IT's a pretty safe bet that if any body part becomes purplish black, it should be taken as bad news. Two nights earlier, the hotel we were staying in wasn't air-conditioned, so I opened the window to let in some fresh air. I woke up the next morning with eight mosquito bites, including one on my left thumb. And yes,

---

* Time check: 10:45 A.M.

ha-ha-ha, I'm sure it was a *mosquito* that bit me, ha-ha-ha.* Vampires have been known to attack their victims on the chest, wrist, tongue, and neck—but I've never read of an undead bloodsucker who preferred to draw from an opposable digit.

I didn't think much about the bites until the following day, when I noticed a distinct change in the color of my thumb, with hints of yellow, black, and blue appearing in the swollen pink, almost as if it were a bruise. If I was home in Washington, I wouldn't have considered this a big deal. But here in the most rural parts of central Romania, the consequences could be dire. I remembered a coworker who told me that after her son passed out during a trip to Romania, the local doctors wanted to perform surgery—for high blood pressure. Shortly before the vampire tour, Ralph had applied for life insurance. He aced the physical and other screeners, but saw his quote double when he mentioned he planned to take a vacation to Romania. Still nursing his dog-bitten leg, I'm sure he was thinking a lot of the same things I was.

As the bus climbed through the mountains, all I could think about was infection spreading through my body, forcing me to go to see a doctor who didn't speak the same language, perhaps be admitted to a hospital (for God knows what treatment), and have to beg off the rest of the tour. In my racing mind, the Marines would have to stage a Jessica Lynch–style rescue mission to save me from imminent torture and cruelty.

As the day went on, I checked on it about every ten minutes. As much as I wanted to deny it, the bite was getting puffier and darker. Despite my usual level of travel fussiness, the only quasimedicinal items I packed were one Band-Aid, half a bottle of Tums, and the hand sanitizer Katherine wanted me to pack. The one Band-Aid was starting to look worse than the bite itself and the sanitizer (of questionable medicinal value, I know) had run out a few days ago.

---

* I suffered through that witty joke no less than eleven times, usually after answering the question, "What the fuck happened to your thumb?"

If it got worse, I'd be especially bummed, because I'd miss the next stage of the tour; the part that I'm sure everyone came here for—a trip through the Carpathian Mountains, retracing the steps of the characters in Stoker's *Dracula*.

In *Dracula*, Jonathan Harker arrives in the city of Bistrita via train. Count Dracula had instructed him to stay in the Golden Crown Hotel upon arriving in the city, where Harker had a dinner of Robber Steak, cheese, salad, and wine. He then spent the better part of the next two days traveling through the Borgo Pass to Count Dracula's castle high in the Carpathians. While Stoker didn't know much about Dracula, and not much more about Transylvania, he was a meticulous researcher about the train and sea voyages taken by his characters. In his notes for the novel, Stoker completely mapped out Harker's initial trip to Transylvania and back, as well as the characters' rush back to Transylvania at the end of the book to kill Count Dracula. Stoker's itineraries even included departure and arrival times, train numbers, and approximate costs. While he had no problem offering an undead fifteenth-century prince who can turn into mist and alter weather as his novel's villain, Stoker didn't want to push believability by thinking someone caught an uncannily quick connection in Rome.

After a day filled with more old churches, more quaint towns, more pine-covered mountains, and more clay roofs, we arrived at the Golden Crown Hotel in Bistrita and made plans to hook up an hour later for dinner. The quite modern-looking Golden Crown we stayed in probably wasn't around in 1987, let alone 1887, but that didn't dampen the enthusiasm of the highly excited vampire geeks.

"I can't believe we're actually here," I heard one exclaim.

When they started to notice the built-in plumbing, central air, and pictures of the original Golden Crown Hotel in the lobby (which bore no resemblance to this place whatsoever), they began to rationalize.

"Well, perhaps it's been renovated."

"Maybe it's the original owners!"

Whatever.

The hotel's restaurant was decorated with some cheap, hand-made wooden coats of arms, a portrait of Dracula, and about two dozen taxidermied animals. There were your standard stuffed fare: deer, wolf, and elk. However, this collection also included squirrels, wild birds, a ferret, and what I thought might be a house cat.

"It is lynx," the waitress said when she saw me staring at it. I'd seen lynx before. Well, I'd seen a lynx on television before. Regardless, a lynx does look just like a cat, but it's about four times the size. While a lynx can be four feet long and weigh forty-five pounds, this little fella was maybe eight or nine pounds before he was stuffed. Further, lynx have very pointy ears and a bobtail—this wall-mounted feline here had normal cat ears and a long tail.

"That's a cat," I replied.

"No, lynx," she replied with a smile.

"No, you have a stuffed cat on your wall."

"Lynx . . . cat . . ." she said before shrugging her shoulders and moving on.

The next morning we all met up in front of the Golden Crown to begin our trek through the Borgo Pass. Well, everyone except Elaina and Brad. They were late, again.

Fifteen minutes outside of Bistrita, Elaina screamed, "Pull over the bus! Pull over the bus!" We couldn't stop. Taking a full-size bus through these roads was distressing enough, but pulling over was just asking for a car to eventually round a corner and plow into us. Over the next half hour, Elaina threw up all over herself as well as the bus's aisle, back stairwell, and rest room. She then curled up in their seat, leaving Brad to try cleaning up the mess with a handful of napkins. When she started to feel better, she immediately started complaining about having nothing in her stomach, then immediately devoured a bag of Doritos, washing it down with Pepsi.

We eventually found a convenience store and pulled in for a break. The bus driver unsuccessfully tried to clean up the remaining mess, then sprayed some "air freshener" around the bus to cover the smell. The industrial faux-clean smell was so pungent that I would have rather stuck with the mild annoyance of the vomit smell. While Elaina was inside the gas station rest room puking up the Doritos and Pepsi, Jeanette started talking about taking up a collection for Elaina and Brad to take a taxi— preferably back to Bucharest. Elaina overheard her and confronted her in the parking lot.

"We paid just as much to be here as you did!" Elaina screamed.

"Yes, but you are ruining this for everyone!" Jeanette yelled back. "I don't know why you don't take a taxi back to Bucharest so you can eat pizza or whatever it is you do."

"I don't know why all you old ladies on this tour hate me, but I've done nothing to you. I know you're talking about me all the time. I can tell. I can tell."

By this time, Huge, Radu, and Brad had managed to keep them apart and get everyone back on the bus. Elaina got sick a few more times, this time into the grocery bags they'd gotten from the convenience store. After each hurl, she'd eat some of the candy bars, potato chips, or licorice she bought at the store.

It seemed that every time Elaina got ill on the bus, it opened a floodgate of discontent among my fellow travelers.

"Why aren't these castles scary? We haven't been to anyplace spooky at all. You'd think Romania would have scary castles or something."

"Have you tried the toilet paper here? They should call it ass-shredding paper."

"Do these people ever eat anything that isn't covered in paprika?"

"The men here have no tact—I've never had more men blatantly stare at my tits."

"I want to know who kept farting in the bar last night. I don't know what they had eaten, but it definitely wasn't cucumbers and tomatoes."

To avoid the drama playing out around me, I leaned my head against the window and looked out into the Borgo Pass.

When you see a movie adaptation of *Dracula*, they always show the Borgo Pass as a rock-hewn, dark, foreboding passage winding through narrow roads along deadly cliffs. In reality, it couldn't be more different. The Borgo Pass is actually quite idyllic. There are farms, tiny collections of houses, pastures and streams running through rolling hills that butt up against tall mountains. Far from being menacing or harrowing, the Borgo Pass was one of the most beautiful and serene places I'd ever been in my life.

Still, there were little reminders of where we were. More than once, we'd drive past a small country house with garlic hanging in the window. The whole garlic thing with vampires can be confusing. Like so many things about vampire lore and culture, it doesn't seem to have one origin, but many. Tradition says that garlic repels vampires. If a potential victim wears garlic around their neck, strings it over windows and doors, or rubs it on surfaces around them, they're safe. Also, it was common to stick garlic into the mouths of the recently departed to ensure they wouldn't return as vampires. It was thought that a vampire chewed their way out of the grave, so stuffing their mouth with garlic would make it impossible for them to leave their grave. The real question is why people thought this was effective. I mean, why stuff a mouth with garlic? Wouldn't a rock be even more efficient?

Garlic has a heap of holistic lore tied to it—thought to be a cure for heart disease, snoring, acne, fungal infections, high blood pressure, even cancer, impotency, and AIDS. Unlike most miracle substances, garlic's rep may be well earned. Medical research has shown that garlic does stimulate our immune defenses, blocks enzymes that help bacteria reproduce, helps purify blood, and can cut the risk of catching a cold in half.

A recent theory about garlic's connection to vampirism involves rabies. Anthropologists have theorized that some elements of vampire lore can be linked to rabies outbreaks in Hungary and Romania during the eighteenth century. It often manifests itself days or weeks after infection, so the symptoms aren't always linked to the correct source. To make matters worse, often by the time a victim starts showing symptoms of rabies, it's too late to help them.

Like many things, when no rational explanation for rabies presented itself, the eighteenth-century Eastern Europeans just made one up. Vampires had been blamed for everything from impotence to birth defects; why not pile on rabies too?

The resemblances to vampires were pretty obvious. Rabies attacks the limbic system, the part of the brain that affects aggression and sexual behavior. Rabies also affects the hypothalamus, which controls sleep, and can cause facial spasms. As a result, you'd see zombielike people running around at night baring their teeth while trying to bite and/or hump others. Rabies victims develop hydrophobia (an aversion to water, which also causes them to avoid swallowing), and vomit blood, so it wouldn't be unusual for rabies victims to have foam and blood around their mouth. Rabies also causes victims to avoid bright light, mirrors, and strong smells, especially garlic. And worse of all, those they attack would eventually succumb to rabies themselves. Adding further to vampire diagnoses, when someone dies of rabies, like those who die of shock or asphyxiation, their blood is slow to clot and thus, decompose.

After an hour of climbing through the mountains, we reached the top of Borgo Pass. When Bram Stoker was deciding where to place Dracula's castle, he knew there was a medieval castle located at the top of Borgo Pass. In *Dracula*, Jonathan Harker arrives at the castle via stagecoach, meets the count, then is held captive there for several months as Count Dracula plots his move to London.

While the actual Dracula had never lived in the Borgo Pass castle, Vlad did give it as a present to an ally. So the location did have a Dracula connection (albeit a thin one). For most of the past few hundred years, the castle was little more than a few partial walls and a pile of rubble. In another example of Romania's odd perspective on historical preservation, an entrepreneur bought the property in 1976 and decided to build a hotel there. He didn't build his tourist trap next to the ruins or in the proximity of the ruins, but literally *on* the ruins. The resulting Hotel Castle Dracula has sixty-four rooms, a Turkish bath, a restaurant, a bar (located in the castle tower), and a basement wine cellar–meeting room known as Dracula's Vault. The older parts of the castle are easy to pick out. The original rough stone walls stand out in contrast to the bright white of the newer construction.

The view from the castle is even more striking than the trip through the Pass. There are more farms, rolling hills, and even in July you can spot snow on top of the nearby mountains. A hotel brochure written in broken English claims the Hotel Castle Dracula is "the ideal place for the both nature and comfort lovers." It goes on to promote the medicinal benefits of the area: "The region has a tonic, stimulating climate and a strong ozonized air with the highest level of iodine from Romanian. This and other natural factors create a unique healing environment for the exhausted persons, hyperthyroidism convalescents, Basedov illness invalids, improving the general health condition."

After making a note to look up Basedov illness when I got home,* I settled in for a nap. Tonight was the "big costume party in Dracula's castle" and the group was already abuzz with preparations.

Both the brochure about the trip and our pretrip itineraries mentioned the costume party and advised that we bring everything we needed. I just couldn't motivate myself to think of a costume. I suck at costumes. I always rack my brain for weeks trying to think of a costume just to settle on the worst idea that crosses my mind and/or come up with a costume idea that nobody understands. I usually spend an exorbitant amount of time trying to explain my Halloween costumes.

My first idea was to dress up as a George Foreman Grill. This was a Halloween costume idea I'd been sitting on for quite some time. I figured I could cut some white foam rubber into a clamshell shape, decorate it, and wear it like a sandwich board.

"And get this," I said, when trying to sell the concept to Katherine before leaving on the trip. "I cut out a foam rubber chicken

---

* It's a thyroid disease, like Graves' disease, that causes hyperthyroidism. The symptoms include irregular heart rhythms, diarrhea, profuse sweating, and eyelid retraction.

breast and glue it to my shirt, that way when I opened the lid, there'd be food in the George Foreman Grill!"

"So . . . you want to dress up as a George Foreman Grill to go to a costume party at Dracula's castle in Romania?" she said.

"Yes, a grill with a big chicken breast hidden inside."

"This grill will cover your entire body," she said.

"Yes, and I—and the chicken—will be inside under the lid."

"So this grill is cooking you, too?"

"No," I replied, starting to get annoyed that she was getting so hung up on details that she couldn't grasp the genius of this costume idea. "I'll be hidden inside."

"Oh," she replied—pretending to get it. "So tell me, how do you intend to get this giant George Foreman Grill to Romania?"

That was a good question. I hadn't thought about that. In fact, that one question nixed the George Foreman Grill idea for good.

I came back a few days later with a new idea.

"How about I go to the Dracula party as . . . a fried egg?"

I had anticipated the look on Katherine's face.

"Listen, it's so simple," I explained. "I can cut a circle out of yellow felt and then attach it to a white T-shirt. If I wear white shorts with it—I'll look like a fried egg."

"No," Katherine replied. "You'll look ridiculous."

Over the ten years Katherine and I had been together, she had developed this knack for killing off my bad ideas with the exactness of a jujitsu master—a simple and powerful action best measured in syllables rather than sentences or paragraphs. I tabled the costume issue until it was too late for options.

When I first signed up for the tour, I asked Kitty about this and she said that the gypsy bazaars had all the capes, fake teeth, makeup, and squirty blood I could ever want. With her encouragement, I decided to wing it.

The hotel felt like a girl's dormitory on the night of the big cotillion: the buzz of hair dryers, people running back and forth between rooms carrying bits and pieces of clothing, doors quickly closed to prevent a premature view. I stepped out and headed down the hill to a small collection of gypsy stands to check out my options.

I found a glow-in-the-dark vampire mask that cost two dollars. I had a momentary pause about having this potentially toxic mask touching my skin for a prolonged period, but I was a little desperate.

By the time I got back to the hotel lobby, most everyone was gathered together. There were no less than ten vampires, a Beetlejuice, two devils, a handful of witches, a few pirates, a Swedish maiden, and a Cher. Butch wasn't wearing any costume. Natalie, a college-age girl from Utah, was wearing a full-length velvet gothic dress with four-foot black feather-covered wings. I kept staring at her, not because she looked particularly scary or attractive, but I just couldn't imagine how she had managed to get those wings inside her suitcase.

For many women, Halloween is an opportunity to wear all the skimpy, low-cut clothing that they have too much self-respect to wear the rest of the year. This evening's events were no different. Instead of witches, vampires, or devils, most of our ladies were dressed up as slutty witches, slutty vampires, and slutty devils. And like every Halloween party you've ever been to, all my tourmates spent the next half hour acting out their costumes for the polite amusement of the others.

Our festivities started when a three-piece Romanian folk ensemble started playing in the lobby and led us outside and down the hillside to a huge bonfire.

The band, consisting of clarinet, accordion, and a woman who sang occasionally but mostly just stood around looking bored, continued playing as people stood around watching the fire. Whatever creepy mood should have been in place—this being a Halloween party after all—was completely killed by the folk ensemble, who were cranking out these little up-tempo polka ditties one after another. It didn't match the occasion at all—kind of like watching KISS perform Raffi songs.

The bonfire led to dinner, which led to a DJ playing Halloween staples like "Monster Mash," "Bad Moon Rising," and the theme from *Ghostbusters*. As the music segued into 50 Cent and "Thriller"—everyone got out on the dance floor. As the empty Vampire brand wine bottles started piling up, the assembled vampires, devils, and pirates transformed into shit-faced vampires, devils, and pirates. By the time the DJ fired up Don Henley's "All She Wants to Do Is Dance," all my tourmates were on the dance floor, jerking around and singing. Two more cases of wine later, we'd enjoyed not one but two conga lines, a dance circle, and Radu jumping up to belt out, word for word, Queen's "I Want to Break Free."

Judging by the folks gathering beside our bus the next morning, you would have thought they were a group of zombie enthusiasts: blank stares, gray complexions, slow aimless motions, and lots of grunting. Everyone looked tired, hungover, and just about done with all this vampire nonsense. For the first time in a week, people started to talk about their kids, pets, and jobs.

There was only one more stop on our way back to Bucharest to start our journey back home—Vlad Dracula's castle at Poenari. Radu had repeatedly warned us that there was one tiny complication we'd encounter getting to Dracula's castle. Actually, there were 1,500 tiny complications.

"The castle, it is on top of mountain, yes?" explained Radu. "To get up, we take the stairs. Many, many stairs." During Radu's previous warnings about Poenari, as well as my pretrip reading, I'd heard various numbers bandied about—1,000 . . . 1,400 . . . 1,500. We kind of blew off the warning about getting to the castle. After having dealt with dogs, sinking boats, and floods—bring on the damn steps.

When we arrived, Radu lined us up outside the bus and pointed to a barely visible structure that seemed to be closer to the moon than to us.

"If you look up there, you can see castle," he said. "Now we walk up stairs, right? We have a contest—first person to top wins prize, okay?"

Fourteen hundred stairs . . . fifteen hundred stairs—it didn't matter. By the time I had cleared the first seventy-five, I could barely breathe and I could feel my heartbeat in my eyelids. I wasn't alone; everyone was red-faced, panting, and filled with excuses as to why it was so hard.

"It's the elevation . . . how far up are we?"

"Oh . . . I had knee surgery once."

"Man, I shouldn't have eaten eggs for breakfast . . . heavy breakfasts slow me down."

In hindsight, for a group of unabashed vampire enthusiasts to have trouble with such a physical task shouldn't have surprised anyone. Instead of wondering who'd make it to the top first, I was wondering who would be the first to give up and head back down.

After almost an hour of constant stair climbing, I was number eight to the top. Who won? Butch. Almost as soon as Radu issued the challenge, Butch shot up the stairs and stayed so far ahead of us that we forgot that he'd gotten off the bus to join us. Much to everyone's surprise, all of us made it to the top. Even Elaina, who chose to wear heels that day.

We were so busy congratulating ourselves and trying to catch our breath that it took us a few minutes to notice the view from the top of the mountain. The castle was at one of the highest points in the Transylvanian Alps. You could see miles in every direction. To the east, you could see all the way to the Danube River.

You could see why Vlad chose this location for one of his castles. This location was all about strategy. He kept his family and valuables here, only staying here himself when he was in trouble.

This is the castle that Dracula built with the boyar slaves who'd survived the slaughter of their friends, husbands, and fathers, and then were marched here from Targoviste to carry bricks and supplies up the mountain. They were kept here for nine months; many didn't survive. Dracula himself experienced tragedy here as well. When he lost control of the country to his brother, Radu the Handsome, word of his capture reached the castle. Except by the time it reached Poenari castle, the rumor was that Vlad had been killed. Assuming she'd soon be raped, killed, or made a slave, his wife jumped to her death, falling from the castle tower to the river below.

When we judge Vlad against twenty-first-century values, things get sticky. It's the same way when examining Thomas Jefferson's slave ownership or the rights of women in Muslim countries. Our way of looking at the world is just too different to pass clear judgment. While Vlad's reign was gruesome, there were dozens of other rulers who've worked from the same playbook. Regardless of how you view Dracula's tactics, it's hard to discount the fact that, with little resources, he managed to make the world's largest army turn around and leave rather than fight him.

In Romania, Vlad remained little more than a fairy tale for hundreds of years after his death. Interest in him wasn't revived by Bram Stoker commandeering his name. In fact, Romanians have very little interest in Dracula as a pop culture figure. Of the forty-five languages that Stoker's novel has been translated into, Romanian wasn't one of them until just a couple years ago. Romanians know the vampire stuff brings in tourists, but among locals, vampires are a rather routine subject. Interest in Vlad was resuscitated by the Communists. Nicolae Ceauşescu (the only Eastern Bloc leader to be executed by his own people following the collapse of Communism) lauded Vlad as a national hero for keeping the Ottomans at bay and protecting Romania from becoming a Turkish province.

Before heading down the mountain, Radu gathered us together for a group picture. Looking at the picture now, there's a happy look of accomplishment on our faces. It wasn't just satisfaction at climbing the mountain, but in making it through the whole trip. My thumb was even starting to look better after I somehow negotiated clean Band-Aids and antibiotic cream from a pharmacist who didn't speak English.

As we started down the mountain, I heard Elaina calling after Radu.

"Like, do you know where we're staying tonight?"

"Yes, ah, tonight we go to Bucharest. Same hotel as when first you come, okay?"

"Excellent," I heard Elaina proclaim. "Pizza Hut."

IV

PULLING OUT THE FEATHERS FIRST

As our story continues, the author searches for the hidden meaning of Friends, *sees sixteen breasts, and is rocked like a hurricane.*

I t was my dad who first told me about *Bite.*

"You know, they have an adult revue in Vegas about vampires," he offered, almost managing to suppress the smile on his face. "If you are interested in going, I'd be happy to go along with you."

I jumped into the other room to do some quick online research and learned that, yes, there was a topless show in Las Vegas called *Bite.* At least two other times that evening, my dad offered to attend the show with me.

My father is a great guy and I love him a lot, but there was no way in hell that I was going to attend an adult revue with my dad. There are lots of fun things to do with dads: fishing, baseball games, carrying heavy things for Mom, lawn work—the list goes on and on. However, nowhere on that list is staring at naked breasts. Going to a topless show with him just felt creepy. Once I'd heard about it, there was no doubt that I was going—the question was how to deal with Dad.

"Why can't your dad come? When did breasts become creepy?" asked Katherine, who had already decided she was coming too.

"Okay, imagine this," I offered. "You're sitting there watching this show, then you look over at your father-in-law and you see a big grin on his face."

"Ew. Okay, maybe it isn't such a good idea."

Still, I felt if I turned Dad down, he'd be heartbroken.

I brought it up with a few friends, and there were definite camps on both sides of the Dad issue. My friend Patricia headed the "pro-Dad" contingency.

"He told you about it, didn't he?" she reasoned. "Well then, he deserves a finder's fee. Not only should he go, but you should pay for his ticket."

Patricia didn't buy the smiling-Dad theory either.

"Wait a minute, you mean to tell me that there is any chance that you'd be sitting in front of a group of naked women . . . and you'd be watching your dad? I think that's far creepier than letting him go."

I had to give her that one.

This went on for another two weeks, with my father eagerly re-offering to join me every time we spoke. Then his interest was dealt a savage blow. The show started at 10:30 P.M. Even worse, 10:30 P.M. *Vegas time.* My parents are early risers and are usually asleep in their recliners before 9:15. My dad probably hadn't seen 10:30 P.M. since 1978. Not even the promise of naked girls could keep him awake that long. For a minute, I think Dad weighed the possibility of going to bed, then waking up early to attend the show, but alas, the curtain time was a deal-killer.

Before leaving for Vegas, I had gone on a vampire movie binge. Despite all my efforts, my movie viewing total was barely more than eighty and I knew I'd have to seriously ramp things up if I was to have any chance of working through the entire list.

I was watching vampire movies in the morning before work, in the evening before bed, and at least two a day on weekends. In just the few days before we left for Vegas, I'd watched *Bloodsucking Redneck Vampires, House of Dracula, Dracula Has Risen From the Grave, Dracula Rising, The Return of the Vampire, Dracula* (the 1979 Frank Langella version), and *Horror of Dracula.* Basically, if you wanted to be around me during that period, you'd better be prepared to watch some vampire movies. Even though I'd felt like the last embers of my social life were slowly fading from red to gray, my binge had moved me forward barely 2 percent.

Right before leaving, I went into Netflix.com to reorder the movies that would be waiting for me when I came home. Once I'd signed in, I noticed something very curious: I had recommendations. The fact that Netflix offered me recommendations wasn't that interesting or unique, it's what it might contain that intrigued me. In order to keep *some* level of separation from my normal life, I'd created a separate Netflix queue just for vampire movies. There were always several dozen movies in there, with additions, subtractions (catching movies on cable), and rearrangements happening on an almost weekly basis. Every time I'd watch a movie, I'd rate it on Netflix's one-to-five star system (after months of watching vampire movies, I had only assigned one movie above a "three"— the clever and beautifully rendered love letter to the original *Nosferatu*, E. Elias Merhige's *Shadow of the Vampire* starring Willem Dafoe and John Malkovich). Eventually, I must have rated enough movies that Netflix's recommendation engine started pumping out suggestions based on my vampire movie viewing.

Now, considering the movies I'd viewed and rated, you'd expect that it would suggest *other* crappy vampire films, correct? If not, you'd expect to see other complementary monster movies of a similar caliber.

Wrong.

What did Netflix suggest? *The Goonies, Wayne's World, The Outlaw Josey Wales,* and the fourth season of *Friends*.

Needless to say, I scratched my head over this one for days. Among all the questions I'd been asking myself, one had consistently risen to the top: why the *fourth* season of *Friends*? I mean, why not the third, seventh, or any of the other nine seasons? I did spot the DVD set of the fourth season in a store and found out that this is the season when Phoebe becomes a surrogate mother, Chandler spends Thanksgiving in a box, Monica and Chandler hook up (though obviously not on Thanksgiving), and Ross marries Emily but pulls the greatest wedding faux pas ever at the altar!

Damn, sounds like a wacky show. Of course, I've never seen *Friends*. Well, that isn't true. I think I watched four episodes in its first season, but it was kinda like sniffing glue. Every time I watched, I could feel my brain cells slowly dying, causing a somewhat delirious effect that some might confuse with humor.

The Goonies I could almost understand, because some of the bad guys are a little weird and the story has a semisupernatural element to it. But *The Outlaw Josey Wales*? *Wayne's World*? And what did these recommendations mean? I was flummoxed.

After a few phone calls and e-mails, I got a hold of Neal Hunt, the chief product officer at Netflix. In English, he's the guy who came up with the recommendation system. He explained that Netflix's recommendation system was solely based on statistical probability: If you like movie A, you'll probably like movie B. Netflix takes in data from user ratings of the movies the user has seen. They extrapolate the findings based on the results from their three million other users and come up with a prediction of what movies you might like. They run the results through an accuracy matrix (whatever the hell that means) and boom—you have recommendations based on your previous ratings.

This just made me more flummoxed. I wanted to know what these recommendations mean. I immediately rented both *Wayne's World* and *The Outlaw Josey Wales* and can say with certainty that neither contained any vampire subplots or themes whatsoever. So, if the recommendation doesn't say anything about the movies themselves—what does it say about the people who rent them? In other words, if someone loved *Vampire Sisters* and also loved *Wayne's World*—does his or her multiaffection reveal anything about them as a person?

"Yeah, it's a pretty useful profile of people's tastes and interests," said Neal. "It may seem like the two movies are disparate things, but what they apparently have in common is that the same people like them. So, yes, on some level I suppose it has to mean something."

"Yes, but what?" I asked. "Let's say you meet a person—and that person viewed nothing but terrible vampire movies—"

"Well," Neal interrupted. "I'm not sure I'd want to meet that person."

"Good point."

While we were talking, I remembered a time when I was sitting in a bar waiting for a friend. There was an older guy sitting nearby watching the news on television. There was a story on about people who lived near the Mississippi River. Their homes had slowly flooded (and in some cases washed away) in the wake of some heavy rains. Eventually the guy got out of his chair, looked toward me, raised his finger to the television, and said, "You know, in order to skin a chicken you've got to pull out the feathers first." Then he walked out of the bar without saying another word.

I spent the next several days and weeks trying to figure out what that guy meant. I was trying to line up the metaphorical relationships between chicken skin and rivers and floods and feathers and houses. Venn diagrams couldn't reveal the connections, yet I was obsessed. I theorized that he was talking about removing houses from the riverbank. I certainly understand why people live beside bodies of water. However, besides dousing your furniture with gasoline and lighting a match, there are few more surefire ways to destroy everything you own than to build a home along the edge of a river, ocean, and so on. Hurricanes, floods, erosion, tsunamis—it's a crazy gamble that many people lose. Perhaps my chicken-skin-and-feather philosopher meant to imply that there was no way to fix the situation until the houses were gone. Regardless, I never figured it out.

That is, assuming there ever was anything to figure out. The guy could have been (a.) totally nuts or (b.) deliberately trying to fuck with me. As a prank, it borders on pure genius. Get up, look at a stranger, say something weird yet potentially deep, and walk away. Of the thousands of things I've heard strangers utter in bars that is the one thing that has always stuck with me. I forget most of the conversations I have with friends, family, and coworkers—but that one sentence from a stranger has lingered ever since.

It came to mind during my conversation with Neal mostly because I kept wondering if trying to find meaning in my vampire movie Netflix recommendations was tantamount to drawing connections between floods and chicken feathers. He was very patient with me as I tried different ways of asking him something he either couldn't tell me or didn't know. Neal reminded me several times that, because of its privacy policy, Netflix doesn't keep an eye on individual accounts and therefore, he doesn't know a lot about the patterns of individual customers.

"However, we do sometimes aggregate information," Neal shared. "When you look at it that way, we've often found geography shows distinct tendencies. For example, you could have predicted the 2004 president election—red states and blue states—based solely on the reactions users had to *The Passion of the Christ*. In states where *The Passion of the Christ* received high ratings—they voted red. The states that voted blue didn't like it as much."*

Neal said that the example holds up state by state across the entire electoral map. Of course, they didn't notice this until after the election, but it is still a pretty amazing match. If anything, Neal's Mel Gibson/George Bush correlation just got me more amped. There had to be some meaning in this vampire/*Goonies* business somewhere.

"Who knows," Neal said. "Maybe there are people who are *Friends* people on Monday, Tuesday, and Wednesday—then they become vampire people on Thursday and Friday."

"I can verify that," I offered. "I've met a few."

Neal chuckled, not realizing I was actually serious.

---

* While on the subject of elections, here is a vampire non sequitur for you: Both George Bush and John Kerry are related to Vlad Ţepeş. According to ancestry.com, the connection goes back thirty-four generations to Prince Vlad III (a.k.a Vlad Ţepeş, Vlad Dracula . . . I think you know who I'm talking about). The site also pointed out that both men were ninth cousins, twice removed.

"You know, there's a pattern to these kinds of shows," said Tim Molyneux, creator of *Bite*. "First off, you have an opening number and you show some boobs. Curtain closes. Then you have your comedian, juggler, or magician come out. Then more boobs. Curtain closes. Then another juggler, magician, or comedian comes out. Then more boobs. Just that . . . over and over again. That's pretty much it. But with *Bite*, we've got vampires."

Tim is giving me a tour of the set for his "erotic and sensual topless review based on deliciously evil vampires with a simple story line of sin, sex, and seduction" (thus sayeth the *Bite* Web site). We only have a few minutes for our tour, since *Bite*'s crew only has twenty minutes to set up after the celebrity impersonator revue, *American Superstars*, wraps up its 8:30 show.

Bite runs six nights a week in the Theater of the Stars in the Stratosphere Hotel and Casino in Las Vegas, a space it shares with two other shows. Starting at 10:30, it's the last of the day. Standing on the stage, you can see how much of the show's setup and design is based on the logistical considerations of the theater. Tim is used to unusual setups. Before coming to Vegas and creating *Bite*, Molyneux Entertainment's specialty was shows for large cruise ships, where size and space are huge issues. *Bite*'s staging is designed to go around the sets and equipment for the two earlier productions. What looks like a brick wall actually hides a drum kit. A backdrop of da Vinci's naked dude on a wheel conveniently covers the lit up *American Superstars* logo.

The theater itself is a typical showroom. The stage is tiny, with minimal wings and backstage. The ceiling is tall for a restaurant or club, but low for a theater. The room is definitely outfitted to serve food—its filled with tightly packed round tables and booths. Transforming such a space from a dinner theater to a spooky den of the undead—and doing so in less than twenty minutes—is a sizable task. Molyneux managed to pull it off pretty effectively with some strategically placed colored lights and murals.

"The hotel wanted a topless show," Tim explained. "It wasn't something we would have thought to do but it was a challenge.

What I did was attend every topless show in town and see what was entertaining . . . see what people tend to like and not. Bringing in vampires gave me the license to do the things I wanted to do—superhuman strength, dancing, flying. With this theme, our show could be sexy, seductive, and powerful without having to build in a big script. Vampire lore embraces these things. People come to the show expecting to see cool kinds of things because of vampires.

"This is a nice touch here," Tim said, pointing to the crotch of a gargoyle at the side of the stage. "During the show, one of our dancers slides out from a trapdoor between the statue's legs. It's pretty neat. Unfortunately, you won't see that in tonight's show. That dancer is off today."

"That's too bad," I said, nodding my head with a disappointed look on my face. "Couldn't another dancer come through there?"

"Well, many of our dancers have specialty things that they do. We try to honor their unique styles and skills." I couldn't help but think that dancer's parents must be proud—not only does their daughter appear in a topless Vegas revue but she's the only one with the talent and skill to eject herself from the crotch of a plaster gargoyle.

Looking around the set, I started to wonder if all this was really necessary.

"So, you've got these beautiful women," I said.

"Yeah."

"And they're topless."

"Yeah."

"Why do they need fangs?"

"That's a good question," Tim replied, looking like he had to think about that one for a second.

"I mean, if you've got naked women on a stage," I said, "why fix what isn't broken?"

"I guess while you can go see boobs on stage anywhere, we're the only one with fangs," Tim answered. "People like spectacle and something different in Vegas. The vampire element adds an intriguing draw. Topless show . . . classic rock . . . vampires . . . how can you go wrong?

"You say 'vampire' to that guy over there or those women over there, you know they will all have a reaction," he said. "People of different generations, all over the place, they all have a reaction to vampires . . . they all know what it is. I could see this show going on tour: *Bite* Miami, *Bite* New York, *Bite* L.A., *Bite* London. Because people know and love vampires everywhere."

Despite its portability—it's appropriate that the show is in Las Vegas. If you ever need evidence that most people are gullible—and happily, willingly gullible—go to Vegas. People travel to Vegas under the notion that *they* are different. However, the over-the-top grandness of Las Vegas wasn't built by giving money away to winners. The casino odds are no secret (in fact, most publish and advertise their odds), yet people still go under the (misguided) belief that *someone* has to win, so it might as well be them. Sure, the odds are two million to one, but *there is still a chance.* Total nincompoopery.

What everyone knows and no one admits is that Vegas is a façade. It's like a movie set—everyone knows that if they view it from an angle, they can see its fakeness. Yet if they keep themselves pointed forward, they are transported into a world of style, elegance, and glamour that otherwise would have nothing to do with them. In Vegas, people are given the illusion of transformation—they can be lucky, sexy, fun, and classy. The price for this dream? Whatever cash you happen to have access to.

While we often place a handsome and debonair man's face on our mental image of a vampire, Vegas proves that sometimes vampirism can also be characterized by neon lights, exploding volcanoes, white tigers, and Wild Cherry slot machines.

In all honesty, despite how nice Tim was and *Bite*'s promises of a "nightly party of erotic rock and roll revelry," "superhuman stunts," and "sensual nibbling"—our expectations were . . . low.

The show opens with a long recorded narration that sets up the basic story line of the show. This monologue, delivered by a guy with a voice so deep you imagine his testicles must drag on the ground, is the only dialogue in the entire show. (This helps keep production costs down, as union rates for stage actors are generally based upon the number of spoken lines.) The setup is this: The show's central character, the Lord Vampire, lost his true love centuries ago and is doomed to search the world until he finds the next Mrs. Lord Vampire. To aid him in his search, he has collected a cadre of topless dancers, known as the "coven of Rock Angels," which the show's Web site describes as "gorgeous, talented, and sexually uninhibited."* Each night they search for the perfect girl, kill a few others, and do a lot of dancing—which occasionally features their naked mammae flopping about. After the introduction is the first big dance number where each of the Rock Angels (a.k.a. Cat, Tush, Ice, Fire, Pain, and Shimmy) is featured by name and does a bit of a solo dance. Afterward, there is a group routine and in some flash of smoke and noise, the tops disappear for the first time. There is so much going on across the stage and it happens so quickly, you don't notice the exposed breasts at first. You have this brief "Oh, my God, I can see her boobs" moment, then realize that it's on purpose.

In an odd way, there is a sense of relief when this happens. The focal point(s) of attending this performance is the breasts. Once they are out in the open, you realize they are just . . . breasts. No angelic chorus sang or blinding beams of light emitted when they unfastened their tops. The Coven (and the other actresses/dancers who disrobe during the show) are simply sporting sixteen fairly normal boobs.

Following their big opening number, the Lord Vampire appears and does some fancy tricks with fire. He then sends the Rock An-

---

* The show's Web site also misspells the dancers' moniker, instead calling them the "coven of Rock Angles."

gels out into the audience to look for potential true loves. Unknown to the audience (except me) is that there are several plants in the crowd—actors and dancers who were selected (along with several legitimate audience members). The Lord Vampire walks among those that the Rock Angels have brought onstage, sends back a few, taps a few semifinalists, and then disappears so that everyone has a chance to dance around for a while.

Regardless of the hokey premise and our low expectations, the show's dancing and sense of spectacle were pretty amazing. The small number of effects the show was able to pull off in the space were incredibly effective. Instead of dialogue, *Bite* is choreographed against a variety of classic rock songs that had at least some modicum of a thematic tie to the action of the show. When the Lord Vampire first appeared, the sound system blared Guns N' Roses' "Welcome to the Jungle." As a newly turned vampire couple did a slow dance while suspended from the ceiling, Nazareth's "Love Hurts" blared as the accompaniment. *Bite* managed to wedge in "Maneater," "Born to Be Wild," "Living After Midnight," "Pour Some Sugar on Me," and about a dozen other tunes into the vampire story line.

The show had a very rapid-fire, no-attention-span vibe, with different things happening constantly—people dancing, things exploding, actors flying above the stage, fire, and Rock Angels suggestively crawling across the stage and one another. And despite its billing as a topless revue, there were surprisingly few topless moments in *Bite*. Yet, because there was so much going on, you hardly noticed the low breast count.

For the next hour, there was more dancing, more flying, more Rock Angels grinding against one another, and more pyrotechnics. It was actually a really good time. After the Lord Vampire had found his new love and all was right with the world and the ticket-paying mortals were sent back out to the casino, I sat down with Anthony, who played the Lord Vampire. When I first started kicking around the idea of interviewing cast members, Tim's assistant tried to steer me away from talking with the dancers themselves.

"To them, this is just a gig," she said. "The fangs, they're just a prop. They aren't really . . . deep thinkers . . . about the theme of the show, that is . . . you know what I mean?"

Yes, I did.

Everyone involved in *Bite* was pretty insistent that I speak with Anthony. Anthony is really into vampires, they told me. It's a spiritual thing, others added. According to his coworkers, Anthony was the real deal.

"I hear he even sleeps in a coffin," Tim added.

Anthony is well over six feet tall, with slightly receding black curly hair that hangs down past his shoulders. He has a bodybuilder's physique and uses makeup to hide the tattoos on his arms. For the show he wears a sleeveless black knee-length coat, glow-in-the-dark beady-eye contact lenses, and a set of custom-made fangs. He paints a pretty foreboding image. Backstage after the show, he couldn't have been sweeter, yet still a muscle-bound giant with glow-in-the-dark eyes and fangs. It's odd to have someone so scary-looking be so nice to you.

I told Anthony that I'd heard he had some actual vampire connections.

"Well, you know I am from Transylvania," he said, leaving a beat before adding, "That is . . . Transylvania County, North Carolina!"*

Anthony came to Vegas looking for work as a fire performer—a line he's been in since he was a child. He was that kid that every neighborhood has—the one who's always lighting things on fire. Things only got out of control once, when he started a large fire in his best friend's backyard and destroyed a large amount of property. Like fire, vampirism is an extension of his own spirituality.

"For some people, they take the Hollywood version," he said. "For me, I think our souls are eternal and rather than drink blood,

---

* There is, in fact, a Transylvania County in North Carolina, a lovely little spot of earth with waterfalls and rolling hills, and home to a rare variety of white squirrels.

I feed off energy. Some do it because it's cool. For me, the energy of the vampire is the eternal soul and connecting with everyone. I've always been interested in the darker aspects of things."

Sitting here listening to this huge guy with glowing eyes and fangs, the more I tried *not* to stare at Anthony's teeth and eyes, the more obvious it was that I was trying not to stare at them.

"I hear you like to sleep in a coffin," I said.

"Well, yeah. I sleep in a coffin sometimes," he said. "I like the whole idea—the energy of it. It's not as weird as it seems."

"I think that most people would argue that sleeping in a coffin wouldn't fall into the conventional definition of normal," I counter.

"Hey, it's comfy. I'm not claustrophobic, so being boxed in is comforting. I guess it *could* be an attraction to death, it could also be restful and secure."

Sure, it *could* be—but again, I'm pretty certain most people would agree that it is creepy. Anthony and I sat around talking as the tech crew tore down the *Bite* set and got the theater ready for the first *Viva Las Vegas* show tomorrow afternoon. I kept trying to ask Anthony what *Bite* meant—not in a literal way, but in a junior year philosophy way. No matter how I approached it, Anthony wasn't seeing it.

"So legend says that vampires don't cast reflections," I offered. "But in many ways, they do—they reflect us. They reflect our values and our fears and what turns us on. If that is true, what does something like *Bite* reflect?"

"Eternal love."

"That's too easy."

"Well, I don't know, why does it have to reflect anything? Or maybe what it reflects is that people really like beautiful women and rock and roll."

"Surely this has to mean something—this show, in this town."

Anthony scrunched up his face, then reached in his mouth, and pulled out his fangs. This, to me, indicated he had something important and profound to offer to our conversation, kinda like when

Grandpa takes off his glasses before dispensing some yarn of folksy wisdom.

"Vegas is such a transient, dark town," he said. "It shouldn't surprise anyone that there are real vampires here. They are mortgage brokers and car salesmen and police officers and nurses. There are a bunch of people who know what they are—and a bunch who don't. They go through life thinking they are normal, but they have to stop and ask themselves why they are drawn to this kind of place."

I asked Anthony what those real vampires think of *Bite*.

"When they meet me, they know I'm coming from a very positive space," he said. "Many love the idea that I'm in the show because they know that I won't play on the Hollywood image of what they do."

I told Anthony that I had trouble believing that. If vampirism was, as he suggested, an extension of his spirituality, wouldn't *Bite* itself be a kind of sacrilege?

"I don't get what you mean," he said.

"Sure, there is a lot of energy and it's very exciting," I said. "But I'm sure that someone must think you are pimping yourself out."

"Are you suggesting—"

"What I'm suggesting is that if this is a legitimate expression of who you are, couldn't others like you look at your participation in this show as tantamount to a black guy starring in a minstrel show?"

Anthony huffed. I could tell he was upset that I would suggest this kind of connection. It was a bit of a cheap shot, but a legitimate question.

"You have to give the leeway that we are in Vegas and this is a Vegas show. And the main draw is the girls and the dancing," he said. "People come to Vegas to experience things they have never or will never experience otherwise. We're just one of those things. One of the great things about this show is that people don't know what's going to happen. They get chills through their body and smiles on their face because they anticipate what *might* happen.

People find this attractive because the doorway of death is the continuation of life. Sure, vampires celebrate death, but in a weird way, they celebrate the value of living, too.

"Plus, we have a lot of 'girl on girl' stuff. That doesn't hurt, either."

THE NEXT MORNING I was having breakfast with some friends and sharing stories about *Bite*, Transylvania, and spooky vampire enthusiasts. My stories of Romania even featured a few updates. My swollen and dark bug bite had left a visible scar (still noticeable to this day), which I always point out to illustrate why a mosquito bite became such a concern (and yes, ha-ha-ha, I'm *still* sure it was a *mosquito* that bit me, ha-ha-ha, that's a good one!). After returning from our trip, Ralph made a trip to the doctor for a dog bite-related tetanus shot. Radu had called back to the monastery before we left Romania to see if the dog was showing any signs of rabies (it wasn't). Nonetheless, Ralph's doctor wanted him to get rabies shots, which he initially refused. The doctor insisted he talk to a specialist, who put the fear of God into him. Ralph then endured a painful series of shots over the following month.

Also, about two weeks after we returned, I'd received an e-mail from Tina asking if I had seen Elaina on A&E earlier that week. Curiosity piqued, I caught a repeat of the show the following weekend. The program was called *Intervention*. It's a reality show where tragic people with tragic problems in their totally tragic lives are confronted by friends and family to get some help. It turned out that Elaina was a compulsive gambler and had burned through more than thirty thousand dollars in the past two years playing quarter slots. Brad was in the show too, begging her to get help. There was snow in several of the scenes, so I guessed that the episode had been taped long before we met in Romania. At the end of the episode, Elaina refused to get treatment for her gambling addiction.

After hearing about Romania, injections, and reality TV, my

friend Chuck decided to throw down a challenge to my wicked vampire insight skills.

"You know what you said about how difficult it is to go through a whole day without seeing a reference to vampires?"

"Yes," I politely responded.

"Actually, I think you're wrong. It's very easy to go through a day without seeing a reference to vampires."

"I'm not just talking about specific references to vampires—which is almost enough on its own—but also when you hear metaphorical references like sucking the life out of something or crossing your fingers in front of someone as a gesture to keep away. There's also 'bite' references like 'bite me' or 'this bites.' And don't forget gesundheit."

Everyone at the table gave me a strange look.

I went on to explain that, in all likelihood, the German phrase for "good health" originated as a protection against vampires. According to several vampire stories, a sneeze was either a sign that someone was vulnerable to a vampire attack or that a vampire had just begun to attack them.* These stories also say that being wished "good health" would prevent the vampire from attacking further. Thus, the practice of saying "gesundheit" when someone sneezes.

Chuck was still feeling skeptical.

"Well," I responded, "in order to skin a chicken you've got to pull out the feathers first."

Several of my breakfast colleagues nodded their heads in agreement as they went on eating their pancakes and omelets.

THE PHONE RINGS. Jeanne picks up immediately.

"Hello?"

---

* When considering this, it's important to note that not all vampires attack by biting. Some attack psychically or somehow convey sickness upon their victims.

"Dr. Youngson? It's Eric Nu—"

"So, you want to understand vampirism?"

"Yes, that's right. I do," I quickly answered. "I want to—"

"Well, I guess that depends on how you define vampirism, doesn't it?"

"Sure, well I—"

"I mean, Colonel Parker vampirized Elvis, didn't he?"

"I guess so," I replied. "What I really want to know is why people are so attracted to vampires and—"

"Hey, do you know much about rats?"

That's a verbatim transcript of the first time I spoke with Dr. Jeanne Keyes Youngson, a vampire expert from New York City. After that, she proceeded to tell me about her "rat kick"—her current obsession with rats . . . for the next ten minutes.

"They are pretty amazing creatures actually. You know, Stoker's *Dracula* has several scenes in it with rats and I remember saying to myself, 'Hey, what do you know about rats?' So I started to do some reading about them and I really can't seem to stop!"

Dr. Youngson has a pet rat named Frank. She tells lots of stories about Frank. Frank seems to get around a lot.

"I was just visiting some friends in Chicago and took Frank along. I got them to pose for a picture with him."

"You took your pet rat to Chicago?"

"Why yes, I took him to London recently, too."

"How did you manage to take a pet rat through customs? Let alone on a plane?"

"Well," she said with a giggle. "Here's a secret. Frank is made of rubber."

"So Frank isn't real."

"Oh, of course he's real."

Jeanne runs the Vampire Empire, a membership club for enthusiasts of vampire movies, literature, and research. Until 2000, the organization was known as the Count Dracula Fan Club. She changed the name to Vampire Empire so they could cover more territory. Jeanne is ground zero for vampires—there is almost nothing that goes on relating to vampires that has more than one degree of separation from her. She knows everyone—every author, filmmaker, professor, you name it. They all come calling, just like me.

She got started with vampires in the early 1950s while working at the Museum of Modern Art, one of the few places in New York that presented silent movies. One afternoon, she slipped in to see a bit of the film that was currently showing: F. W. Murnau's *Nosferatu: Eine Symphonie des Grauens*. She was hooked. The museum gave her a twenty-minute afternoon tea break, so she staggered her break times each day so that she could sit and watch different parts of the movie.

In the early 1960s, her husband Robert (two-time Oscar winner and writer, director, and producer of more than three dozen films) suggested she find a new hobby that wouldn't require her to be away from the home. At about the same time she took a tour of Romania and heard stories about the barbaric Romanian prince who became the namesake of Bram Stoker's novel. Right then Jeanne turned to an Australian widow sitting next to her and said she was going to go home and start the first Count Dracula fan club. The widow insisted on becoming the first member.

Soon after, as she puts it, vampires and Dracula took over her life. She started the club out of her Greenwich Village apartment in June 1965. Except for a few years following her husband's death, when she was splitting her time between London and New York, the Vampire Empire and the massive archive of materials Jeanne has collected have always operated out of her home.

The club itself is a somewhat byzantine organization. Jeanne has the club divided into fifteen divisions, including: The Research Library; the Vampire Bookshop; Dracula, Vampires, and the New Age Vampire; the Golem Group; the Lugosi Legacy; Vampires in the Media; Supernatural Spirits; Maggie's Morgue; the Werewolf in Fact, Fiction, and Fantasy; the International Vampire Information and Database; the Monster Menage; the Tepes Alliance; Special Interest Division; Rats, Bats, and Mysterious Cats; and Friends of the Library. In addition to running the Vampire Empire, she also runs the International Frankenstein Society; the Bram Stoker Memorial Association; Fans of Oz; and the International Society for the Study of Ghosts and Apparitions. As an extra value, membership in the Vampire Empire also includes complimentary membership in the other clubs as well. The Vampire Empire even publishes many of its own books written by Jeanne and others.

After a whiplash-inducing conversation through some questions I had, I asked her about finding some modern-day vampires.

"Do you mean something underground?" she asked.

"Well, sure," I replied. "I want to find someone who practices—"

"Oh, dear, you don't want to have anything to do with those people," said Jeanne. "When you stick to research, books, and movies, you'll learn a lot and have a lot of fun. But those people—they are thrill-seekers. Thrill-seekers in the worst way. There are plenty of other ways to get thrills.

"We stay away from underground organizations . . . as far as possible. If something about them was in the paper, I wouldn't even cut it out. They're very dangerous. You won't learn anything from them."

"Maybe I should find that out for myself."

"Well, I won't have anything to do with it. You get nothing but trouble with those people."

"But I've tried, and it's almost impossible—"

"You've still got a lot of ground to cover before you have to worry about them," she said, then informed me that our conversation had to end—she had to get ready for her upcoming trip to England to hunt theater ghosts.

"And watch out for those scary people," she said. "You don't want to have anything to do with them. Be careful, okay?"

"I promise."

V

FROM WAMPYR TO WHITBY

In which the author travels to England to find exploding graves, great bargains at Top Shop, coffin-shaped candy, and gay men spilling into the streets.

I WAS SITTING on a bench near a cliff overlooking Whitby Harbor. It was almost 9:00 P.M. exactly, so my timing was perfect. I flew across an ocean and took a five-hour train ride to get here for some insight into one question: how could someone so mediocre do something so extraordinary?

Bram Stoker sat here the evening of August 19, 1890, at exactly 9:00 P.M. and wrote some observations in his journal about his latest obsession: an idea for a new novel. It was a horror story entitled "The Undead," featuring an evil vampire from Austria named Count Wampyr. From that location near the cliff, you can see all the places mentioned in Stoker's notes. Most prominent is Whitby Harbor where the count's ship crashed during a storm, its entire crew dead. There are the 199 steps leading from near the water's edge up to the top of the cliffs on the opposite side of the horseshoe-shaped harbor that the vampire ran up in the form of a wolf. There's the old graveyard where he hid during his first few weeks in England. There are the rows of beautiful waterside cottages and houses in which the human characters stayed while in Whitby, much like Stoker did for three summers. It was later during one of those summers that he'd come across a small six-page pamphlet that would change the course of his novel as well as that of his life and legacy. Even though Stoker had already started to outline the novel, he was so affected by what he read in the pamphlet that he went back and changed every reference to the novel's evil count, including a scratched-out revision to the title of the novel itself, so that both would bear the name of the pamphlet's protagonist. The pamphlet began, "In the year of Our Lord 1456 Dracula did many dreadful and curious things . . ."

The fact that Stoker stumbled across this 450-year-old tale of an evil Wallachian prince had less to do with Vlad's prominence in European history than it did with an event that occurred about the same time as Dracula's reign—the commercialization of the printing press.

Shortly after the printing press was invented in 1450, as well as a process for cheaply manufacturing sufficient quantities of paper, early publishers realized the commercial potential of printed books. Even considering that the affluent were the only people who could actually read in the late fifteenth century (let alone afford books), the sensational stuff always sold best. At about the same time, German monks living in Transylvania sent home tales of Vlad Dracula, which were quickly turned into considerably trumped-up pamphlets. Even back then, Dracula was a publishing sensation. At the time, the Bible was the only book that outsold tales of Dracula's exploits. While the monks printed four volumes of Dracula tales as fund-raisers, eventually more than sixteen different volumes were published, often under unwieldy titles such as *The Frightening and Truly Extraordinary Story of a Wicked Blood-Drinking Tyrant Called Prince Dracula*. In them, Dracula was often cast as a ruthless murderer and tyrant who thought nothing of killing hundreds or thousands simply for his own sadistic amusement. Each was widely reprinted and revised over the centuries. One English-language translation of these stories eventually ended up in the Whitby library and into the hands of summer resident Bram Stoker.

If it's been a while since you read the novel *Dracula,* or you're familiar with the film adaptations but never read the book itself,* here's a quick overview:

The novel tells the story of a young solicitor named Jonathan Harker who is sent to Transylvania to complete a real estate transaction with a count interested in buying several properties in London. Once Harker arrives, Dracula—actually an ancient vampire—imprisons Harker for several weeks (with the help of his three vampire "wives") while Dracula prepares to move to England. After Harker escapes from the count's castle (nearly dying in the process), the novel's focus shifts to England. Count Dracula's ship (containing him and more than fifty boxes of Transylvania dirt), arrives in the coastal town of Whitby. There, Dracula hides for several weeks in a cemetery while beginning to infiltrate the lives of the novel's two female characters: Mina Murray and Lucy Westenra. As the group relocates back to London, Lucy is repeatedly attacked by Count Dracula. A group of men (including her fiancée, two former suitors, and Dr. Abraham Van Helsing—a mysterious professor who specializes in the supernatural) rally together in an attempt to save Lucy from Dracula. Eventually Lucy succumbs and is temporarily turned into a baby-snatching vampire herself, until she is re-killed by the posse of "protectors." The count then turns his attentions to Mina. Things backfire this time and Dracula is driven from England by Van Helsing and company, commencing in an 1890s version of a high-speed chase back to Transylvania. The vampire killers, now joined by the reunited Jonathan and now-clairvoyant semivampire Mina, follow Dracula back to Transylvania and kill him.

Dracula defined the gothic horror novel. Yet at its core, the book is more than a great horror story or a loosely adapted story of vampirism and a deceased brutal prince—Stoker wrote of the deepest human urges and desires that were (and still are) shared almost

---

* You might feel a little weird reading a book about the history and cultural influence of vampires, and admitting that you've never read *Dracula.* Don't feel bad—when I started working on this project even *I* had never read the entire book before.

universally. *Dracula* opened up the possibilities of abandoning the distinction between need and want. The count could have anything he desired. All that was required of him in return was to follow a few simple rules: drink blood from the living, avoid religious icons, sleep in his coffin, and some other miscellany.

Dracula was filled with tantalizing, emotionally charged action, exotic settings, and erotic undertones. While Count Dracula's terrifying activities were truly frightening, readers were equally taken with the dark romance of it all. Even the novel's characters were drawn in by Dracula's allure. In *Dracula*, the count had to be invited in to a home before entering. So while Dracula was a horrific presence, his victims asked him to come into their world.

Dracula's legacy can be attributed to always being in the right place at the right time. When the novel was published, English society was at a turning point. Literature and theater were just starting to break away from their classical roots, and the Victorian era, where behavior and morality were exceptionally restrained, was winding down. London was just coming to terms with the notion that Jack the Ripper, who had driven the city into a panic at a time just before *Dracula's* publication, would never be caught. The entire foundation of human nature was being reexamined in the wake of Charles Darwin's *Descent of Man*, published just a few years prior. *Dracula* captured all this, embodying not only the magnetism of fear, but the allure of desire.

MY TRIP TO London and Whitby was the first time that Katherine had accompanied me on a dedicated vampire outing. From the minute we arrived in the U.K., she made it quite clear that she was here for the free trip, not for research. In fact, Katherine had gotten to the point that she'd be happy to go along for just about anything, as long as it had nothing to do with vampires. By this point she'd sat through dozens of movies and countless stories—so I couldn't really blame her.

When we arrived in London, Katherine politely declined my invitation to look up some of the locations in *Dracula*, opting instead to "help out" by shoe shopping on Oxford Street.* We met up later so we could take a tour of one of the few *Dracula*-related spots in London that did intrigue us both—Highgate Cemetery.

Highgate Cemetery is considered to be one of the most organically creepy places on earth. Walking through the front gates, even at 11:00 A.M. on a sunny summer morning, I had no problem accepting this as fact.

Highgate has a contentious place in *Dracula* history. Stoker's rep for exactness and research takes a weird turn when the novel's characters arrive in London. Most of the places Stoker mentions in London are real, however some have had their names or exact locations changed. In a few instances, Stoker completely made up locations (such as Carfax Abbey) that had no real world equivalent. Many *Dracula* experts think that Highgate was Stoker's model for Kingstead—the location where Lucy Westenra was buried, comes back to life as a vampire, and where Professor Van Helsing and his merry men re-kill her. The problem is that there is no cemetery called Kingstead.

Some claim Stoker's Kingstead is actually Hendon Cemetery, less than a mile down the hill in Hampstead Heath. In the novel, the Van Helsing posse gathers at an actual pub called Jack Straw's Castle (still there), then heads out to Lucy's grave. Looking at a map, Hendon Cemetery would have been closer to both the West-

---

* Katherine had no idea what she was missing! Beside the decaying (and completely fictionalized) Carfax Abbey, Dracula's main hangout in London (and a stash for nine boxes of Transylvanian dirt), was a house he purchased across from Green Park. According to Stoker's description in *Dracula*, it was located near the "Junior Constitutional Hotel" (known as the Junior Athenaeum Hotel in the real world) on the corner of Down Street and Piccadilly. This house is also significant because it is located in the area where most experts thought Jack the Ripper resided (a detail that wouldn't have been lost on Stoker). With the help of the doorman at the Junior Constitutional (who said, "Never heard of Dracula living on the block, but I've been standing here since time began, so I should be able to help"), I located the building that Stoker designated as Dracula's house. In something that must resemble irony, it is now a Hard Rock Café.

enra family home and the pub. While geographically convenient, that theory doesn't make much sense. A family with the social status of the Westenras would never have buried their daughter in such a distinctly less-than-vogue cemetery. For well-to-do northern Londoners, it would have been Highgate or nothing.

Following years of overcrowding and disgusting conditions in London's church graveyards (not to mention a nasty little cholera epidemic), seven private cemeteries were opened in London in the early nineteenth century. Highgate was arguably the grandest of these and among its largest. The cemetery was opened in 1839, with an expansion across the street a dozen years later (now known as the East Cemetery). Highgate was an immediate success and became the fashionable location for burial in London. At its height, there were dozens of burials in Highgate every day. The cemetery was designed to be a grand open park dotted with mausoleums and markers, employing thirty-five landscapers and gardeners. Located at the highest point in London, the cemetery afforded views of the entire city.

However, early in the twentieth century, Highgate slowly began to encounter problems. Specifically, Highgate ran out of prime plots, which led to a reduction in cash flow and a crowding of grave sites. Thus, things slowly started to fall apart. By the 1970s, Highgate had crammed 169,000 burials into its 51,000 original plots (with an average of more than three burials per plot it was common for family members to share the same plot, stacked on top of one another). The markers and monuments were practically touching one another and squeezed into almost every available inch of space at odd angles. The staff of thirty-five caretakers had been reduced down to two elderly guys who basically sat around watching TV and never ventured out into the cemetery at all. The older, western part of the cemetery had gone completely wild, with self-sown trees, ivy, and other weeds and plants growing over the entire property. In many parts of the cemetery, paths had been completely grown over and were almost impassable, and many graves and mausoleums had deteriorated to the point that they had fallen over or come open. This resulted in Highgate's unfortunate reputation for exploding graves. The combination of unexpected fresh air, moisture, poorly maintained grave sites, and tightly sealed lead-lined coffins caused gas buildups, which routinely caused caskets to explode like watermelons stuffed with firecrackers.

In its ruined state, with no security and the opportunity to see exploding, decomposing body bits, the cemetery was a popular spot for all sorts of late-night activities. Newspaper reports in the late 1960s and '70s claimed that locals were routinely spotting ghosts walking in the cemetery at night. In all likelihood, these spooks were drunken teenagers in search of a tree to pee behind.

In 1975, the cemetery went bankrupt and was taken over by a nonprofit group wanting to preserve Highgate as a historic ruin. The newer East Cemetery is in pretty good shape, with burials continuing there even to this day. The old West Cemetery is closed off and only accessible by guided tour (only held on certain days and limited to very small groups).

While we waited for our group to assemble inside the gates, I asked our tour guide, a soft-spoken guy named Bob, why it was necessary to only take small groups inside the cemetery.

"Well, first, you can get lost," he answered. "Secondly, because of its condition, there are lots of sinkholes popping up around the property. Since many of the graves can be several meters deep, we'd hate for you to be admiring the scenery then drop in on someone, eh?"

I found it difficult to believe that you could get lost inside a thirty-seven-acre cemetery. That is until Bob took us through the gates and into the cemetery itself.

It was as thick as a forest—dense with graves, wild trees, and green leaves from almost every variety of wild plant and weed you can think of. Outside of clearing the paths and growth away from some of the markers and monuments, the volunteers running Highgate have kept it pretty much in its natural state. Wild trees grow up in between plots—with the occasional tree root or wild trunk knocking the lid off of an aboveground grave. Ivy covers everything. What makes the sights of Highgate so incredibly creepy and odd is that all this wild decay surrounds some of the most ornate, beautiful, and unusual grave markers you'll ever see. The Victorians were infatuated with death and funerary bigness. As a result Highgate is like a living museum of Victorian burial fashions. Grand, opulent markers sit next to deliberately humble and subdued ones. Some eras favored statuary; others either avoided or gaudily embraced religious icons. Egyptian symbols were obviously popular at one time (including several pyramid-shaped markers large enough to be a child's playhouse). England's largest freestanding mausoleum is here as well, a stone and marble monstrosity the size of a two-story house. Highgate's pièce de résistance is the Circle of Lebanon, located at the highest point in the cemetery. It's a group of intersecting rings of mausoleums, giving a townhouselike effect to the dozens of adjacent crypt doors. It's up here that Lucy Westenra would have been buried and where, in 1970, the Highgate vampire was hunted down and killed.

In 1967, the usual Highgate ghost sightings seemed to grow exponentially, along with reports of mutilated animals and some questionable evidence that groups had been practicing witchcraft on the cemetery grounds. Rumors began to circulate that Highgate was now housing a vampire, who had moved beyond drinking the blood of trespassing teens and was venturing out into the adjacent neighborhood.

Enter Sean Manchester and David Farrant. Up until this time, Farrant was a freelance occultist. Manchester was prancing around England in tuxedoes, frilly gothic suits, and big blow-dried hair trying to make a name for himself as "Britain's No. 1 Psychic."* He was kind of like a combo of Miss Cleo and Geraldo Rivera (minus the mustache). When the vampire rumors reached a crescendo, Manchester announced he would lead an expedition into Highgate to hunt down and kill its vampire. Manchester set the hunt for the

---

* A title and ranking that Manchester gave himself.

evening of Friday the thirteenth in March 1970. At 6:00 that night, he and Farrant both appeared on live television at the north gate of Highgate detailing their plans for the evening. By 8:00, Highgate was a mob scene, with hundreds of amateur vampire hunters and gawkers stopping by to assist Manchester and Farrant hunt for the undead. Despite the police showing up to control the crowd, Manchester, Farrant, and about one hundred others entered the cemetery and proceeded to the Circle of Lebanon, the alleged site of the vampire's lair. Unable to open the door to the mausoleum, Manchester had himself lowered down into the tomb through a hole in the roof.* The crew found no vampire, but Manchester did leave cloves of garlic and some crosses in some empty coffins he stumbled across.

These raids on Highgate continued until, according to Farrant's accounts, he was eventually arrested for putting stakes through the chests of corpses and Manchester eventually announced that he'd hunted down and killed the vampire. Despite all the hubbub, no one ever did provide any proof that there was a Highgate vampire (shocking, I know) or that he had ever attacked anyone, let alone proof that said vampire had been turned to dust. I guess we just have to take Manchester's word for it.

If there ever was a Highgate vampire, it was probably Manchester or Farrant—though not in the literal sense. In the more than three decades since, both Farrant and Manchester have repeatedly engorged themselves on the Highgate vampire's notoriety. Both have published books. Both have tried to take credit for finding the vampire.

These days, Farrant is still running a Web site and selling magazines about the Highgate vampire. After the Highgate vampire had been dispensed with, Sean Manchester decided to branch out into general exorcism. Since, according to canon law, only a bishop

---

* Manchester claimed this was a sign that the vampire knew he was coming and was trying to protect itself, as Manchester had easily gained access to this crypt on a previous preliminary visit.

can perform exorcisms, Manchester decided to become ordained in a church he founded, the Church of the Holy Grail. He now walks around in a bishop's outfit and has a corner on the market for exorcism-conducting, vampire-killing, psychic bishops.

WHILE *DRACULA* IS the best known of vampire stories, it wasn't the first. In the 440 years between the invention of the printing press and the publication of *Dracula,* there were six English-language novels about vampires. In the 110 years since *Dracula,* there have been more than a thousand. The nineteenth century was a good period for vampires. Previously, vampires had been a part of folk history and traditions, but it wasn't until the early 1800s that the vampire truly emerged in formal literature.

The first modern Western vampire story was written by the poet Lord George Byron—sort of. Byron never intended to publish a vampire story. While a vampirelike character did appear in Lord Byron's 1813 poem "The Giaour," the character was largely based upon the Greek mythology surrounding the vampirelike demons known as vrykolakas rather than the prevailing vampire myths of Europe. In 1816, Byron was forced to divorce and flee London because of his "eclectic" sexual interests. While staying with some friends in Geneva, he came up with an interesting idea for them to entertain one another: Everyone would spend the evening writing a ghost story to share with the group. The most famous outcome of Byron's challenge was *Frankenstein,* written in rough form that evening by Mary Shelley. Byron's contribution was a story fragment called "The Vampyre," based upon some of his research for "The Giaour." Byron never thought about his vampire tale after that evening until he came across a copy of *New Monthly Magazine* in 1819, containing a story—attributed to him—called "The Vampyre." It appeared that another of the gathering's guests, John Polidori, had fleshed out the story and submitted it. The magazine was confused by the story's lineage and gave the byline solely to Byron.

The tale featured a villain named Lord Ruthven (who bore more than a passing similarity to Lord Byron) and was loosely based on the story of Arnod Paole (you might remember him from earlier—the eighteenth-century Serb who died after falling from his horse and was blamed for sickening and killing half his village). In it, Lord Ruthven was killed while traveling through Greece. His killers left his body in the moonlight, which became the source of Ruthven's vampire power. Once Ruthven returned to England, he lived an apparently normal life among humans. However, once Ruthven encountered the light of the full moon, he'd become a blood-drinking vampire who would prey upon his friends and neighbors, with a particular taste for the young ladies. Byron and Polidori's tale was more than the first Western narrative about vampires, it was also the first to make the vampire into a complex, calculating character who abandoned his morality right along with his mortality. Ruthven used his vampire powers to his advantage, often selecting his victims based upon the potential benefits their demise might bring him.

Because the story was attributed to Byron, it got much more attention than it would have otherwise. It was translated into several languages and was adapted for the stage in three countries. After it was first published, Byron wrote letters denying his authorship until he learned that his friend Polidori had adapted his story. Afterward, both Polidori and Byron worked to correct the error. Because of the popularity of Byron, all publications of the story carried Byron's name until the error was finally corrected for good—in 1945.

The first full-length vampire novel was John Rymer's *Varney the Vampire or The Feast of Blood,* published in 1847. Despite its rather corny title, *Varney* was a popular horror story. Even if you harbor any guilt about not reading *Dracula,* you should feel total absolution for skipping *Varney the Vampire.* My copy is printed in three volumes, the shortest of which is 298 pages long. *Varney* is a painful read. Treading through it, you might think that its rambling and verbose prose was an indication that Rymer was paid by the word. You'd be right.

Varney originated in weekly serialized newspaper installments and, gathered as a novel, is both unwieldy and repetitious. Writing like this is so tedious that I wouldn't be surprised if we couldn't find anyone who's actually read the entire thing. Instead of saying something like "Daylight can have an effect on how people see the world," Rymer opted for: "What wonderfully different impressions and feelings, with regard to the same circumstances, come across the mind in the broad, clear, and beautiful light of day to what haunt the imagination, and often render the judgment almost incapable of action, when the heavy shadow of night is upon all things. There must be a downright physical reason for this effect—it is so remarkable and so universal. It seems that the sun's rays so completely alter and modify the constitution of the atmosphere, that it produces, as we inhale it, a wonderfully different effect upon the nerves of the human subject."

Like Lord Ruthven, Varney had amazing powers and could walk about in daylight, but unlike Ruthven he didn't need large quantities of blood to survive. Varney could even go several nights without feeding. He could be wounded and even killed, but then he completely revived once in contact with moonlight. Unlike Ruthven and traditional vampires, Varney was more like a superhero, a complex mixture of power and honor. Varney empathized with his victims (often young women), repeatedly bumbling his feedings, and getting caught in the process. Varney was so endearing that more than once he was saved by living humans who befriended him.

The next major work of vampire literature featured a creature much more sinister and evil than her predecessors—Sheridan Le Fanu's 1871 novella *Carmilla*. Not only was Carmilla literature's first female vampire, but she was also the first literary vampire required to sleep in her native soil at night, to be dispensed with by a stake through her heart, and to be a person returned from death (rather than an corpse possessed by evil spirits). Carmilla's choice of victims was both incestuous and erotic (with some strong lesbian overtones). Carmilla was also the first vampire whose bite would not kill her victims or seal their future fate as vampires. Carmilla's attacks would only weaken her prey; repeated attacks and/or drinking of Carmilla's blood were required to turn her victims into vampires themselves.

Carmilla was inspired by a true-to-life story that occurred in Hungary three hundred years earlier. Elizabeth Bathory, a.k.a. the Blood Countess, sadistically murdered dozens to hundreds (depending on which version of the story you hear) of young women.* Around the time of *Carmilla*, Bathory's exploits were repopularized by claims that she bathed in the blood of virgins thinking it would keep her eternally young. Beyond the scandalous stories, there is no real evidence that Bathory believed this or ever attempted to bathe in blood. According to what evidence does exist, Bathory punished minor transgressions by her domestic staff with brutal beatings, maiming, and bloodletting, killing many in the process. Truth aside, its whole "blood of virgins" routine does make for a good story.

The mother lode of all vampire stories would come two decades after *Carmilla*, when a middling theater manager and failed novelist sat on a cliff in Whitby and started to piece together his masterpiece. After its publication, every vampire tale to follow, anywhere in the world, would have to answer to it.

WHITBY, ENGLAND, IS probably the least likely place on earth to be the "birthplace of goth." If you didn't know better, you'd probably never find out about Whitby's role in vampire and goth history. Stoker and *Dracula* are a sidebar in Whitby history, literally. In guidebooks and tourist brochures, Whitby frames itself as a serene seaside former whaling town—an ideal summer getaway. Stoker and the evil count merit a few sentences of mention, if that.

---

* The Bathory legend also inspired nine films, including the 1970 Hammer Films flick *Countess Dracula* starring Ingrid Pitt and *Immoral Tales* starring Pablo Picasso's daughter Paloma.

You can't blame them, really. The town is quite pleasant and peaceful. Going there, I expected to find a gray place, with howling winds, cold waves crashing against rocky cliffs, and unhappy/fearful locals scuttling about. The rocky cliffs are here, and it seems like a heavy fog or good rainstorm are never far off. Otherwise, I couldn't have been further off the mark.

Twice a year, Whitby does embrace its gothness, when the Whitby Goth Weekend rolls into town. In April and October, the teeny town is taken over by an influx of more than one thousand pilgrims coming to goth mecca. Attendees basically hang out, wear black, drink, and avoid the sun for the weekend. Clothes, accessories, books, comics, and crafts are sold at the daily Bizarre Bazaar. Several bands, with names like DeathBoy, Screaming Banshee Aircrew, and Psychophile, play in the Whitby pubs during the evenings. On Sunday, the Whitby churches conduct special goth services.

Otherwise, Whitby is a quiet place with a modest tourist industry on top of its port traffic. Getting to Whitby is a bit of a chore. It's a little fucking far out of the way. Unless you drive, it involves a five-hour trip from London on three separate trains—each progressively less posh than the ones before. The last stretch of the trip was on a diesel train that felt more like a bus on rails.

Once we arrived, I suggested a walk before dinner to check things out. Rain was forecast for the next day and there were some hard-to-reach places I needed to visit. I wanted to take advantage of the clear afternoon and sunlight. I'm a big walker—I'll happily do it for hours and hours. I like walking so much because taking in the world at a walking pace nicely matches my mental ability to cognate my surroundings.

Unfortunately, my friends and family don't seem to be as down with long walks as I am. Living in Washington, D.C., it's easy to sucker visitors into a walk, say, from the White House to the Lincoln Memorial, then over to the Capitol Building. On a map, it seems totally doable. Counting stops along the way, it can easily drag out to three or four hours on your feet. "Good for the soul," I say. "More like a death march," say my disgruntled companions.

"As long as we can be back in time to have fish and chips for dinner, I'll go," Katherine said.

I just wanted to hike up to the Whitby Abbey and then find the Stoker Seat. That's all. An hour tops.

STOKER WAS DESTINED to write *Dracula*. As a boy he was surrounded by death. He was born in the small town of Clontarf, just outside of Dublin, during the height of the Irish potato famine. During the 1840s, more than one million of Ireland's eight million people died from starvation. Many of those who didn't die wandered the streets looking like the living dead. However, Stoker didn't see this firsthand. He was bedridden for the first seven years of his life, the victim of a mysterious disease that seemed to leave him unable to walk. His mother, who had a bizarre habit of telling her son horror stories while he was confined to bed, often regaled him with graphic stories of the devastation caused by the famine (Stoker later assembled many of these stories in a collection of horror stories). After he was miraculously healed of his affliction, Stoker would often play in a cemetery near the family's home, which was used to bury suicides and other outcasts and undesirables.

My journey to Whitby actually began in Philadelphia, on a street filled with towering nineteenth-century row houses that no one I know could ever afford to live in. In the middle of all these homes is the Rosenbach Library. It's such a subtle presence that if you weren't looking for it, you'd probably walk right by. The Rosenbach isn't a "get on the wait list for the latest John Grisham book" kind of library. It's more a "big building filled with very precious and rare shit" kind of library. The Rosenbach has tons of cool stuff—a large collection from *Where the Wild Things Are* author Maurice Sendak, the original manuscript of James Joyce's *Ulysses,* and the sole surviving copy of the original *Poor Richard's*

Almanack, printed by Benjamin Franklin himself. The Rosenbach Library is also the owner of Bram Stoker's notes and outline for *Dracula.*

When I arrived at the Rosenbach, I was greeted with polite and professional skepticism. I don't blame them. I show up, a complete unknown, claiming to be writing a book about vampires. I guess it's a testament to their open-mindedness that they let me in to the rare documents room at all.* Once I was signed in and properly identified and documented, the librarian brought in a large black box, filled with smaller black folios, each filled with plastic protective sleeves for every page of Stoker's notes.

The original manuscript for *Dracula* was thought to have been lost forever. (The manuscript did resurface in 2002 when it was offered in a Christie's auction. Despite the intense interest in the manuscript, it didn't sell for its reserve price.) The same was thought of his original notes for the novel, until Radu Florescu and Raymond McNally, two Dracula researchers known for popularizing the connection between Vlad Dracula and Count Dracula, went to the Rosenbach to view a Vlad Dracula woodcut in its collection. While viewing it, one of the library's staff remarked, "Would you like to see Stoker's notes for *Dracula?* We have them around here someplace."

A little more than a year after his death, Bram's widow Florence auctioned the contents of his library to raise some cash. The collection was purchased by an American book dealer, who promptly lost the *Dracula* notes for more than twenty-five years. They emerged in several auction catalogues in the late 1930s and early 1940s, and then disappeared again until 1970, when they were found discarded in a barn owned by a collector. The Rosenbach Li-

---

* I don't want to give you the impression that the Rosenbach folks were stuffy clichés—quite the opposite. They do have some fun with their most famous acquisition. Every Halloween they have a series of public events, including a small parade with giant vampire puppets that seems to perplex the library's neighbors.

brary bought them, catalogued them, and pretty much forgot about them too until Florescu and McNally showed up a few years later.

The Rosenbach's collection of notes provides copious, fascinating *Dracula* trivia. They also demonstrate how almost accidental the novel's greatness was.

Perhaps it's just me, but when told I was going to view the handwritten notes for one of the most influential novels of all time, I expected something a bit more grand than what I saw. Stoker's notes are packed on small slips of paper, written in tiny, tight, and sloppy cursive that made my hand hurt just looking at it.

According to his notes, Stoker originally envisioned *Dracula* as a Sherlock Holmes–style mystery thriller.* In a listing called "Historiae Personae," what became Dr. Abraham Van Helsing started off as three separate characters—a detective, a "psychical research agent," and a professor from Germany (switched to Austria when molded into Van Helsing).† Stoker had also penciled in and then abandoned, a "deaf-mute woman" and a "silent man" as servants in Count Dracula's castle, as well as an undertaker and his assistant, though with no indication as to how they were supposed to fit into the story (outside of, most likely, dealing with some dead bodies at some juncture).

Other curiosities include a list of scenes that never made it into the book—a large dinner party for most of the novel's characters as well as a prelude to the novel's eventual opening scenes that had other characters visiting the count in Transylvania before Harker's arrival. Stoker also had copious notes about vampire lore, including lists of powers he contemplated for his count. Among those he

---

* This is particularly interesting since during the time Stoker was working on *Dracula,* Holmes author Arthur Conan Doyle wrote a story called "The Parasite" that featured Holmes battling against a psychic vampire. It's even more interesting when you realize that there was a connection between Stoker and Conan Doyle at the time. Stoker and Henry Irving acquired the rights to Conan Doyle's first play, eventually performing it more than three hundred times at the Lyceum. The two authors even became friends.

† In addition to sharing a first name, *Dracula*'s physical description of Van Helsing matched Stoker's own attributes, leading many Stoker experts to think that Bram very consciously molded Van Helsing to represent himself.

eventually decided against including were sensitivity to music and an obsession with numbers.

Stoker also took meticulous notes about the action of the novel and the movements of his characters. Among his notes were calendar pages from 1893 (the year the novel takes place). Stoker filled in the calendar with the details in the story, assigning specific dates for every point on his outline (though this level of detail is never shared in the novel itself). For example, Harker arrives at Castle Dracula on May 5, Dracula arrives in England on August 7, Van Helsing shows up to save the day on September 10, and the whole mess is cleaned up by November 1. Stoker went as far as to list the specific trains or boats, arrival and departure times, and the costs for every journey taken by any character. He even had notes taken from reading a book entitled *Fishery Barometer Manual*.

The most obvious changes to the novel's construction were its title and the name of its protagonist. At various points he had considered "The Undead" and "The Dead Un-dead." Originally, Stoker had wanted to call the count "Wampyr" and wrote the character into the outline itself for the first ten chapters. Once he discovered the tales of the evil Wallachian prince, he crossed out every mention of Wampyr and replaced them with Dracula. He was so taken with the name that he wrote it repeatedly throughout his notes, like a teenage girl writing the name of her current crush on the cover of her notebook.

"WHAT DO YOU do with it?" Katherine asked.

"You eat it, I guess," I replied.

"No, I think *you* eat it."

We were both staring at a large piece of candy in my palm, called a Dracula's Coffin. Walking through Whitby to reach the 199 steps leading up to the abbey, we passed dozens of quaint tourist trap gift shops, selling a variety of kitsch with no discernable useful purpose. Among the stores hawking jet jewelry and dream catchers, I spotted a building painted black with bright red trim. It was a candy store with a banner advertising: DRACULA'S COFFINS SOLD HERE. Three pounds later, I was the proud owner of two Dracula's Coffins. They were little brown chocolate coffins, about the size of a candy bar. As a little added touch, each had a cross painted on top in red icing. This was one of only three businesses in town with *any* kind of goth, vampire, or Dracula-related merchandise or mentions.

After deducing that the point of buying a candy bar was, in fact, to eat it, I bit in. The bar was filled with red nougat, which I assumed was supposed to be strawberry-flavored, but tasted more like wet powdered sugar. I caught myself thinking afterward, "Why strawberry?" Strawberry is something I associate with Care Bears and My Little Pony, not undead evil. It seemed that if you wanted to pursue the whole "candy blood" thing, you'd pick something with a bit more kick—like wild cherry or tropical punch. Maybe that's just me. Regardless, the taste in my mouth cleared up any debate (albeit nonexistent) as to whether Dracula's Coffins were sold for their novelty value or confectionery excellence. Mixed with the chocolate, the Dracula's Coffin tasted more like Dracula's ass.

I still had the "strawberry" taste in my mouth by the time we reached the plateau containing the ruins of the abbey, which dramatically sits atop a cliff overlooking the entire town. Whitby Abbey has a brief unspecific mention in *Dracula*, but was more than likely the inspiration for some of its more famous locations. The abbey was originally built in 657 by St. Hilda, then was attacked by the Danes, and pretty much destroyed 200 years later. It was rebuilt in the eleventh century by a guy named, seriously, William the Bastard, and remained in operation until it was shut down by Henry VIII in the sixteenth century and abandoned. The remains of the abbey were in better shape during Stoker's day, but most of the fifty-foot northern walls that formed the front and left sides of the abbey still stand.* During *Dracula*'s London scenes, Count Dracula's main hangout was a dilapidated Carfax Abbey. As I discovered while roaming around London, there is no real Carfax Abbey (or anything similar). However, from its description, it bears a strong resemblance to Whitby Abbey. Considering how the abbey rises so grandly above the town below that it almost seems majestically out of scale, you can imagine some influence on Stoker's vision for Dracula's Transylvanian castle as well.

Just outside the abbey grounds is St. Mary's Church and its adjacent cemetery. The roof and some other bits of the abbey were used to complete St. Mary's Church after it was shut down by Henry VIII. (Henry also ordered that the church bells be shipped to London. The locals were pretty pissed off by this move, but were cheered up when the boat carrying the bells sank soon after leaving port. Supposedly, the bells still sit in the waters off Whitby Harbor and, according to local legend, can be heard ringing on occasion.) The gravestones go back to the mid-1700s. The wind and salty air have left their surface blackened and pitted, looking like they are covered in noodles rather than details of the locals buried underneath. With the juxtaposition of the North Sea, the abbey ruins, and the town below, the cemetery has an eerie and mildly spooky vibe to it. Standing in the midst of it, you can see why it would make a great strategic location for the count to hide.

On our way back into town, we passed several pubs, most of which advertised fresh fish and chips. Katherine looked longingly at them, then at me, hoping I'd notice.

"Only one more stop before dinner," I added. "We need to go find the Stoker Seat, then we're good."

The Stoker Seat was an official memorial to Bram and his book that was (purportedly) located near a statue honoring former

---

* German bomb attacks on Whitby during World War I leveled several sections of the abbey. In the years since, preservationists have "rebuilt" part of the ruins—to help it stay ruined in a more authentic way. This is a concept that strikes me as incredibly British.

Whitby resident Captain James Cook. Supposedly, when you sit on it you get a panoramic view of all the Whitby locations mentioned in *Dracula*. The only problem was that I had no idea what the Stoker Seat was, where it was located, or what it looked like. I hadn't let Katherine in on this lack of specifics, but figured I could wing it.

BRAM STOKER'S LIFE was going exactly as planned until he attended a performance of *Hamlet* in 1876. After graduating from Trinity College with a degree in mathematics, he followed his father in civil service. During his postcollege years in Dublin, his creative output was limited to a four-part serialized short story called "Jack Hammon's Vote" as well as work on his first book, the self-explanatory 248-page *The Duties of Clerks of Petty Sessions in Ireland,* a guide to civil service procedure and policy. A page-turner, it is not.

His initial ambitions in life weren't literary. While in college, he had harbored dreams of becoming an actor, but his family's disapproval, along with an unfortunate lack of talent, forced him into the wings. To stay connected to the theater, he took an unpaid position writing byline-less theatrical reviews for the *Dublin Mail* (which was owned by *Carmilla* author Sheridan Le Fanu).

While reviewing *Hamlet,* Stoker was blown away by the lead, Henry Irving. Stoker would go on to write three reviews of Irving's *Hamlet.* Irving was so impressed by Stoker's praises of him that he invited the critic to dinner. That night the two men struck up a deep friendship—eating, drinking, and conversing late into the night. In his biography of Irving many years later, Stoker wrote of that evening, "Soul had looked into soul! From that hour began a friendship as profound, as close, as lasting as can be between two men." They continued to spend massive amounts of time together on Irving's return trips to Dublin as well as during Stoker's visits to London.

They began their friendship at the same time that Irving's star was rising. During this age, an actor who reached the pinnacle of success would set up his own company in his own theater. When Irving came into such an arrangement in 1878, he asked Stoker to move to London and manage his theater, the Lyceum. Bram didn't think long before accepting Irving's offer. He rushed his courtship to a local girl, Florence Balcombe, and was off to London with his new wife less than two weeks later.*

Stoker's work at the Lyceum was difficult and consuming. The theater rotated different productions (all starring Irving) throughout the season, with most summers taken up with tours. However, his position opened up a new world to Stoker. Because of his generous compensation and Irving's status (he was by this time considered England's greatest living actor), Bram and Florence enjoyed a lifestyle and social position they would never have had otherwise. Through his Irving connections, the Stokers mixed with royalty and high society, eventually befriending artistic heavyweights like James McNeill Whistler, Alfred Lord Tennyson, Mark Twain, Dante Gabriel Rossetti, George Bernard Shaw, and the widow of author Charles Dickens.

Despite the perks, life with Henry Irving had its drawbacks as well. To be succinct, Irving was a mercurial, narcissistic, melodramatic attention-whore. To be even more succinct, he was a huge asshole. It was Irving's world—Stoker and the rest only lived in it. While Irving craved attention and adoration, he was less than quick with praise and acknowledgment of others—especially Stoker. Over the years, their close friendship morphed into something in between codependence and servitude. Stoker was perpet-

---

* One of the most curious of Stoker's many connections to other literary figures of the time involved his rival suitor for Florence's hand—Oscar Wilde. Bram and Oscar had become acquainted during their years at Trinity, with Stoker forming a strong bond to Wilde's father, Sir William Wilde. Oscar Wilde was the antithesis of Stoker, which is probably the reason Florence tired of waiting for Wilde to settle down and instead married Stoker. Oscar and Florence would continue to correspond and remain friendly throughout the rest of their lives.

ually devoted to Irving and the responsibilities entrusted to him. He was Irving's protector, sounding board, wingman, and cleanup crew. Stoker's talents at running the theater also made Irving a very rich and successful man. Irving, however, never missed a chance to ridicule Stoker or to make sure that the pecking order of their relative status was apparent to everyone.

Other elements of Stoker's life slowly became unraveled as well. His marriage to Florence turned cold after the birth of their only child. He mustered the time and energy to write three novels, all of which failed. After what seemed to be such a bright start filled with potential, Stoker slowly settled into an unhappy, unfulfilling, and mediocre life. Then, in 1890, he started to outline a new novel, one that would take him six years to conceive and write: his story of an undead count from the east and the band of brothers that would come together to rise up and defeat him.

Stoker jokingly claimed that the story of *Dracula* came to him one night in a dream after eating too much dressed crab. In truth, he spent three years outlining and taking notes before starting to write the novel during a summer vacation at Cruden Bay, Scotland. Stoker immersed himself in constructing *Dracula*, far beyond his efforts for his previous books. Stoker's son, Noel, remembered that during the times Stoker was writing *Dracula*, he was extremely testy and difficult. Florence once commented, "When he was at work on *Dracula*, we were all frightened of him. He seemed to get obsessed by the spirit of the thing. There he would sit for hours or wander alone up and down the sandhills, thinking it out."

The first thing that strikes most people when they spend time with *Dracula* is that the count in the book is so much different than what we recognize as the iconic image of Dracula. If asked to describe the count, most go for Lugosi: a regal, European aristocrat with flawless hair, strikingly handsome looks, and wearing impeccably tailored evening wear. Stoker's vision of Dracula, especially in the beginning of the novel, is quite different.

Stoker describes the count's general look as "one of extraordinary pallor." Stoker's villain looked old and pale, with white hair that "grew scantily round the temples but profusely elsewhere," a thick mustache, and large nose. During their first evening together in the Transylvanian castle, Jonathan Harker noted the count's "particularly sharp teeth," pointy ears, bad breath, and his hands, which had squat fingers, long nails, and hair in the palms of his hands.

There's been quite a bit of speculation about Stoker's inspiration for the count's look. Obviously there are some elements that comport with European vampire lore, but such a striking and specific presence begs for a better story. Yet like so many other things about Stoker and *Dracula,* if there's any deeper meaning, Bram left few clues. One clue might be a brief name check by Mina of Italian criminologist Cesare Lombroso. In Lombroso's work on degeneration theory, he described the "delinquent type"—a physical profile that was typical for criminals and other degenerates.* Other researchers have theorized that Stoker modeled Dracula's physical characteristics after Henry Irving's portrayal of Mephistopheles.

One of the most unusual (yet totally plausible) theories about Dracula's physical origins involved the man who was probably the largest influence on Stoker's life—poet Walt Whitman. Save the hairy palms and pointed teeth, Stoker's physical description of the count closely resembles Whitman.

Stoker discovered Whitman while a student at Trinity College. Bram was big into a debate society called the Phil and spent an inordinate amount of his time arguing for Whitman's genius. Debates were a way for Stoker to command a stage and audience. At the time, Whitman was a hot topic. Some thought his themes of "robust love" and male camaraderie defined masculinity; others saw Whitman as a barbaric deviant who "offended modern sensitivities." Though the concept of culturally defined sexual identity still

---

* Lombroso's work is also considered to be profoundly racist, which wouldn't help *Dracula* overcome recurring criticism about its own racist overtones.

hadn't jelled by the late nineteenth century, Whitman was a con-flicted homosexual, a theme that was core to his work.

Stoker's intense interest in Whitman continued to grow after college. So much so that Stoker wrote a two-thousand-word letter to the poet in February 1872. Reading it today, it reads like a mash note. He wrote that he wanted to talk with Whitman "as men who are not poets do not often talk." He continued, "You are a true man, and I would like to be one myself."

"I am writing you because you are different than other men," he penned. "You have shaken off the shackles and your wings are free. I have shackles on my shoulders still—but have no wings . . . I have to thank you for many happy hours, for I have read your po-ems with my door locked late at night."

At times, the letter veers toward sounding like a personals ad description: "I am six feet two inches high and twelve stone weight naked . . . I am ugly but strong and determined and have a large bump over my eyebrows. I have a heavy jaw and a big mouth and thick lips—sensitive nostrils—a snub-nose and straight hair . . . I am equal in temper and cool in disposition and have a large amount of self-control and am naturally secretive to the world."*

He concluded (several pages later) by humbly acknowledging that Whitman probably received many such letters from fans of his poetry and might never see Stoker's letter. "Even if you do not read my letter it is no less a pleasure to me to write it. . . . How sweet a thing it is for a strong healthy man with a woman's eyes and a child's wishes to feel that he can speak so to a man who can be if he wishes father, and brother and wife to his soul."

After reading this, you are probably having the same reaction I did when I first discovered it: The letter really makes it hard to ar-gue that Bram wasn't totally gay. However, it's just another ex-

---

* One explanation for this peculiar description is that both Stoker and Whitman were big fans of phrenology—a fad in the nineteenth century that used head bumps and shape of the forehead to predict character traits. Stoker probably included these details to clue Whitman that he was a fellow head-reader.

ample of the enigmas that surround Stoker. He wrote one of the most erotic, metaphorically laden novels of his time, yet more than likely was completely clueless as to how powerful his characters and story would become. Further, earlier in his life he began a longtime gushing correspondence with one of the most iconic gay writers of all time, yet was probably unable to comprehend his own feelings. One of the reasons it is so difficult to understand Stoker is because Stoker didn't understand Stoker.

Whitman almost didn't get a chance to read Stoker's letter. After writing it, Stoker stuck the letter in his desk drawer. It sat there, Stoker too nervous to send it, for more than four years. Then, after attending a debate over the merits of Whitman's "Children of Adam" poems, he went home, fished out the yellowing letter, and posted it.

Whitman loved receiving letters from young men moved by his work. He kept and often commented on Stoker's letters, especially enjoying Stoker's description of Whitman as "father, brother and wife to his soul." Whitman wrote back to Stoker, igniting a correspondence between the two men that would continue until Whitman's death.

Whitman influenced *Dracula* in many profound ways. In his writing, Whitman often celebrated a somewhat bizarre mixture of blood, death, and sexual euphoria. The novel's plot hinges on a Whitmanesque view of masculine power. In the novel, Count Dracula goes about with his plans relatively unchecked until a group of men come together to challenge him. Through their camaraderie, their heroism emerged. After spending the first part of the book being confused or bumbling around trying to understand what to do next, once they come together as a group, their true potential surfaces. Only then are they able to uncover the evil protagonist's plans, save the virtuous woman, and then kill the offender. In subtle ways, Whitman taught Stoker that love and sex were so powerful that even death was a fair exchange for finding them.

The bottom line is that if you were to hold up images of the count and Whitman—you'd be looking at the same person. Stoker imagined Dracula as the perfect human. His monster was an example of the ultimate masculinity, the quintessential male. When Bram Stoker thought of the perfect man, he thought of Walt Whitman.

Stoker was empowered by Whitman's acknowledgment. Within a few months of the Whitman correspondence, everything in Stoker's life would change. His father would die. He changed his name from Abraham to Bram, quit his civil service job, abandoned writing criticism, started writing novels, and left his life and family behind to follow Henry Irving to London.

As Whitman would later point out, when Stoker started writing to Whitman, what Bram really was doing was writing to himself.

AN HOUR LATER Katherine and I had crossed over the Esk River and hiked up to the plateau on the west side of Whitby, visited the Cook statue, another monument to Whitby's whaling industry, a gazebo, and at least a half dozen other structures that, at a distance, mildly resembled something official-looking. We had asked for directions in two hotels, a gift shop, and a bar. With one exception, no one had even heard of the Stoker Seat, let alone knew what or where it was. The one guy who claimed to know (a hotel clerk) pointed us toward an area of a park that contained an abandoned tennis court, a trash can, and a large mud puddle—but no memorial to Stoker. The only thing approaching undead status was me, as whatever grace I had with Katherine slowly evaporated after our third or fourth dead end. I had resorted to triangulating our position based on the Whitby Bay and the abbey (now a distant tall-looking thing on the other side of town), but I was getting nowhere fast.

"This thing is in Whitby, right?" Katherine asked.

"You bet. I've seen a picture of it, it's here."

"Maybe it's a joke," Katherine offered. "They pull this prank on people researching vampires. They lead you around town, then just when you are about to collapse from exhaustion or eat your own foot from hunger, they show up and let you know it doesn't exist."

In truth, I hadn't really seen a picture of it. I'd seen a picture of the dedication, which was a bunch of people in suits standing around shaking hands (no memorial in the picture). I'd also seen a picture of the plaque attached to it. Again, I decided to keep this bit of intelligence to myself.

I noticed three older people chatting on the street corner, two of whom were leading dogs. For some reason (probably the odd number of them and the presence of dogs), I was convinced they were local. I walked up and asked about the Stoker Seat.

They looked at one another, then back at me.

"You mean the bench?" one asked.

"I guess," I replied. "I really have no idea what it is."

"There's a bench around here with a plaque on it. It's green I think."

I looked out at the line of forty or fifty green benches that run along the cliff every twenty yards or so for as far as we could see.

"Any idea which one?" I asked.

"No," he replied. "But if you plan to find it before sundown, you'd better get started now, shouldn't you?"

"Right. What happens at sundown?"

"Vampires, lad," he said, curling his fingers and baring his teeth. "The vampires come out to get ya."

He laughed; we didn't.

* * *

READING MEANING INTO *Dracula* is difficult—mostly because it is so easy to do. The problem with understanding the novel's subtexts is that so little is known about Stoker's intentions. Because of this, scholars and critics have a tendency to dump what little is known about Stoker into the book, assuming that there has to be some

sort of connection. There doesn't. *Dracula* could have been a vehicle for all sorts of dark creepiness running around in Stoker's
brain. Equally, it could have no meaning at all.

A tremendous amount of ink and brainpower has focused on
the subtexts, metaphors, and allegories contained in *Dracula*.
While *Dracula* is a Rosetta stone of the Victorian psyche, the book
has become a thematic dumping ground. That's the unifying force
among all vampires—literal and figurative: They are vessels. Be it
fear of change, sex, political turmoil, untimely death, immigration,
war, AIDS—the vampire always appears, embodying everything
that terrifies, titillates, and confuses, then feeds off that fear to create its power.

Chief among these themes are the issues of eroticism and sexuality that underlie *Dracula*. The Victorian era was a time of extreme sexual repression, especially for women. Any woman in
Victorian literature who expressed interest in sex, even married
women, were portrayed as hussies. Of the five female characters in
the novel, four of them wind up as vampires (with the fifth saved
from undead status at the last minute). If you accept vampire
blood-sucking as a metaphor for sex, the message is pretty clear:
Death and eternal damnation wait for those who succumb to
tingly feelings. Women are also shown as sexual predators bent on
the undoing of men. As vampires, the female characters attempt to
seduce and corrupt the men around them, tempting them down
their own virtueless path. During his captivity in Transylvania,
Harker is visited by the count's three vampire wives for a little
four-way vamp action. Harker has a more sensual and intimate relationship with the count's wives on one page of *Dracula* than he
does with his own fiancé throughout the rest of the book.

This scene also sets the stage for the other chief sexual theme
often pegged to *Dracula*—homosexuality. When things are getting
hot and drippy among Harker and the vampire ladies, the count
bursts in and orders the vamps away proclaiming, "Back, I tell you
all! This man belongs to me!" If you combine this declaration of
dominance and ownership with the theories of who Stoker mod-

eled the count after—Whitman and Henry (both men that some critics have strenuously argued Stoker was in love with)—you can quickly see why this scene is thought to set the tone for *Dracula's* perceived homosexual themes.

Right behind the sex stuff are gender issues. Specifically, the differences between the two female lead characters, Mina and Lucy. Critics often complain that the female characters in *Dracula* are two-dimensional and rather wooden stereotypes. Two responses come to mind. First, look in just about any piece of fiction with two female central characters. Almost universally, one is painted as a virtuous princess, the other as a promiscuous, rebellious slut. From Desdemona and Emilia to Ginger and Mary Ann, Betty and Veronica, and Thelma and Louise—right or wrong, it's kind of the default archetype for multiple female characters. It didn't begin or end with Bram Stoker. Secondly, the shallow characterization goes beyond Mina and Lucy. Given, the central male characters in *Dracula* are rich, complex, and multidimensional. Beyond that, when you look at *every* Stoker character in every one of his novels, they all (male and female) are terribly dull, flat, and uninteresting. Still, Stoker had a pretty hard-line view of women. One bad move and an upright, virginal good girl became a deflowered, adulterous, unredeemable slut. There wasn't a lot of gray area in between as far as Stoker was concerned.

Having sat through more Lyceum-produced Victorian drama and Shakespeare than anyone should have to see, it's no surprise that many see some of those thematic structures emerging in Stoker's work. Count Dracula has a strong resemblance to Faust's Mephistopheles (a role Irving performed hundreds of times). The Transylvanian castle's supernatural occurrences and allure parallel with those in *Macbeth*. The dangers of female sexuality can be seen in both *Dracula* and *Othello* (Lucy even name checks Desdemona in a letter she writes to Mina).

Count Dracula himself is the poster boy for Darwinism. Pitting Van Helsing and crew against the evil count amounts to a showdown between man and nature. Further, during the Industrial

Revolution science was considered a tool to control and manipulate nature (Dracula's pursuers make use of a variety of cutting edge turn-of-the-century technology such as phonograph cylinders, telegraphs, and typewriters).

Others have pointed to *Dracula* as a rejection of science and technology, embracing it as Christian allegory. Not only are vampires repelled by Christian symbols, but as Professor Van Helsing gathers together his vampire hunters, he tells them they are "ministers of God's own wish"—setting out on a crusade to save the innocent from evil. Stoker's London is on the verge of moral collapse, and the vampire killers embrace righteousness and the power of the Church to save their friends and neighbors.

Still others see *Dracula* as an embrace of occultism and worship of the supernatural. Beyond the living undead able to turn into rats, wolves, and mist, it has been long rumored (and largely undocumented) that Stoker was involved in an occult society in London. At the time, spiritualism was quite a fad in Europe and many people (Stoker included) participated in parlor spiritualism of one sort or another.

These suggested themes are just the beginning. Countless deep thinkers have viewed *Dracula* as testimony for Marxism, cultural xenophobia, conscious-altering drugs, classism, anti-Semitism, war, sadomasochism, and on and on.

Despite what you've read over the past few pages, all of this was lost on the critics of the time. When *Dracula* was released, the reviews were polite and tepid (this was actually a *good* critical reaction for a Stoker book). While some critics found the book grotesque, not a single one picked up on any deeper themes or metaphorical taboos. A large but not overly impressive 3,000 copies were printed for sale in England. *Dracula* sold better than other Stoker books, but was far from a hit.

During this time, authors regularly staged tedious read-throughs of their books on stage in order to protect their dramatic rights. Stoker was no exception. Stoker did openly fantasize about *Dracula* being staged at the Lyceum, with Henry Irving in the lead. Despite his repeated attempts to interest Irving in staging the story, Irving never took it seriously. During the read-through of *Dracula,* Irving was seen looking in from the back of the theater. When asked what he thought of Stoker's new story, Irving gave a simple and clear response, projected loud enough to echo through the entire theater.

"Dreadful."

"Excuse me, have you ever heard of the Stoker Seat, or a bench dedicated to Stoker, or anything to do with sitting and *Dracula*?" I asked an older man we passed. Since encountering our first group of Whitby seniors, we'd walked down past every bench on the west shore of Whitby, then back through to double-check. The sun was setting and by this time we'd been walking several hours.

"Sure," he replied, as if it was something he was asked every day. "It's that one right over there."

I should have been excited that he was pointing to a bench less than thirty yards away. However, to get there, we'd have to walk down a set of stairs along the cliff, across a road, up another set of stairs on the other side, and past five other benches. There sat a green wooden bench which looked slightly different than the others.

"Can—"

"Let's just go," Katherine interrupted, offering a weary but assuring smile.

Down the stairs, across the road, back up, and down the row. There it was.

In the middle of the bench was a small plaque about the size of a snapshot:

THE VIEW FROM THIS SPOT
INSPIRED BRAM STOKER (1847–1912)
TO USE WHITBY AS THE SETTING OF PART OF HIS
WORLD-FAMOUS NOVEL
DRACULA

As we sat there seeing Whitby pretty much the way that Bram did more than one hundred and fifteen years ago, I point out all the features to Katherine. Down below us is the site of an actual shipwreck in 1885 that inspired Stoker to use the scene for Dracula's arrival in England. Rising out of the bay are the famous steps that Dracula and Lucy dart up toward the cemetery. Directly across is where Mina and Lucy lived. I felt a little silly because I was talking about the novel's events as if they had actually happened. But being in a location like Whitby makes the book come alive in an unexpected way. It felt oddly natural to mix fact and fiction together, making you appreciate the elegant perfections of the story. Sitting on that bench, I had no problem understanding why *Dracula* has become a classic. I could literally feel the power of the novel, its weight and gravitas.

DESPITE THE EVENTUAL reach and success of *Dracula*, Stoker saw few returns during his lifetime. After its publication, his life went on as normal for several years, until the death of Henry Irving in 1905. As testament to how much the relationship between the two men had changed, Irving's will didn't contain any mention, thanks, or bequest to Stoker. Afterward, Stoker learned how much his position in society was tied to his former employer. Many of his former acquaintances, especially his famous and high society acquaintances, had little use for Stoker once Irving was gone.

After closing up Irving's affairs, Stoker tried his hand at management again with an opera production. It closed in two months. He bounced around among several other projects before suffering a stroke in 1907, which made walking difficult and permanently affected his eyesight.

Dracula remained in print throughout his lifetime, but didn't earn much in royalties. During this period Stoker complained to his brother that his royalties were only about one hundred and sixty dollars a year. For additional income, Stoker turned back to writing. In addition to cranking out novels and a two-volume memoir-biography of Irving,* Stoker wrote profiles for several newspapers in London and New York. If *Dracula* brought any benefits to Stoker during his lifetime, it was to open doors for profile subjects, such as a young Winston Churchill (who was a fan of the novel). To cut down on expenses, Bram and Florence downsized their home.

Stoker made some quiet references to creating a *Dracula* sequel that would bring the count to America. In *Dracula*, the count wasn't killed by a stake through his heart, burned and reburied, or other traditional vampire-slaying methodology. The Van Helsing posse killed the count via decapitation. Given Stoker's research into vampire lore, and the "correct" methods used to kill off Lucy earlier in the book, it's doubtful Stoker created the flubbed death by accident. Further evidence of a potential *Dracula* sequel lies in Stoker's edits to the original manuscript. Originally, Dracula's castle was to be destroyed in a volcanic explosion following the count's death. Just before publication, Stoker deleted those passages.

Stoker continued to write books during his remaining years, at one point stating his goal was to publish a new novel every year (more for the meager advances he received rather than the artistic outlet). He released three more supernaturally themed novels. None were very good or attracted a fraction of the modest attention given to *Dracula*. All three of these novels had plots involving evil women, including his last book *The Lair of the White Worm*. If any of Stoker's novels contained a metaphoric relationship to Stoker's views on women, it was *Lair*. Reading it, you'd think that Bram thought the vagina was the most hideous and repulsive contraption ever devised. When writing about the lair of the novel's two-hundred-foot, two-thousand-year-old vampire-like worm character Lady Arabella, Stoker described her as having

---

* Most of the known biographical information about Bram himself is contained in these volumes.

a "snake's hole" that smelled like "the drainage of war hospitals, of slaughterhouses, the refuse of dissecting rooms." Yum.

Stoker died in April of 1912 at the age of sixty-four, about a week after the *Titanic* sank. Like so many things about Bram's life, the cause of his death is less than certain. The official cause of death was kidney ailments. However, there is evidence that Bram may have died of complications from syphilis.* Stoker scholars get in a lather over this issue. The truth is that it is almost impossible to conclusively prove, or disprove, either argument. The only thing certain is that Stoker's life ended much like the rest of his life was lived—it was murky, unremarkable, and unfulfilled.

ON THE NIGHT before we went home, Katherine and I headed out to poke around the one nearby London neighborhood that we hadn't yet explored—Soho. The warnings about Soho given in most tour guidebooks were the very reasons we were interested in going— Soho is the West End home for many of London's "seedy and fringe cultural elements."

Walking down Old Compton Street we passed dozens of restaurants and gay bars. Even though it was only 8:30 on a Tuesday evening, most of the gay bars were overflowing onto the sidewalks. After walking for several blocks with an intense look and her mouth slightly ajar, Katherine looked at me and said, "I wish my cell phone worked here."

She didn't need to explain any further; I knew exactly what she meant. Whenever Katherine and her girlfriends have something

---

* This hypothesis came about in 1975 when Stoker's grandnephew had Bram's medical records examined with hopes of illuminating some of the disorientation and looniness found in *Lair*. The primary argument for syphilis is the fact that Stoker's doctor prescribed arsenic for him during the last two years of his life. Arsenic was not used as a treatment for stroke or kidney ailments, but it was a common treatment for syphilis. Further, some of the ailments that plagued Stoker at the end of his life (locomotor ataxy—a degeneration of the nervous system) were common side effects of prolonged syphilis.

"important" to discuss right away—such as relationship advice, bad shoes on a mean coworker, or a major delivery at Loehmann's—they text message one another. Katherine's comment indicated her pain that she couldn't immediately share this discovery—hordes of well-groomed gay men (complete with British accents) literally spilling into the streets. Katherine and her girlfriends love gay men. In fact, they love everything about gay men. They all dream of having their very own gay boyfriend for shopping trips, dishing, and late-night clubbing.

"I don't think I've ever seen so many hot guys in one place in my life," she said, her attention darting from the bass thump emitting from a dance club to a group of skintight-designer-T-shirt-wearing guys enjoying a chat over double mocha decaf lattes before going out for the evening, then back over toward a rowdy group drinking pints on the sidewalk in front of a pub.

Even though we'd visited the birthplace of goth and arguably one of the creepiest places on the planet in the past few days, it's this moment that was the trip's most revealing to me about vampires, Bram Stoker, and all this associated nonsense.

One of the reasons Katherine and her friends lionize gay men is because they are a safe outlet, an easy, living metaphor. Our culture tends to frown upon married women having deep relationships with other men—unless they are gay, of course. Finding other men attractive, going out to nightclubs, long and intense discussions—all enjoyed guilt-free with her gay male friends. Expressing these feelings through gay men is so acceptable she can even discuss them (and her desire for them) with *me*. People approach vampires the same way. Vampires are a metaphoric release, a channel for desires, fears, biases, anger, and longing that would be taboo otherwise. The point isn't that people have these thoughts and feelings, they just need a safe way to express and comprehend them.

The Highgate vampire could be seen the same way. The reports of Highgate ghosts and undead creatures happened to occur at a time when London's baby boomers were just coming of age and doing lots of reckless things (like hanging around in dangerous abandoned graveyards). Attempts by the locals to destroy the un-dead could be metaphors for trying to control the crazy young hippies.

Whatever Stoker was trying to work out, *Dracula* doubtlessly served the same purpose for him as well.

Months later, when I asked Katherine about my theory about our Soho visit, she responded, "Huh. Well, I guess you're probably right. I really hadn't given it much thought." Her vibe—mildly in-teresting, but not interesting enough that she'd ever cared about it before.

If you could ask Bram Stoker about whatever flavor-of-the-month thematic *Dracula* deconstruction you happen to favor, he'd probably respond in the same blasé manner. Whatever Count Dracula represented to Stoker—sex, race, evolution, xenophobia, encroachment of technology—it just kinda happened because it . . . happened. Despite the years of effort he put into charting the actions of his novel, he more than likely didn't put in any time to examining his own motivations.

In fact, if Bram Stoker saw what we've done with his count, he probably wouldn't recognize him. If he did, he'd laugh. In the more than 110 years since Count Dracula made his voyage west, we've taken Stoker's original vampire and made him into a heinous rat-looking thing, a dapper gentleman, a karate-chop-wielding de-fender of Jesus, a rock star, an alien from another planet, a woman, and hundreds of other iterations. Our Draculas have been molded for our times.

Stoker would probably be outwardly flattered by all the fuss. In-ternally, though, he'd probably be confused.

VI

GOD IS DEAD AND NO ONE CARES

In which the author meets many vampires and two rats,
then refuses to dress like a gay pirate.

"CHECK OUT THIS one," I said, while pulling out a black shirt dotted with spikes, eyelets, and about a dozen buckles that apparently held together little besides a faint sense of sinister coolness. "If I were drunk, I'd wear this."

"Mmm. I see where you're going," said my friend Shauna. "But I still think the frilly stuff makes a clearer statement."

Shauna and I were browsing at a store named Trash and Vaudeville in Greenwich Village. We'd originally met up for lunch while I was in the city, but Shauna decided to accompany me on my shopping trip. Shauna is one of my dearest friends and a beautiful, stylish woman. However, she wouldn't be my first choice for a goth fashion consultant.

I was in town to attend a gathering of "the vampyre society of greater New York," called The Court of Lazarus. I was totally prepared for just about anything to happen that evening. The only problem was my clothes. In order to keep some sense of privacy at this semipublic gathering, The Court of Lazarus has a dress code. Specifically, a dress code calling for "formal gothic attire." Now, take a moment to look at the author photo on the cover of this book. As should be quite obvious, my round face and boyish looks are about as far from goth as you could get, save for someone wearing a set of Mouseketeer ears.

This caused me an embarrassing amount of duress. I wanted to fit in (let alone *get* in), yet I felt that if I wore something overtly sinister, I'd be faking it. I couldn't imagine finding anyone willing to speak to me in an obvious "costume." Originally I planned to just wear a black shirt and pants. However, after seeing pictures of previous Court of Lazarus gatherings, I was a little panicked. I arrived in New York with a list of goth shops, most along St. Marks Place. Shauna and I were working our way down the list.

After visiting about half a dozen shops, things weren't going well. So far, a bunch of the stores on my list had gone out of business. Others were more tailored toward fetishists or wannabe rock gods, so unless I wanted something skintight or made of rubber and designed to allow easy orifice access, my pickings were slim. There were a fairly substantial variety of slutty goth girl clothes, but for guys the only option seemed to be Victorian shirts with puffy sleeves and lace around the collar and cuffs.

"No, I think that's a terrible idea," I said.

"Why?" she replied, pulling a white frilly shirt off the rack. "It's pretty gothic-looking."

"On me it would be gay pirate–looking. That's not the variety of scary I think they're looking for."

"It could look rather sexy," she offered.

"Or it could look rather stupid," I replied.

Shauna held the shirt against my chest and took a step back. The look on her face is one you'd expect from a mother when her four-year-old tries on a pumpkin costume for Halloween—not the reaction I had in mind.

"Okay, hold up the red one instead," she ordered.

I did.

"You know, you're right. You do look like a gay pirate."

With each disappointment, we got more desperate. However, at Trash and Vaudeville we hit the jackpot.

"Ew, look at that," Shauna said, as I pulled down a heavy black cloak and hood. "It looks pretty scary."

"Yeah, but that's too Anakin Skywalker *Attack of the Clones* scary. Maybe even Grim Reaper scary. On me, it would look like Friar Tuck just walked in the room."

"No!" Shauna exclaimed.

I was holding up a four-inch silver crucifix pendant, complete with a tiny Jesus nailed to it.

"Why not?" I asked.

"Eric, I worry about your eternal soul," she answered.

"What does my soul have to do with this?"

"That doesn't strike you as a bit blasphemous?"

"It's not like I'm going to take a shit on it or something. I'm going to wear it around my neck."

The Court of Lazarus gig was a big deal to me. Other than this, the success of my vampire hookups had been limited. More dead ends, more unanswered phone calls. Even my D.C. vampires had pretty much abandoned me. After our get-together at Jillian's, I had exchanged some phone calls and e-mails with several of them, but all had eventually faded away. I went to the bookstore where Loren worked. They told me he'd quit and had no idea where he was now.

That's something I've noticed about all self-professed vampires. They sure like declaring their undead status, but questions or probing (of the questioning variety) are definitely not welcome. Perhaps vampires are actually quite shy, or perhaps these people hadn't put a lot of thought into the details of their fantasies, but rarely would I get anything beyond an initial e-mail or a phone message saying, "Yes, Mr. Nuzum, I am, indeed, undead." This strikes me as odd, because you get the impression that a large number of these folks simply want attention. Yet when you give them a little, they run and hide. Either that or you almost immediately realize that they are nothing remotely close to what they claim. For example, I found one Web site put up by Rolando—a tall vampire with long dark hair who said he had a circle of human slaves/donors who kept him knee-deep in fresh blood. He offered that he'd been alive for one hundred and forty-five years and his site was filled with stories about the trail of bloodless bodies he'd left across America since becoming a vampire in his twenties.

My first clue that Rolando's story was kinda fishy (as if I needed any indication that his story was kinda fishy) was a claim that he had fought in the Civil War. Now, I know things got nasty at the end of that war, but I doubt they were drafting toddlers (do the math—according to Rolando's claimed age, he would have been in diapers during the Civil War). Rolando's story fell completely apart when I received a phone call from a very irate father in Minnesota who asked me to stop e-mailing his fourteen-year-old son, Roland, asking how he became a vampire.*

This same scenario played out dozens more times (minus the thinly veiled child molester accusations). Self-outed undead I'd found through Web sites, magazines, and various leads. All would answer one e-mail or phone call (if that), then slowly peter out and disappear. Vampirism seems to be a one- or two-sentence expression—no questions, please.

My most recent rendezvous with a self-declared vampire really made me feel I was running in circles. For some reason I've never quite figured out, many of the vampires that I come across have a fondness for chain restaurants. In this case, Ruby Tuesdays. I was supposed to meet the head of a Virginia vampire group who called himself Blacula. Learning from my previous meeting with vampires in restaurants, I asked Blacula for some details so that I could pick him out.

"How many black vampires do you think you'll find at the bar of a Ruby Tuesday in Fairfax on a Tuesday night?" he asked.

I'm sure he thought he was making a strong point, but I asked for something to go on.

---

* Rolando's Web site was taken down soon afterward.

"I'm black. It's Fairfax, Virginia."

Blacula was the first nonwhite person I'd encountered since getting off the highway on my way over, let alone in the restaurant. However, he would have stuck out in an A.M.E. church as well. He had large black tattoos up and down his muscular dark arms, several facial piercings, and his black hair was bleached—leaving it a faint orange color. Despite the cold weather, he was wearing a leather vest with no shirt underneath. Judging by the packed ashtray in front of him, he'd either been there for hours or chain-smoked.

"Blacula, right?" I asked.

He exaggerated a look around the restaurant, then opened his arms and smiled.

"Where's the rest of your group?" I asked.

"They'll be here soon," he said. "Just you and me for now."

"And your name . . . is Blacula?" I asked, taking the seat next to his.

"Nah . . . my name is Juno. I've got a few nicknames."

I told him about my previous encounters and meetings with other self-declared vampires. He told me that he knew of CrimSol and had spoken with her on the phone.

"You've never met her?" I asked.

"No," Juno replied. "Vampire groups . . . they're really cliquish. They don't tend to mix well. Plus, those guys are all 'psy' vamps anyhow."

I asked what was good or bad about psy vampires. Juno told me there were actually three types of vampires—psy or psychic, posers, and lifestylers. He said most people who tell you they are a vampire, and aren't completely full of shit (his clarifier), are probably psychic vampires. Juno correctly pointed out that many vampires found in historic lore were undead creatures that drew from the life energy or soul of their victims.

"A psy can suck the life right out of you, sometimes they draw so little that you don't even know it's happening. But if you piss one off, they can hit you time and time again and really fuck you up."

"So they don't have to bite you?" I asked.

"No, man," Juno replied. "Sometimes all a psy has to do is think about you to attack you.

Juno told me that lifestylers were people who consider themselves vampires trapped in human bodies—or think they are, indeed, actual vampires. They live life as if they were vampires: They only go out at night, they dress in gothic clothing all the time, only fraternize with other lifestylers, and some wear makeup and fangs full time to complete the effect. Some even claim to drink blood. Posers are those who dress up like vampires to go out to clubs and parties, but otherwise live a "straight" life. The difference between posers and lifestylers is kind of like the difference between cross-dressers and transsexuals—one is just going for a look while the other is trying to fundamentally change themselves.

Juno was much more interested in talking about other vampires than about himself. He'd rattle off lists of nightclubs, books, music, and films that I had to check out, but whenever I'd ask him about his attraction to vampirism, or how he got so involved in the scene, he quickly changed the subject. Juno made several allusions to fetish clubs that were "hot," but otherwise, Juno had very little to offer about Juno.

I explained my luck with vampire hookups, and he wasn't surprised.

"You know, there are a lot of fucking dudes who like to say, 'Ew, look at me, I'm a vampire.' They think it makes them cool . . . or not uncool. But they don't even go out to clubs or talk to other people, they just sit at home, play video games, and jerk off.

"Then there's the RPG kids who just hang around the boards because they want to 'take it to another level,'" Juno offers, using sarcastic air quotes.

"You know, I bet that ninety-eight . . . ninety-nine . . . almost everyone who says they're into this is nothing but bullshit."

When you search the Internet for the word *vampire* a surprising percentage of the hits you get back are sites solely devoted to the game *Vampire: The Masquerade*. I purchased the basic rule book, which runs for 308 pages of ten-point type filled with rules, instructions, and backstory that govern game play. After reading the book cover-to-cover twice, I still don't understand how this game is played.

Vampire: The Masquerade is an RPG (role-playing game), similar to *Dungeons and Dragons, Magic: The Gathering, Highlander,* or *Pokemon.* The first edition of *Vampire,* released in 1991, was like other RPGs: Players build character profiles by following instructions in the rule books, then create attributes using cards or rolling multisided dice. They create maps and game scenarios and then play through them using more cards or dice rolls to determine the outcomes of their actions. Each game has a leader (known as a Dungeon Master in *Dungeons and Dragons* and a Storyteller in *Vampire: The Masquerade*), who narrates the action and makes judgment calls on rules and how the game progresses.

Two years later, the second edition appeared, and with it an entirely new world of geek game play. It was created as part of a new wave of RPGs, known as LARPs—or live-action role-play games. In LARPs, character résumés and game grids are replaced with live action in parks, abandoned buildings, nightclubs, and houses. LARPs are more like improvisational theater than anything else. The new edition of *Vampire* encouraged players to break away from the basement card table and bring the game to life, coming complete with plastic fangs and blood capsules.

Vampire: The Masquerade is one of eighteen different RPGs created by White Wolf Publishing, a Georgia company founded by brothers Stewart and Steve Wieck.* Since then, the game has become so popular that our contemporary *Dracula*-inspired vampire lore has been changed by the game's premise and story line.†

The game is played by manipulating copious amounts of infor-

---

* *Vampire: The Masquerade* was their original game and is still, by far, their most popular title, having sold more than 5.5 million games and books.
† Two recent vampire movies, *Underworld* and *Van Helsing,* have both incorporated *Vampire: The Masquerade*'s contentious relationship between vampires and werewolves.

mation, rules, exceptions to rules, and rule subsets. In addition to the basic rule book, there are a litany of other books, each several hundred pages, containing game scenarios and additional rules. There's *The Vampire Storytellers Handbook; The Vampire Storytellers Handbook Revised Edition; The Guide to Caramilla; The Guide to the Sabbat; Kindred of the East; Kindred of the Ebony Kingdom; Dark Ages: Vampire; Lair of the Hidden; Giovanni Chronicles IV: Nuova Malattia; Clanbook: Malkavian Revised; Succubus Club: Dead Man's Party; Blood Sacrifice: The Thaumaturgy Companion; Havens of the Damned;* and more than three dozen others (as well as several dozen serialized novels and graphic novels based on the game). It's hard to fathom how anyone could write all this stuff, let alone read or comprehend it all.

Vampire: The Masquerade starts with a few pages of backstory, explaining how vampirism started with Caine, the son of Adam and Eve who was exiled by God for killing Abel. According to the rule book, this turned Caine into a vampire—the world's first bloodsucker. Caine discovered that he could pass his gift on to others with "the Embrace" and soon created the first generation of "childer."* Caine eventually realized that filling the world with vampires was a bad idea and forbade his childer from creating more childer, then disappeared. The childer acted like any other child would when left alone—they did the opposite of what they were told. The childer created bunches of vampires, who soon divided themselves into clans and sects based on their lineage. Each generation of vampires was less powerful than its undead ancestors, with most vampiric powers petering out by the fourteenth generation.

At first glance, the people you see playing *Vampire* are a collective definition of goth—disaffected punks, nerds, skaters, wallflowers, geeks, artsy intellectuals, gay and bisexual kids, and other various square pegs. However, there is a significant distinction be-

---

* "Childers" are the vampire version of offspring or children. The vampire who offers "the Embrace" to a vessel (a human who gives blood to a vampire) is called their sire.

tween your run-of-the-mill goth and *Vampire* players. It's like the difference between an Eagle Scout and a Green Beret: They may dress the same and talk the same—but while one is escorting old ladies across the street, the other is gutting Charlie with a bowie knife. Or in the case of the "vampires" playing the game, pantomiming their way through a gutting in a way that looks frighteningly cathartic.

When players create their characters, they decide what clan and sect they want the character to be. There are the gangsterlike rebels known as the Brujah; the shape-shifting wilderness-loving Gangrel; the Malkaviar, who are all insane and subject to psychotic episodes; the hideously ugly Nosferatu; the vain and artsy Toreador; the witchlike Tremere; the ruthless and regal Venture; and the Sabbat, the baddest of the baddest. Each clan has different strengths and weaknesses and all are subject to the roll of the multisided dice to determine how they rank in strength, linguistics, hypnosis, intimidation, etiquette, and intelligence (among two dozen other traits). There are also a few nonvampire roles in the game, including human vampire hunters as well as various fairies, ghouls, and zombies.

After the opening story setting up all this complexity, the book features a prominent "Inevitable Disclaimer" before getting into the rules of the game:

> *Vampire: The Masquerade* is a game. It's a game that requires imagination, effort, creativity, and, above all, maturity. Part of maturity is realizing that *Vampire* is only a game and that the situations depicted in these pages are strictly imaginary. If you beat somebody at Monopoly, you don't go out and foreclose on their house. If you sink someone's Battleship, you don't go down to the Navy Yard and start throwing Molotovs at the boats. The same principle applies to any role-playing or storytelling game.
>
> In other words, you are not a vampire. When a game session ends, put away the books, pack away the dice, enjoy the rest of your life and let other people enjoy theirs.

For the 99.9999 +% of you who are sufficiently well adjusted not to need such a ridiculous disclaimer, have fun.

Despite its irreverent tone, it's clear what the game's creators were thinking when they wrote this: The chance that game play may get a little out of hand.

It's not an unfounded fear—when *Dungeons and Dragons* rose to popularity in the mid-eighties, there was a rash of violent incidents blamed on overzealous gamers.

A study on *Vampire: The Masquerade* was published in the journal *Psychological Reports* in 1998. It basically established that role-playing gamers are no more or less well adjusted than the rest of the population. However, that hasn't stopped critics from blaming the game for several vampire-themed murders committed by gamers.

In 1996, a group of teenaged *Vampire* players from Kentucky took the game too far, eventually cutting themselves and drinking one another's blood. The group became so convinced that they were developing actual vampire powers that their ringleader decided to attack one of their friends' parents. He bludgeoned the adults with a crowbar, drinking their blood before finishing them off.

Four teenagers in Dallas also moved from game play to drinking one another's blood. They then progressed their way from vandalism to spray painting racial slurs, eventually going as far as burning down a church before they were caught.

In 1996, Marcus Noren, a Swedish *Vampire* player was found decapitated. The media speculated that his devotion to the game might be connected to his murder.

The number of game-related crimes pales in comparison to vampire-inspired killings that have nothing to do with any role-playing. In 2001, twenty-year-old Perry Cerf of Bergenfield, New Jersey, hired a hooker, got high on coke, beat her to death, then drank her blood. A Corpus Christi, Texas, man became convinced that his vampire-obsessed girlfriend had become the real thing, so he stabbed her while she was sleeping. In 1995, a Virginia Beach man recruited a group of thirteen-to-sixteen-year-old girls into a vampire cult that involved him biting them while wearing a black cape, white makeup, and fangs. That same year an Exeter University student was attacked at a school dance by a man in a white dinner jacket who repeatedly attempted to bite her neck.

In 1994, a young man returned home from a screening of the film *Interview with the Vampire* and attacked his girlfriend. He stabbed her seven times after warning her, "I'm going to kill you and drink your blood."

In 1985, a man named John Crutchley abducted a female hitchhiker in Florida, then repeatedly raped her and drew her blood, claiming it was slowly transforming him into a vampire.

The most sensational vampire crime in recent history happened in 1989, when four young women in Queensland, Australia, developed an interest in the occult. One of the women convinced the others that she was a vampire and led them through a series of self-mutilations and crimes meant to turn the other three into vampires as well. The group eventually picked up a local man outside a bar with the promise of group sex, lured him to a remote area, and stabbed him to death. Two of the women did consume the victim's blood while one of the others ran to the police and confessed. The trial (where two of the women were convicted, one pleaded guilty, and the fourth was found innocent) was one of the most widely covered criminal proceedings in Australian history.

The one thing that all these crimes have in common is that the perpetrators were (a.) all outsider teens or young adults, and (b.) obsessed with the power of vampirism. These characteristics could also be used to describe the people who gravitate to Juno's group.

Or don't.

After sitting there smoking and drinking beers for more than an hour, it was still just the two of us. Juno did offer that even though there were more than one hundred active participants on their Web site, turn out at group gatherings was generally . . . light.

"Dozens of people promise to show up," he said. "Then when the actual night gets here, it's usually just a few." In fact, if everyone

Juno thought would actually show up that evening came, it would be the largest public gathering of this group ever: four people.

"If Dawn shows, you'll like her, she's into all kinds of shit. I have no idea where these fuckers are at."

As if on cue, someone walks up behind Juno and jokingly puts his hands around Juno's neck. After exchanging some greetings with Juno, the guy introduces himself to me as Jason. The two of them spend the next twenty minutes gossiping and exchanging war stories about late-night drinking and girl chasing. The stories were really entertaining, but I wanted to steer the conversation back on course. When Juno got up to go to the bathroom, I took my opportunity.

"So, Jason," I asked. "What attracts you to all this vampire stuff?"

"I'm not into vampires," he flatly replied.

"You're not?"

"No."

"But isn't this a vampire group—a bunch of people who are into vampires?"

"Yeah, sure . . . I guess. I just hang out."

It seems that Jason met Juno through some mutual friends a few years ago and they started hanging out together. Jason started to visit the Web site and come to the gatherings just for fun. I probed a bit, thinking that Jason was joking or trying to cover up a deep interest in vampire culture.

No. The more I asked, the more I realized that Jason found the whole vampire thing kind of corny and boring.

"You know, I bet it works for some people. It just isn't my thing," he offered.

"But you come to the meetings and post on the Web site," I said.

"Sure, but we hardly ever talk about vampire stuff. We talk about drinking and horror movies and shit. That's about it."

To me, that seemed a lot like joining the Jehovah's Witnesses because you like wearing starched white shirts, but I let it slide.

Juno was back and it was pretty obvious that Dawn—or anyone else—was not going to be joining us this evening.

"Dude, the other night I bought drinks for a dude who bartends at that place by my house," Jason said. "He told me that if we stopped by tonight we could drink for free—get totally fucked up. Let's go."

"I'm game, man," Juno answered, gathering his keys and cigarettes from the bar. "Hey, you want to come with?" Juno asked me.

I thanked them but declined, using my drive back home as an excuse for not getting totally fucked up for free. We exchanged good-byes and headed to our cars.

Despite more than a dozen phone calls and e-mails, I only heard from Juno once—then never again.

"WHICH ONE IS Frank?"

"Pardon me?"

I had arrived at Jeanne Keyes Youngson's apartment about twenty minutes earlier. We'd sat down in her cramped living room/office/library/storage space to chat.

Jeanne lives in a New York penthouse apartment that she and her husband bought more than forty years ago. Despite the fact that there were other apartments on her floor, I got off the elevator and found her door wide open. Having been the hub of vampire study over the past forty years, her place houses a lot of vampire stuff: comics, dolls, toys, posters, masks, and almost every kind of vampire trinket you can think of. And there are books—thousands of them—literally everywhere. Bookshelves line every bit of wall space. Additionally, piles of books are often stacked in front of the shelves. When I used one of her bathrooms, the tub was stacked up chest-high with books.

She does have several stunning views: her apartment terrace overlooks Washington Square Park, the East Village lies right below it to the north, and an unobstructed view of the Empire State Building looms directly beyond. To the south, there is a large hole in the skyline where the World Trade Center once stood.

Jeanne ushered me in and sat in her desk chair. I sat in a lumpy chair across from her. On a third chair were two rubber rats.

"Of those two," I said. "Which one is Frank?"

"Oh, the little one," Jeanne answered. "The bigger one is his mate, Emma. She's larger, you see!"

This struck Jeanne as quite funny.

"Does she travel with you, too?"

"Yes, but not as much as Frank. She stays home. Actually, she's from London."

I paused, waiting to see if any explanation would come on its own. It did.

"My friend and I were in London touring an old operating room—the oldest in London—you know, one of those tall places with the glass ceiling to let in the light.

"Anyhow. While I was looking around my friend found a little gift shop by a staircase. Then she yelled out to me, 'They have rats!'—which I'm sure they didn't appreciate. I came running over and there were a bunch of rubber rats. Have you ever read Bram's story 'Burial of the Rats'?"

"No," I answered, having answered this same question in every one of our previous conversations.

"It's funny because there are rats in the story, but no rats get buried. That's the thing about Stoker and *Dracula*—there are so many spiderwebs. Well, the more I thought about rats, the more interested I became."

Jeanne is curious about many things: Dracula, theater ghosts, New Orleans, King Kong . . . and rats. She pursues each interest with an amazing amount of vigor until a new interest captures her eye.

"Yes, I remember," I said, hoping to avoid covering the whole rat thing again.

"Well, my friend bought me a rat and told me her name was

Emily. But once I got her home, she told me she preferred the name Emma instead."

"Who told you?"

"Emma did."

"The rubber rat told you?"

"Yes, she told me herself," Jeanne replied, giving me a slight smile meant to indicate that even she knew this sounded a little weird.

"So now you call her Emma."

"Yes."

"Because she corrected you and said that was her name."

"Uh-huh."

I decide to just let that one sit there for a minute, then thought it best to change subjects and ask if I could have a copy of her best-known work, "The Vampire in Contemporary Society via a World-wide Census."

When Jeanne decided to conduct a census, she somehow came across more than 900 names and addresses of people who claimed to be vampires. This shouldn't be that surprising. Since Jeanne is such a focal part of vampire research in the United States, she gets mail from all kinds: People wanting to find vampires, claiming to be vampires, wanting to become vampires, and so on. She got 713 questionnaires back. These formed the basis of her census.

Outside of asking "Are you a vampire?" and some other basic questions—the list of potentially revealing questions you'd ask vampires gets a bit thin. As a result, the census starts off sounding like a demographic summary and ends up more like a *Playboy* bunny profile of turn-ons and turn-offs. Ninety-six percent of the respondents indicated that they were, in fact, vampires. Seventy-one percent reported that they drink blood—some from various types of willing donors, others from packaged meat, farm animals, and "self." The types of vampires broke out into twenty-three percent that claimed to be psychic vampires, forty-one percent that said they were "true vampires" (lifestylers), and thirty-six percent that called themselves "vampirelike" (posers). Two-thirds stated they had a special "vampire name."* Eighty-four percent reported being sensitive to sunlight and about half said they wear fangs.

Most report they are sensitive to aromas. Good smells include leather, lilacs, musk perfume, fresh-brewed coffee, and new car interiors. Bad smells include plastic curtains, untended cat litter boxes, foot odor, semen, and old urine. Listed hobbies include riding motorcycles, amusement parks, collecting jewelry, and computer games. Their occupations (besides being a vampire) were reported as security guard, chef, theater usher, mechanic, librarian, and beautician.

Among the reported verbatim comments:

From a retired university professor: "Anyone who steals the essence of another to feed his obsession or ego by way of money, power, blood, semen, youth, or energy could rightfully be termed a vampire."

"If vampire 'wannabes' are not hurting anyone or interfering with others' rights," said another respondent, "why not let them do their thing?"

"We exchanged menstrual blood and I also sliced open my arms with a razor so she could lick the blood," wrote one woman who had a vampire/lesbian thing going on. "She felt guilty about what we did so we both went into therapy."

Wrote another young woman: "I probably would not have thought of it had the questionnaire not come along, but I now realize my boss is a vampire. He sucks our juices, figuratively speaking, by nagging us to do extra jobs at work."

"Let me tell you what I don't get, Jeanne," I said.

"Okay."

"You don't want me to hang around with vampire groups because you say there is nothing interesting to learn from them. That they are 'thrill-seekers' and into 'kinky sex.'"

---

* Including Countess Noir, Thundergod, Sangrita, Lord Death, Princess Moonbeam, Renaldo the Wolf, plus two Vlads, and eight Countess Draculas.

"Yes."

"Yet you conducted this huge survey of these people."

"Yes."

"That doesn't strike you as a bit contradictory?"

"Well, when I started out on the project, I didn't realize what kind of responses I was going to get," she explained. "I'd been hearing from wannabes for years. When I finally started learning more about what they were doing—pretending to be vampires and such—I became less and less interested. So often they were just bored with their life, have bland jobs, unhappy marriages, and latched onto vampirism as a way to make themselves more interesting, to perk up their lives, or to rise above the ordinary.

"There were some situations that were excruciatingly painful for me to read . . . like the fellow who was placed with his uncle's family and had to sleep in the barn. He is the one who sucked blood from cows. I am just trying to recall a couple of the stories that turned me off the whole scenario."

Jeanne told me that after the census was originally published she was overwhelmed with letters from people who wanted information on vampires. Things came to a boil after a popular nonfiction book about vampires mentioned, erroneously, that Jeanne was trying to start a pen pal club for people who thought they were or wanted to become vampires.

"You know, prison libraries must have lots of old books in them," she said. "Because I'm still getting letters from inmates who want to join . . . and I mean lots and lots of letters every week. That book must be in every slammer in the country!"

"Did you get one of these?"

"No, I didn't," I said. "I'd love one, thank you."

The little guy standing in front of me crinkles up his nose as he pulls a small stack of stapled papers away from his chest and hands it to me. I forgot. Being in a room full of vampires and hard-core goths, declaring how much you'd "love" something probably isn't the best way to express interest.

I take the stapled papers from him. On the front is an illustration of a gaunt, barely dressed woman in a dungeon. The top reads THE COURT OF LAZARUS NEWSLETTER: A NEWSLETTER FOR THE VAMPYRE SOCIETY OF GREATER NEW YORK.

"Thanks."

The guy rolls his eyes as he walks along to the next person. I guess being thankful is also gauche in this crowd. Newsletter Guy had an interesting look going on. At first glance, I momentarily thought he was (a.) from that area in southeast Russia near Japan where all the people look like they've been holding their breath too long, (b.) has a mild case of Down's syndrome, (c.) has a liver ailment that makes his skin dark purplish, or (d.) a combination of the above. Even considering this, the one thing that really stuck out was the frilly white Victorian shirt and coat he's wearing, making him look like a combination of the vampire Lestat and Paul Revere. Shauna would be so proud.

I'd first heard about the Court of Lazarus from a friend who sent me a link to their Web site along with a note that read, "I saw a vague mention about this on the calendar for the Slipper Room. I thought these were your kind of people."

The Slipper Room is usually a burlesque club, but on Sunday nights a few times a year, they host the Court of Lazarus gatherings. From a quick perusal of their site, I learned that these semi-private parties were meant as a get-together for New York City vampires to mix and mingle. The site's photo gallery featured a variety of the sinister-looking unholy rickets-prone people in a variety of cool-yet-intimidating-scary poses and conducting some type of service or ritual.

Outside of the photos and a mention of the event (and the dress code), there was very little information on the site about what *actually happens* at the Court of Lazarus. I had sent e-mails to several of the group's organizers hoping that I could meet them before the gathering or chat on the phone. No replies.

I tried again the week before heading up to New York. Nothing.

When I walked up to the Slipper Room that evening I was greeted by a doorman with red contact lenses, dyed black hair teased out a good twelve inches from his head, who was wearing a knee-length skirt.

"Hey, is this the place for the Court of Lazarus thing?" I asked.

He didn't say a word. Just smiled, revealing three sets of fangs.

I figured I was in the right place.

After moving on from me, Newsletter Guy wordlessly exchanges nods with the guy sitting next to me and hands him a newsletter. I'd been trying to figure out this guy next to me since he came in.

First off, my attire for the evening hadn't been an issue at all. I'd worn a red skull shirt and my new crucifix, but I felt so silly when I walked in the door that I took the crucifix and hid it inside my shirt. Outside of a general fondness for black, most of the other patrons that evening were wearing everything from Calvin Klein to spiked knuckle covers and assless leather chaps. There were even two people wearing those big heavy cloak and hoods we'd seen earlier.

The guy next to me was a standout. He looked like a thinner version of the actor Christian Bale, with a tiny beard following his jawline. He was decked out in a red turtleneck sweater and a brown tweed jacket, complete with elbow patches. Outside of exchanging greetings with a few others around the room, he'd spent the entire time clutching a drink and staring, usually at whatever wall was directly in front of him. On one occasion, I leaned in to make some conversation, but he didn't even acknowledge my presence.

Even though the event was supposed to start at 8:30, it was almost 9:30 and nothing had happened yet. The bar had about forty or so people sprinkled about. Over in the corner, I noticed a young woman pull out something that looked like an X-Acto knife or razor blade. She took the hand of her male companion and stuck his finger with the object. She periodically sucked on his finger throughout the evening. Otherwise, most people were staying to themselves or the others they came with—not a lot of mingling going on. This actually made sense to me.

Once the initial visual shock is over, you start to notice things about these people. First, vampire goths seem to come in two varieties—the emaciatedly thin and the profoundly obese.

Secondly, once you strip away the finger armor, black lipstick, hair extensions, and leather, you are left with the same square pegs that got stuffed in their lockers in high school. The captain of the football team never seems to end up thinking he's a vampire. It's the unnoticed geek in the corner who eventually ends up declaring himself undead.

None of this should surprise anyone; it's pretty obvious when you are around these folks that one of their fundamental attractions to vampirism is its ability to shock and empower. Outside of the Slipper Room, where the smokers congregated, not a single person went by—on foot or in a car—that didn't do a double take and stare at the assorted vampires out on the sidewalk. In their prevampire days, none of these folks would have turned a single head. Many of them claim they don't want the attention of "normals"—yet if they truly wanted to disappear from society, all they'd need to do is leave the leather coat and fangs at home. Considering their pasts, it's easy to mistake these people as harmless. However, I tried to remind myself that these particular geeks and outcasts might be fantasizing about drinking my blood.

To kill some time, I looked through the newsletter. When you're as secretive as these people, there really isn't a lot of "news" shared in the newsletter. Instead it contains a few ridiculous poems about slow death, dark blood, and penetration. Half the newsletter is devoted to an article by "Catherine of the Night" called "The 'Reality' of Vampires." The article puts forward the argument that vampirism is actually a virus, which she calls V5. Catherine claims that the V5 virus is well known to medical scientists as having the ability to alter human DNA to make someone crave blood in order to survive (unfortunately for Catherine and any other validity-seeking blood drinker, outside of a few mentions on vampire message boards, I couldn't find a single reference to a virus called V5 anywhere—referring to vampirism or otherwise). The newsletter's other feature was an advice column called "Dear Vampy," where assistance for the undead is dispensed by Priscilla Blueblood. In this edition of the column, "Awkward in Park Slope" writes in that his or her blood donor wants to bring another donor for a little bloodletting three-way. Awkward doesn't like this idea and isn't sure how to deal with the situation. Priscilla Blueblood responds by urging Awkward to "speak up and feel empowered." She says if Awkward is only comfortable in a monogamous blood exchange relationship, then he or she should "make a stance and be as firm as your fangs." "Mundane in Bronx" was worried that a recent trip to Starbucks after watching Larry King on TV was indication that she was becoming lame. Priscilla advised that Mundane shouldn't get too worked up over nothing—one decaf latte was nothing that a little trip to the dungeon wouldn't cure.

Whenever I'm in a bar and I want to talk with as many strangers as possible, I always sit at the bar next to the place where most people go to get drinks for their table. They're stuck there for a few minutes, making them easy marks for some chatting.

The first thing I learned is that these vampires *love* Bloodbaths. A Bloodbath is basically a Cosmopolitan made with red wine instead of vodka (specifically, they use good old Vampire wine—even looking at the bottle makes me think of goat-cheese-and-egg pizza). The result is very sweet and packs all the punch of a wine cooler. Considering the price of cocktails in New York, it doesn't offer a great deal of bang for your buck. Yet once one vampire gets one, they *all* have to have one. The bartenders can barely keep up.

One girl came to the bar and ordered a Bloodbath, then looked over at me, mostly out of boredom while the bartender mixed her drink. She was wearing a tight black dress, had hair the color of red Kool-Aid, and dark, thick eyeliner around her green eyes.

Oh, and she had two sets of fangs.

I introduced myself. She said her name was Jenny. We shook hands and I told her what I was doing.

"Oh, you should interview me," she replied.

"So I assume you are a vampire?"

"Why else would I be here," she replied.

"I don't know, perhaps you are writing a book about vampires, too."

"Ha-ha. Could be. You never know."

"So do you wear fangs all the time or just on nights like this?" I asked.

"I wear them when I need to," she replied.

This back and forth continued for a while. From what she was telling me, I came to the conclusion that she was somewhere between a poser and a lifestyler—depending on the question I was asking. She said she was at least part vampire, having been "turned" by a previous lover a few years earlier. She had a "normal life" but once or twice a week she hooked up with one of her "regular donors"—some men, some women—and did a little light bloodletting/drinking. Afterward, they'd usually have sex, or at least cuddle.

"Cuddling?" I asked, acknowledging that an interest in cuddling is probably the last thing I expected to hear from a self-declared vampire.

"Haven't you ever watched a cat play with its prey? Giving life is very intimate, sometimes you want that to linger."

"Then why sex?" I asked.

"Come on," she said, taking a sip of her Bloodbath. "Few things are hotter than tasting blood as it drips off a guy's hard cock."

I paused for a minute when I noticed the expression on her face. Her eyes were big; she was smiling. She was waiting for a reaction.

"You want to know what I think?" I asked.

"Yeah," she said, with a bit of excitement.

"I have this sneaking suspicion that you're telling me this to shock me."

"What do you mean?" she asked.

"I mean that I think you're blowing smoke up my ass."

She looked very confused.

"Meaning that I think you are lying to me," I said.

"What?!" she exclaimed. "I'm not lying!" Which, of course, reinforced to me that she was.

"Give me a break," I said. "Ten minutes ago you didn't even know who I was, now you are telling me that you like to drink blood and cuddle and lick bodily fluids off penises. I haven't even told you what state I live in and you've already fast-forwarded to your status as a sadist dominatrix cuddling vampire."

"What, you don't live in New York?" she replied.

"I'm sorry, I just find this difficult to believe."

"Whatever," she said, picking up the remainder of her Bloodbath and heading back to her table.

At a few minutes before 10:00, a woman walks up to the microphone on the small stage and announces that Nefarious Wrath, the group's leader, would conduct the evening's ritual in a few minutes.

The room went silent and Nefarious Wrath worked his way through the bar toward an open area in front of the stage. He was dressed in a black velvet hood and robe and carried a small sword. There was a small table set up in the open area that held a few large lit candles, an oversized book, a glass of wine, and a pot of burning incense that made the entire bar smell chokingly like a Catholic Mass. Nefarious walked toward the table and opened the book.

Nefarious started reciting a bunch of stuff that didn't make much sense, then pulled out the sword and pointed it over his right shoulder.

"In the name of all that is unholy, from the west, we summon you, Lucifer," he said, raising the sword up into the air. "From the south," he said, pointing the sword in front of him (which was actually north, by the way), "in the name of all that is dark, we summon you, Lord Satan."

At this, the Christian Bale guy in the tweed coat, who was still standing next to me, dropped to his knees, raised his hands above his bent head, and began to mumble some kind of chant in a low voice.

Nefarious continued on, conjuring various demons and dark

spirits from the east and so on. All I could think was that if Shauna was concerned about my eternal soul for buying a metal crucifix, she'd be having a fit right about now.

Nefarious then started uttering a bunch of words that sounded like Latin. Then he called forth a couple I had seen milling around the club since I got there. They stood on either side of Nefarious Wrath, heads bent and hands folded together as if in prayer. Nefarious picked up the glass of wine and turned to the man. He uttered some Latinesque words, which the man did a poor job of phonetically repeating. Nefarious handed him the glass of wine, he drank from it, and handed it back to Nefarious. Nefarious then repeated the process with the woman.

The whole time the Christian Bale dude continued to babble away on his knees next to me.

After putting everything back on the table, Nefarious raised his hands and recited more of his faux Latin. Then he slammed his hands down upon the candles, extinguishing them with the palms of his hands.

Nefarious and his two wine drinkers slowly walked through the crowd and down the back stairs to a smattering of polite applause from the attendees.

After Nefarious was done invoking the devil and chanting, it was time for DJ Jason to start up again with more music about coldness, isolation, and despair. As is often the case with loud clubs with no smoking, the best place for a conversation was out on the sidewalk.

As a former smoker, I'm telling you that the day they find a way to produce cigarettes that won't kill you, I'll be the first in line to buy a carton of nondeath sticks. The birth of my children, winning the Nobel prize, having a national holiday named after me . . . none of these things would bring me more intrinsic pleasure than being able to smoke again. So, you'd think that undead, unkillable vampires would be smoking them two at a time. Not true. In fact, more of the Court of Lazarus vampires complained about having to walk through the clouds of smoke surrounding the entrance to the Slipper Room than were outside on the sidewalk partaking themselves. Nonetheless, the smoker's area was a conversational jackpot.

I was making small talk on the sidewalk when I noticed someone step up beside me.

"You must be Eric."

I turned and saw it was Nefarious—smile on his face, hand extended.

"Yeah, I'm Eric. . . . How did you know?" I said, before realizing that if you walked into the Slipper Room and had three seconds to figure out the one person who didn't belong, it would take you half that time to settle on me.

"Your Web site," he answered. "After we got your e-mail we did some checking up on you. Your Web site has your picture on it."

"Oh," I said, trying to decide on the fly how bothered I should be that they'd spent that much time researching me.

"Sorry about all the e-mails," I said. "I was just hoping I could get a chance to talk when there wasn't so much going on."

"Yeah, I'm sorry no one ever responded," he offered. "We were pretty busy."

Yeah, I thought. Busy digging up stuff on me.

"Nefarious!" A black guy I had seen earlier with Nefarious was calling out from just inside the club. "The Baron is ready to start and he wants you to introduce him."

Nefarious nodded and turned back to me.

"The Baron . . . he's a singer," Nefarious explained. "We try to offer lots of things at our gatherings. We make sure each one has live music of some sort. A lot of the bands in the goth scene are members. How about we talk afterward?"

Without really waiting for my answer, Nefarious turned to walk inside the club. I followed and positioned myself at the bar near the stage. On the Slipper Room's pillbox stage was a five-foot-tall candelabra with six red candles. On the other side sat a guy who looked like Slash from Guns N' Roses, cradling an acoustic guitar that was plugged into a massive amp behind him.

Nefarious stepped up on stage and announced that we had a special treat this evening. Baron Misuraca, lead singer of the band Vasaria, was about to do an acoustic set at the Court of Lazarus. When the Baron first walked out, the first thing I noticed was his hair. It's jet-black (except for one white streak about an inch thick) and long—really long. It's Crystal Gayle long; down past his knees heading toward his ankles. The vampires responded with genuine enthusiasm (something I guess they don't display often).

According to the band's Web site,* Vasaria is "infamous for expanding upon the boundaries of both the metal and goth genres. Vasaria has certainly left its indelible mark (or rather bite), infusing classical and horror film score influences within a rather brooding, riff-laden soundscape as dark poetic lyrics beckon escapism and release. Eloquent yet highly aggressive, to label them would be a disservice." (After I played some Vasaria for Katherine, then read her that bio passage from the Web site, she replied: "I'll label them . . . crap. And that *is* a service.")

Once they began playing, the Baron's songs were a combination of slow minor chord progressions from the Slash lookalike with the Baron (possessing a voice that was a dead ringer for Pete Murphy of Bauhaus) uttering lyrics with plenty of references to pain, God, struggle, darkness, and betrayal. After each song, the vampires would whoop and applaud their approval. Baron Misuraca would introduce the next song, with titles like "Shadows of the Dead," "Release," and "From Cradle to Grave," then launch into a song that sounded exactly like the ones they'd already played. Despite the small venue and crowd, Baron Misuraca was playing for the rafters—big dramatic gestures, lots of finger pointing and head snapping (with accompanying flourishes of moving hair), and painful grimaces. He was really feeling it and apparently wanted us to be aware he was feeling it.

---

* The Web site also features tons of photos of Baron and the band, including a picture of Baron Misuraca posing with Butch Patrick. Small world.

"I stare into outer space as want imprisons my soul," he sang. "I feel that I am dead, or perhaps have never lived."

The Baron also took a few occasions between songs to promote his new comic book, which stars himself as a dark, brooding, misunderstood "blasphemed fourteenth-century musician cursed into vampire undeath." Written by the Baron himself, the comic chronicles his rebirth in New York City, torn between his need for fresh blood and his quest for redemption. However, the Baron is never alone on his adventures, but accompanied by an "awe-inspiring array of all new femme fatale characters."

Before I even had a chance to ponder how a *person* can be "blasphemed," I was distracted by the number of rock clichés that the Baron was rattling off. For example, in between two songs he called out, "Are you having a good time!?" with all the gusto you'd expect to hear at a Mötley Crüe concert. He followed it with, "You've been listening to me—I want to listen to you. Make some noise!" The crowd (of forty) responded accordingly.

Baron Misuraca capped his performance with an emotional dead-on, goth acoustic version of "My Way" delivered without a hint of irony. Afterward, the assembled vampires went totally apeshit. They were on their feet, applauding and hooting their approval as loudly as they could. I kept waiting for him to smile, shrug, or show in some small tongue-in-cheek way that he was joking, or for the audience to do the same, but like everything else he did, he was serious. Very, very serious.

After a few bows, Baron Misuraca and the Slash lookalike left the stage. The woman doing the announcements plugged the raffle again and said that the next performance would be coming up shortly. I headed back out to converse about reality shows with my smoking vampires.

Working my way outside, I noticed that the club was starting to fill up. I mentioned this to a guy I'd met earlier outside on the sidewalk (wearing a long trench coat and white contact lenses).

"Yeah, even though it's Sunday, I'm amazed that they start these things so early. Eight thirty—that's like a breakfast meeting for vampires!"

"True—and who wants to drink a Bloodbath for breakfast?" I added.

"Have you tried one of those things?" he asked.

"No, I haven't."

"It's a pussy drink," he replied. "But, you know, it does taste good."

"Sorry we got interrupted earlier," I heard from behind me. It was Nefarious. "So, what do you want to know?"

"I don't know," I said, scrambling to respond to what should have been a pretty easy question. "Why all this? I guess. What attracts you to all this?"

"Vampirism is an archetype for us," he responded, demonstrating that he'd anticipated this question and thought through the answer ahead of time. "To us, it just makes sense.

"Some people expect us to be crazy. We really aren't. It is just something we all have in common and unites us. We're into all the elements of it. . . . We just use the vampirism as a metaphor."

Nefarious's friend started calling for him again, the next performance was about to start.

The evening's finale was a performance piece by Victor Noirlocke and Misty. After everyone was gathered to watch, DJ Jason started playing Nine Inch Nails' *The Downward Spiral,* really loud.

As the first song, "Mr. Self Destruct," kicked in, Victor walked across the stage in a Victorian suit, smoking a cigarette like he was breathing it. Misty slowly walked out and sat in a chair on the opposite side from Victor, wearing a bustier, fishnet stockings, and high heels. She began a slow striptease-style dance. While she never removed any clothing, Misty did flex and gyrate while her fingers slowly and deliberately grazed across almost every inch of her body, with particular attention paid to the inside of her thighs.

"I am denial, guilt, and fear and I control you," blared from the speakers.

As the CD segued into the next song, "Piggy," Victor lit another cigarette, walked over to Misty, and pulled a fifty dollar note from his pocket. Misty took the money, then continued to dance in front of and against Victor. Victor stood unmoved, just dragging on his cigarette as if his life depended on it.

Misty continued to dance as Victor reached inside his jacket and pulled out a slender dagger about twelve inches long.

"Black and blue and broken bones, you left me here I'm all alone," rang through the room.

Misty was leaning her back against Victor's chest and continued to move back and forth. Victor took the knife and began to lightly brushing it against her stomach, chest and arms. Misty raised her arms and wrapped them back around Victor's neck as he took the knife and started rubbing it in between her legs. Victor slowly bent down and ran the dagger against her tights. As she sensuously moved her hands up and down the outside of her legs, Victor slipped the knife down inside her stockings. As the next song, "Heresy," started up, DJ Jason turned the music up even louder. It was to the point where it was almost painful. Misty grinded her hips against Victor and he started pulling the dagger back up, applying just enough pressure to pop the strands of her fishnet stockings one by one. After removing the dagger, he twisted it through random holes in her stockings, slitting them along her calf and thigh, as the music screeched out of the speakers so loud I could almost smell it.

Victor then took the knife and ran it across her neck. While she wasn't cut, the look on his face and the violent way he jerked the knife indicated that he was taking his performance very seriously. Then Misty began to convulse and softly fight Victor as he pressed his mouth against her neck. Misty's gestures became more frantic and resistant, her convulsions more violent, as Victor pretended to suck at her faux neck wound.

I looked around and noticed that I wasn't the only one who was viewing this and wondering if the girl wasn't acting. As Misty clawed and scratched at her attacker, one couple got up and left. Several others looked at each other not quite sure what they should do, if anything.

"God is dead and no one cares."

Misty's convulsions faded as she began sinking toward the floor.

"If there is a Hell, I'll see you there!"

After Misty's limp body collapsed into a clump on the floor, Victor ran his tongue across the bloodless knife, put it back in his jacket, lit a cigarette, and walked off stage. DJ Jason faded the music and everyone just stood there for a minute, not quite sure what to do. Then one person started clapping, then others, then everyone was whistling and hooting. Victor leapt back out on stage, helped Misty back up to her feet, and they both took bows. Misty gleamed like she'd just done the lead in her high school musical. They both waved and walked off stage arm in arm.

Nefarious had watched the performance right in front of me.

"What did you think?" he asked.

"That was probably the most disturbing performance I've ever seen," I said.

"Yeah, it was pretty cool, huh?"

Nefarious went on to chat with some of the others.

By this time, the club was getting pretty full. However, as the crowd grew, there were noticeably fewer vampires and many more pasty goth kids who looked like they'd been ripped from the pages of the Suicide Girls Web site.

I tried to chat with a few others, but the tone of the evening was shifting. Now that the performances and rituals were over, it felt just like any other night at a club. Given, a club where a large percentage of the patrons were wearing fangs, but you get the point.

White-eyed Guy and I ended up at the bar together.

"So, what did you think of all this?" he asked.

"It was a little . . . odd."

"How so?"

"Oh, I don't know, we can start with invoking Satan and take it from there," I said. "As long as you cover the pantomimed murder, too."

White-eyed Guy chuckled.

"It's all just symbolism," he offered.

"I'd buy into this easier if I hadn't just spoken with a woman who likes to drink blood dripping off of penises."

"Really, who said that?"

"The girl over in the corner with the red hair."

"Oh, her," he said in a tone indicated that (a.) he wasn't surprised and (b.) there was more to the story.

As White-eyed Guy turned away, Jenny looked up and met my glance. She stared at me for a moment, mouthed "Fuck you," and stuck out her tongue.

VII

I MAY BE DEAD, BUT I'M STILL PRETTY

In which the author sits through 144 episodes of Buffy the Vampire Slayer, *sits in the dark with 1,000 people, and cringes a lot.*

I WAS SITTING at my desk when a woman who works on my floor leaned herself against the frame of my open office door. The look on her face was quite serious.

"I hear you're watching all the *Buffy*s," Kathie said.

I explained to her that I had, indeed, begun a new component of my quest: watching every episode of *Buffy the Vampire Slayer* in order, from start to finish. All 144 episodes. A total of 104 hours of viewing.

"How far are you?" she asked.

"I just finished the first season and started the second," I said.

"Oh, so they are still in high school. So you haven't seen the one with her college roommate yet, have you? The one who turns into a demon?"

"No," I replied, trying to hide my desire to cringe.

This is at least the third time this has happened to me: Word gets around that I'm watching this show, a fan comes to talk to me about it, and then promptly drops a spoiler in my lap for an episode or story line I haven't seen yet.

"So, Buffy hasn't hooked up with Spike yet, has she?" asked another coworker, Carlos, when he found out I was watching all the *Buffy* episodes.

"Hook up with Spike?" I reply. "She hates Spike—they're always trying to kill each other."

"Yeah, that's the way it always starts," Carlos said. "You just wait."

Cringe.

I guess I will.

Within forty-eight hours of telling *one* coworker that I was watching *Buffy*, I had received no fewer than *four* e-mails and visits from people at work who were ardent fans. And it wasn't just at work. I was at an out-of-town meeting when a colleague asked how my vampire work was coming. I mentioned *Buffy*. One woman at the meeting looked up and blurted out, "Has Buffy died yet?"

"That happened at the end of the first season," I said. "I'm way past that now."

"Oh, she dies again later," the woman replied. "And this time it's a big deal, trust me. She's dead, buried, and comes back from the grave."

Cringe, followed by polite smile.

Despite the infestation of *Buffy* fans at work, I soon found out they weren't the only vampire-enthusiasts in the building.

"You know Susie in Finance?" asked Patricia. "I heard she and her husband held a vampire dinner party last Halloween. They had hors d'ouevres served in a coffin!"

Turns out the coffin was made of cardboard—a Halloween prop obtained from Toys "R" Us (containing no hors d'oeuvres, but the rest of the story was true). After exchanging some e-mails, Susie and I met up for a beer after work so I could hear about her Night of the Vampires dinner.

If I had to guess which of my coworkers liked to dress up like a vampire with her friends, Susie would have been close to the bottom of the list. When you meet her, she comes across as the definition of a classy businessperson. Definitely not undead material.

Susie and her husband, Stan, belong to a group of four couples who rotate hosting dinner parties four times a year, all of them themed. Susie and Stan's turn was set for November 1, so she thought she'd do something "Halloweenish" and quickly settled on a vampire theme. She sent out invitations (which required that guests attend dressed as vampires), and hit some post-Halloween clearance sales for decorations.

"I decorated my house with cobwebs, spiders, dead flowers, tombstones, and set up my coffin in the middle of the room," Susie told me, gleefully describing the details. "I set the table with a black tablecloth, dead flowers, and took off the labels on all the wine bottles and labeled them with blood types—like AB Negative, Type O, and Type A, you know. We only used candles—no electric lights—to really set the mood."

Susie's main course was Bat Breasts and Wings in Blood Sauce (a.k.a. Cornish game hens in a cranberry sauce). The appetizers were Eyeballs Floating in Blood (meatballs and marinara sauce), then came Tarantula Salad (caesar salad with rubber spiders hanging off the bowls). Their desert was—my personal favorite—Whipped Blood with Clot Chunks (red food coloring added to white chocolate mousse with pieces of raspberries floating in it).

"It was *a lot* of fun," she added. "After dinner, we drank *waaaay* too much Type AB Negative and we all took turns lying in the coffin and getting our pictures taken. Then, at midnight, everyone flew home."

"So," I asked. "Why a vampire theme?"

"Oh, you know," she said. "Vampires are sexy and mysterious. I guess dressing up like one makes you feel that way, too. It gives you permission to dress and act a way you normally wouldn't. Thankfully, it was only for one night. Between the dress and makeup and fangs and all, I can't believe there are people who dress up like this all the time."

"There are."

"That seems like a lot of work," she replied.

"Hey, sometimes 'sexy and mysterious' requires a lot of work."

ORIGINALLY, I HAD blown off the adventures of Buffy Summers completely. As I've mentioned before, I'm not a big TV watcher. This may be odd for a pop culture writer to admit, but even though I don't watch much of it, I stay surprisingly up-to-date. It isn't that I hate watching TV, I just can't stand most of the crap that passes for episodic television: dramas that aren't interesting, comedies that aren't funny—it's just generally boring.

Ironically, I picked up my current TV philosophy many years ago from a vampire movie. In *The Lost Boys*, Corey Haim and Jason Patric move in with their grandpa and learn that he—*gasp*—doesn't have a television. Yet soon after settling in, they notice that Grandpa subscribes to *TV Guide*. The boys ask Grandpa if the presence of *TV Guide* would indicate the complementary presence of a television to guide. Grandpa tells them no.

"I just like to read the *TV Guide*," he says. "You read *TV Guide*, you don't need a TV."

When I first saw this, twenty years ago, it immediately struck me as pure genius and I decided to follow Grandpa's example in real life. Though my periodical of choice is *Entertainment Weekly*, I follow the shows, their story lines, and the characters. I had a similar history with *Buffy*. During its seven-year run, I never saw a single episode. When I started working on this project, I asked some of my TV-watching friends about the show, their universal advice was to blow it off, saying, "*Buffy the Vampire Slayer* really isn't about vampires."

However, the show soon became hard to ignore. Even though *Buffy the Vampire Slayer* was a big show for UPN and the WB networks, it was never a huge ratings hit during its run on television. Nonetheless, the show made a big impression on popular culture. The show has been name checked on other television shows, such as *Will & Grace, Charmed, Smallville, Friends,* and like any touch point in popular culture, been fodder for sketches on *Saturday*

Night Live and *MadTV*.* There is a *Buffy*-themed video game and tons of merchandise and tchotchkes of all imaginable varieties. A recently discovered celestial object, 2004 XR_{190}, was given the nickname Buffy by its discoverers, as a shout-out to their favorite vampire slayer. In September 1998, *George* magazine included Buffy Summers high on its list of the "Twenty Most Fascinating Women in Politics" (she came in at number two, as a matter of fact, second only to Elizabeth Dole). The magazine said, "What she's really taking on is a regular assortment of challenges that threaten to suck the lifeblood out of teenage girls, like a suffocating high school hierarchy and a sexual double standard."

I realized that if the statement, "*Buffy the Vampire Slayer* really isn't about vampires," was true, then it's exactly what would make the show so interesting to me.

Not long into my *Buffy* viewing, I learned that I'd really underestimated this show. While initially I thought that viewing a hundred-plus hours of a show over a couple weeks would be an excruciating experience, I'd actually come to enjoy it.

The show debuted on the WB network as a midseason replacement in March 1997 and ran for seven seasons (the last two moving to the UPN network), wrapping up in May of 2003. The show basically picks up where the original movie left off (albeit with a different cast and location). Buffy and her mother move from Los Angeles to the small sleepy nowheresville of Sunnydale. While in Los Angeles (in the original movie) Buffy learns she is the Slayer—one girl from every generation who is mystically chosen to have the skill and strength to fight vampires and other collective

---

* *Buffy* also influenced a large number of successor shows as well. One thing that creator Joss Whedon set out to do with *Buffy* was turn the stereotype of young blond females on its head. Especially in horror, the young blondes are usually tits on a vacuous stick with little to contribute once they bounce around the screen or lose their virginity (just before being killed, of course) to the film's lead actor. In *Buffy*, the young blond girl is transformed into a superhero, almost always saving the male characters rather than being saved by them. This empowered young female lead emerged in several post-*Buffy* series, like *Joan of Arcadia*, *Dead Like Me*, and *Veronica Mars*.

forms of evil. They move to Sunnydale to start over after Buffy's first major run-in with vampires in L.A. Though Sunnydale seems quaint on the surface, it happens to be the location of the Hellmouth—a gateway to the demon world. The Hellmouth is like a magnet for vampires, demons, ghosts, and other assorted bad guys, resulting in a higher than average number of bizarre happenings and unexplainable deaths. Soon after arriving, Buffy meets Rupert Giles, her Watcher (kind of like a teacher/mentor covertly placed undercover as the librarian in Sunnydale High School), and hooks up with a small group of square peg friends who, for the most part, stick with her throughout the series.

In the introduction to *The Portrait of Dorian Gray*, Oscar Wilde wrote that all art is both surface and symbol. *Buffy the Vampire Slayer* is proof positive of Wilde's argument. On one hand, *Buffy* can be enjoyed as a vacuous teen drama, on the other hand, you can see how the story lines echo the themes of *Faust, The Odyssey,* and the stories of Dickens and Shakespeare.

What makes the show work is that it derives most of its humor, dramatic tension, and subtexts from a series of coexisting parallels. In real life, there is a "teen" world that operates in a parallel (but interconnected) existence with the "adult" world. They occupy the same space, but adults and teens talk differently, dress differently, and care about completely different and divergent things. The "Buffyverse" (as fans call the show's world) exaggerates this separation, but also adds a third parallel—the "monster" world. Also, there are parallels between the deathly seriousness of Buffy's vampire-hunting quest matched against the melodrama in a teenager's normal life. Chaos, death, and the potential collapse of life as we know it are such common occurrences in the Buffyverse that they become almost blasé. On learning about Buffy's true calling, one of her boyfriends commented, "I feel the sudden need to know the plural of apocalypse."

To illustrate how out of touch adults can be, not only don't they understand the teen world, they're often oblivious to the monster world as well. One evening, as Buffy sets out to destroy the Master vampire who's attempting to bring about an apocalypse, Buffy's mother jokes to her, "I know—if you don't go out, it will be the end of the world . . . everything is life or death when you're a sixteen-year-old girl." Clueless adults tend to rationalize their encounters with Sunnydale's monsters, writing them off to a gas leak or gangs of kids on drugs.

When the series starts out, Buffy and her friends are in high school, and—in addition to confronting monsters—have to navigate all the turmoil and drama that is adolescence. In the early seasons, the vampires and demons often sound and act a lot like adults and the battles with monsters are short-leashed metaphors for the trials of teen life. When Buffy sidekick Xander encounters some evil demon hyenas at the zoo, he joins a pack of other hyena-possessed teens who bully and tease other kids at school—behavior equally believable without the influence of mind-invading hyenas (except when the possessed kids eat their principal). When Internet predators were a national obsession, a *Buffy* episode featured a demon who lived inside a computer network, befriended a bunch of computer nerds (including Buffy's other main sidekick, Willow), and eventually convinced them to do bad things.

As the series progresses, the vampires morph into contemporaries of Buffy and her friends. Buffy's transition into adulthood is marked by losing her virginity to her vampire boyfriend Angel (who is a good vampire—he was cursed to have a soul again—he is sent to protect Buffy and the two fall in love . . . it's complicated). After they have sex and Angel experiences true happiness with Buffy, his curse is lifted and he becomes evil again. The story line plays into one of every woman's worst nightmares: Once I sleep with him, he'll become a monster.

Eventually, in the show's final seasons, Buffy struggles to be a grown-up caring for her sister after their mother's death from cancer. She has to battle the forces of evil while managing mortgage payments. Then, the vampires and monsters represent metaphors of Buffy herself (in the final season, the über-villain "the One" often takes the physical shape of Buffy). In these seasons, especially the sixth, the show goes from campy and fun to downright sinister and dark, dealing with addiction, broken relationships, attempted rape, bad jobs, and more deaths in Buffy's inner circle.

Buffy is, in essence, a textbook example of Joseph Campbell's mono myth, where an ordinary person is put into an extraordinary situation, thus bringing out their true potential. At first Buffy resists her calling, confronts it, and faces trials. Buffy even dies in the series—twice—coming back to life after each time. Buffy, as Campbell suggests, finds that coming back afterward is the toughest part of the whole thing. Her experiences have changed her. "Normal" no longer exists.

With the exception of those last few seasons (and an incredibly unfortunate, potentially shark-jumping subplot involving a secret government demon-catching program called "the Initiative"), the series is very clever in its humor. A perfect example is an episode that centers on a "fear demon" trying to cause mass chaos. Once he appears in the flesh, the demon is only about four inches tall and is quickly squished by Xander during the episode's last few seconds.

A few days later, Carlos called me at my desk to ask how things were going.

"Have you seen the part with the Initiative yet?"

"Yes, I have," I responded. "It was some of the worst television I've ever seen—all of a sudden *Buffy the Vampire Slayer* gets transformed into a Schwarzenegger movie."

"Yeah, that was pretty out there," Carlos remarked. "And then you find out later that the Initiative still exists and Riley runs off to rejoin them."

Cringe.

"No," I said. "I haven't seen that part yet."

"Oh, sorry."

"He meditates . . . 'Damn these racing-thought stories . . . it must be post-traumatic stress syndrome!'"

Actor Chris Pennock pauses, anticipating a laugh. He looks up at the assembled crowd. A few people politely giggle.

"He gardens . . . 'How the hell do you know the difference between a weed and a non-weed.'"

He looks up again, more people laugh this time. He smiles and continues reading.

"Works out at the fitness center . . . 'Uh! Uh! Oh!' Attempts to act with a community theater group . . . 'Uh-um, oh, line please!'"

More polite laughter. Pennock seems encouraged and continues.

"Reads poetry at the Café Aroma . . . 'Roses are red . . . violets are blue, shitty ass rat fuck cunt blow screw!'"

The room grew silent for a moment, and then there was some uncomfortable laughter.

Chris Pennock is an actor in his early sixties with longish wavy hair, a deep tan, and surprisingly—no, shockingly—smooth skin. Over the years he'd shown up in small parts on dozens of television shows, including *Melrose Place, Baywatch, Simon & Simon, Dynasty, General Hospital, Cagney & Lacey, The Guiding Light,* and even an episode of *The Love Boat.* But the reason he's here is because of a show he appeared on more than three decades ago—*Dark Shadows.*

The deft prose that Chris Pennock was reading came from a comic book. A comic book he wrote and illustrated with crude black-and-white drawings. A comic book he wrote less than ten days earlier. A comic book he was selling (autographed) for fifteen dollars a pop.

At that moment, Pennock was standing on a stage in the Hollywood Renaissance Hotel, reading his new comic book cover-to-cover (including describing all the action and acting out—badly acting out—the various parts) in front of 1,000 adoring attendees at the twenty-second annual *Dark Shadows* Festival.

Dark Shadows was a daytime soap opera that ran on ABC from 1966 to 1971. The show originally centered around a young woman named Victoria Winters who was hired by the creepy Collins family to serve as governess to their ten-year-old boy. The

Collins clan lived on a massive estate called Collinwood abutting a rocky cliff near the fictional town of Collinsport, Maine.

Billed as the "first gothic soap opera," the series chugged along with little notice for its first few months and found itself teetering on the verge of cancellation. With little to lose, the producers decided to add some characters and plot lines to make the show scarier. They added a séance to an episode and saw a bit of a ratings boost. Then they added a ghost into the story and the ratings bumped up again. In April 1967, the producers went for broke when they added Barnabas Collins (portrayed by actor Jonathan Frid), a one-hundred-and-seventy-five-year-old vampire ancestor released from his chained coffin in the family crypt—and the ratings exploded. *Dark Shadows,* with its new vampire star, went on to become the most successful daytime soap at ABC, at its peak commanding an audience of almost five million vampire soap-watchers every day.*

The success of their experiments encouraged the producers to throw other elements into the mix, eventually working several other vampires, a werewolf, and a bunch of ghosts into the show, as well as several forays into time travel and parallel universes. No matter how odd things got, the show continued to grow and grow.

The cast members were instant celebrities and throngs of people waited outside the studio daily for a chance to get autographs and meet the actors. In addition to being a huge hit on television, the show eventually spawned thirty-two novelizations, two feature films, a daily newspaper comic strip, and countless other toys, memorabilia, and knickknacks.

Of course, all this success shouldn't be interpreted as meaning that the show was any good. It wasn't. The acting was simply terrible. The story lines were sometimes difficult to follow and took

---

* Even though Barnabas the vampire became the show's signature character, for some reason they were reluctant to call him a vampire. Instead, they'd say things like "He's one of the undead," or "He's not alive!" It wasn't until the 410th episode—more than a year and a half after Barnabas first appeared—that the word *vampire* was used on the show.

months, if not years, to resolve (and sometimes did so inside a single episode). One of the things that contributed to *Dark Shadows'* quality issues was the fact that the cast and crew produced a new half hour show every weekday on a shoestring budget. The show wasn't live on television, but was recorded live to tape. That meant no retakes, second tries, or editing; any snafu that occurred during taping was there for eternity. If a prop gravestone toppled over, a wall or set piece collapsed, actors called other characters by the wrong name or forgot their dialogue, cameras cut to the wrong scene, special effects misfired, or a prop man wandered onto the set—they all stayed that way for posterity.*

Despite all its success, the franchise seemed to have run its course by the release of the second feature film in 1971. However, much like *Star Trek* (which debuted on television the same year as *Dark Shadows*), *Dark Shadows* gained its foothold on popular culture through syndication. In 1975, *Dark Shadows* became the first daytime soap opera to be redistributed after its initial run. It remained in syndication, on and off a variety of networks and stations, for more than twenty years. It was around this time that fan newsletters started to emerge, along with *Dark Shadows* conventions and fan festivals like the one I was attending.

The convention had actually started two days earlier when the weekend's emcee opened the festivities by saying, "Good evening and welcome to the *Dark Shadows* Hollywood Weekend. Get set for one of the most exciting weekends of your life."

Looking around the room—a sea of many hundreds of people—I had no problem believing that statement would be true for a large number of the attendees. They didn't seem like the type of folks who got out much. For them, this was about as exciting as it got.

The convention was largely a collection of oddballs of every stripe. Of course, there were "normal" folks there, but they weren't

---

* Every one of these things happened in the show—some many times.

taking the day percentage-wise. Lots of people would dart about, seemingly unaware (or terrified to death) of the fact that there were groups of people around. People would laugh, really loudly, at inappropriate moments. One guy two rows behind me kept loudly mumbling to himself. There were many people using wheelchairs, canes, and crutches. It was like a Noah's Ark of disability and dysfunction. (I talked with one attendee who said, "They should sell *Dark Shadows* inhalers here, they'd make a fortune.") The crowd was so odd that every time I'd run across some average-looking person with a convention name tag, I'd watch them intently just to see what tic would eventually emerge.

Outside of occasional question-and-answer sessions and presentations, the convention itself was, basically, 1,000 people sitting in a dark ballroom watching TV. Each session began with a short presentation, then the lights would go out, and the attendees would watch a video on a large screen. They'd talk about bloopers. Lights go down. They'd watch bloopers for an hour. Lights go up. They'd have a presentation about *Dark Shadows* actors who'd passed away in the last year. Lights would go down. They'd watch scenes with said actors for twenty minutes. Lights go up.

Friday's big event was a session featuring three surviving actresses of *Dark Shadows*. After watching scenes for a half hour, the lights came up and the emcee announced the actresses would take questions.

The line at the microphone was twenty yards deep in an instant.

First question: "In that last scene, where you are all together, do you remember what you were thinking when you filmed it?"

All three actresses said they didn't remember anything about filming that scene. To break the uncomfortable silence, actress Diana Millay remarked, "I always loved playing the bad guy. Nobody wants to be the goody, sweet, nice girl. We all want to wield the power and glory. We want to be the one making everyone else squirm. If I was thinking anything, I guess I was thinking that."

The audience loved the answer and applauded enthusiastically.

The second questioner started by remarking that all three of the actresses looked just as lovely as they did forty years ago—if not lovelier. Then asked: "What did it feel like to make *Dark Shadows* knowing that it would be so popular with so many people for so long?"

Answer: "At the time, we had no idea it would be popular."

Silence and shuffling while the next nervous and excited questioner walked to the mike.

"If there was a *Dark Shadows Next Generation* . . . would you want to play your old characters or would you want to play new ones?"

I couldn't pay attention to the answer. It was so obvious that these fans kept this show in such high regard, that they couldn't appreciate what these roles must have meant to these actresses: It was simply a gig. They were young, B-rate actresses trying to find work in New York when *Dark Shadows* came calling. It wasn't deep. It didn't mean anything. Just as the guy renewing your driver's license presumably doesn't spend a lot of time looking for deep meaning in his work, they surely didn't look for any either. It was a paycheck.

Out in the hallway, I tried to make acquaintance with some attendees milling around the hallways. If they didn't pretend not to hear me or walk away without answering, they tended to offer less-than-revealing information.

A typical exchange went something like this:

Me: "So, what makes *Dark Shadows* so interesting to you?"

Attendee: "Because it's good."

Me: "What makes it so good?"

Attendee: "I don't know, 'cause it is."

End of conversation.

Another typical repartee:

Me: "Tell me, why do you think *Dark Shadows* is still so popular with these folks thirty-five years after it went off the air?"

Attendee: "I never thought about it, I guess."

Me: "Well then, why do you like it?"

Attendee: "Excuse me, I need to go to the bathroom."

I even tried hanging out in the merchandise area—figuring that the people browsing merchandise, and laying down serious money for mint condition copies of the serialized novels, would be more likely to talk about their interest in a vampire soap opera.

While I was browsing for interview subjects, I looked around at the merchandise for sale. In addition to the expected DVDs, videos, books, photos, T-shirts, and comics, there were *Dark Shadows* calendars (including those for past years), *Dark Shadows* action figures, and even *Dark Shadows* underwear. Several of the books were packed with a numbing amount of minutiae about the series. One such book had a section featuring all the misspellings in the episodes' end credits. There were also a wide variety of vanity publications from the actors themselves—autobiographies, memoirs of working on *Dark Shadows,* and just about anything else they could think to print and manufacture. It seemed that many of these actors had realized long ago that anything they put out that was connected to the series would have an instant market with these fans.

I did strike up a conversation later that afternoon in the hotel bar with an attendee named Ralph (though his conference badge identified him as "Henry"). He offered a theory about why a thousand people would come to Los Angeles to sit together in the dark for three days.

"You know, for a lot of people, vampires are all about sex, but I think it's deeper than that. I think all this stuff is really about power."

"How so?" I asked.

"You notice all the sick people at the convo?" he said. "During the whole *Dark Shadows* series Barnabas is a vampire in search of a cure for his curse," he continued. "A *cure* for his *curse,*" he added for emphasis. "It seems pretty obvious that we're talking about a bunch of people happy to fantasize about someone finding a cure for their curse, eh?

"These are people who don't identify with the human characters—they identify with the freaks. In *Dark Shadows*, the monsters are always conflicted, always looking for a way out. They struggle. These con folks, they know what it's like to live like that."

I could hear a roar of applause coming from the ballroom that indicated the question-and-answer period was wrapping up. Soon after, the lights dimmed and the next video started. This cycle continued . . . until 3:00 A.M.

IN FRONT OF me was a black box and in that black box was a ring.

"Can I pick it up?" I ask.

"Sure."

I lifted it to my face for a closer inspection.

There are two pieces of jewelry associated with Bela Lugosi's portrayal of Count Dracula in the iconic 1931 film *Dracula*. A silver medallion and a large signet ring. In the movie, Lugosi is often seen walking with his bent arms extended slightly in front of him, as if the ring was leading the way. The medallion is currently buried six feet under with Lugosi. The ring is nested in the box in my hands.

"How did you ever get this?" I asked.

"Well, he gave me a few things himself, but the ring was given to another friend," replied Forrest Ackerman. "Then the friend thought it would be better kept with me."

People have entrusted a lot of precious things to Forrest (who most people just call Forry)—incredible rare and valuable pieces of movie memorabilia—given for him to display in the "Acker Minimansion," a.k.a. his house, in Los Angeles's Los Feliz neighborhood. The bungalow is tiny, probably no more than 1,200 square feet, and every room is packed with items from his collections. Lugosi's ring is above the mantel. Life masks of Bela, Lon Chaney, Tor Johnson, Vincent Price, and Boris Karloff hang above the doorway into the dining room. The false teeth and top hat worn by

Lon Chaney in the now lost film *London After Midnight** sit near the kitchen door. An alien hand used in the original *War of the Worlds* is sitting on top of a cabinet. Prop pieces from *Metropolis* sit in his front study. I notice two masks on top of the refrigerator that look like the Creature from the Black Lagoon.

"What's the story with these?" I ask.

"Well, the one on the left is from the original and the one on the right is from the first sequel," Forry replied.

"These are the *original* masks?"

"Yup."

"Sitting here on top of your refrigerator?"

Forry giggles. "Yes."

Forry is credited with coining the term *sci-fi* to describe the monster, science, and outer space movies, magazines, books, and comics that he adored. Forry first got hooked on the fantastic when he could barely even read. He stumbled across a copy of *Amazing Stories* magazine when he was nine years old (which he still owns and displays in his house), devoured its collection of weird tales, and was hungry to find more. By the time he was thirteen, he was corresponding with more than 120 other fans, had coined several pre-sci-fi phrases to describe the genre (including *scientifiction* and *imagi-movies*) and was contributing to early science fiction magazines. Since, he's been a literary agent, film producer, comic book creator, writer, prolific movie extra, and creator/editor of the seminal sci-fi magazine, *Famous Monsters of Filmland.*

For as impressive as his collection is, it used to be much bigger. Forry's full collection used to fill a larger house in the Hollywood Hills. When health and finances forced him to downsize a few years ago (he is nearing ninety and now lives alone), he held a yard sale to get rid of some of his 300,000 science fiction and horror items. He donated 120 pieces to the Science Fiction Museum and

---

* This film, helmed by *Dracula* director Tod Browning, was the first U.S. film with a vampirelike character.

Hall of Fame in Seattle and has a few others here and there. The remaining items are here in this house. Every Saturday morning Forry opens his house to anyone who wants to stop by and look at his things. He's done this every Saturday since 1951.

"You're interested in vampire stuff, aren't you?" he asks.

"You bet."

Forry launched into a mini-lecture about how he views the appeal of vampires. According to Forry, vampires have much more appeal to women than to men.

"I think a lot of ladies in their love life occasionally get bitten a bit by their lovers and they can imagine it going just one step further," he said. "I think that Bela Lugosi and Christopher Lee had a lot to do with spreading an international interest in vampires. Ladies would see these dashing sophisticated gentlemen. Sure, they had an evil side, but that only added to the attraction."

Forry pointed his finger toward a glass-fronted cabinet.

"Get over to that bookcase and bring me the yellow book there," he added.

I could see the bookcase, but getting to it would be a challenge. There was about four solid feet of stuff, chest-high, separating me from the bookcase. I slithered along the wall containing some of the original paintings that graced the covers of *Famous Monsters of Filmland* and some of the original hand-drawn panels for an issue of *Vampirella*—a comic that Forry created.

For someone who believes that vampire fans are primarily women, I kinda want to ask him to explain *Vampirella*. The character Vampirella is a dominatrix-looking, tits-and-ass, leather-clad hottie in a space suit it looks like she outgrew when she was eleven.

In addition to being a comic book, *Vampirella* is also the worst vampire movie I've ever seen.

Vampirella combines Forry's two favorite things: outer space fantasy and vampires. Vampirella lives on the planet Draculon and travels to Earth to avenge the death of her father. The murderer was another vampire and Draculon exile named Vlad, portrayed by Roger Daltrey, lead singer of The Who. Once on Earth, Vampirella hooks up with a guy named Adam Van Helsing, who is part of a paramilitary group called PURGE that hunts vampires (a precursor to *Buffy*'s the Intitiative). The movie is so poorly acted, so poorly shot, so poorly directed that it seems too easy to make fun of it. The biggest question you have while watching *Vampirella* is how Roger Daltrey got twisted up with this crap ball. Given, his "acting" is limited to widening his eyes and hissing, but you think that he would have rather used some of his rock 'n' roll money to buy the rights to the film and have it destroyed, rather than experience any well-deserved shame for having any association with this flick. Even easily forgiving horror fans complained about the film (many suggesting that Vampirella Talisa Soto wasn't busty enough for the role).

In the film, Vlad has, of course, decided upon the low-key profession of rock star, thus forcing Daltrey through the indignity of lip-syncing some terrible songs written for the movie while wearing some oppressively '80s clothes and makeup (especially odd seeing that the movie was shot in 1996). In the meager crowd at Vlad's concert, you notice one guy really enjoying the music: Forry.

Once I positioned myself as close to the buried bookshelf as I could, I was able to reach my fingers inside the glass doors on the bookcase and retrieve the yellow book. Once I handed it to Forry, he opened the front cover, turned it around toward me, and handed it back.

"Look."

The book itself was a first American edition of *Dracula*, signed by Bram Stoker himself as well as many people associated with *Dracula* over the years: Christopher Lee; Vincent Price; Carla Laemmle; Ferdy Mayne; Vampira; Raymond McNally; Lon Chaney, Jr.; John Carradine; Bela Lugosi (who signed it twice); and several others that I couldn't make out.

"And come over here," Forry said, pointing toward the bay window at the front of the house.

There stood a short black mannequin—the top of its head barely reaching my shoulder—wearing a cape. It was Bela Lugosi's cape from the Broadway stage version of *Dracula*. The cape Lugosi wore in the movie *Dracula* has been the subject of several urban myths. Unlike most of these tales, one of the most bizarre versions of this story is actually true: Bela Lugosi was buried wearing a cape. Despite decades of trying to escape from the role, Lugosi had indicated that he wanted to be buried in his *Dracula* costume. The mythical part kicks in with stories that claim the cape was later found hanging in Lugosi's closet—suggesting that somehow it had returned from the grave. It wasn't the same cape. Considering the number of times he portrayed Count Dracula (among many other vampire characters), Lugosi had several.

TWELVE YEARS AFTER Bram Stoker's death, his dream of seeing his novel come to life on stage was realized. The only problem was the play bore little resemblance to his novel.

The reasons no one had been willing to stage *Dracula* were that the novel takes place in two different countries and dozens of locations. It would require a large cast, expensive effects, and would be difficult to pare down to a reasonable length. Despite all this, when English theater producer and actor Hamilton Deane approached Florence Stoker about rights, she really didn't care what he did with the book as long as she got paid. In order to secure the stage rights, Deane had to turn over 90 percent of the royalties to Florence.

When the play debuted in August 1924 at the Grand Theatre in Derby, England, critics hated it; audiences loved it. After two successful seasons in Derby, Deane moved his play to London, where it opened in February 1927. Again, critics blasted the play, but it was a sellout for five solid months. To add even more spectacle to the production, Deane positioned a nurse inside the theater for every performance of the play. Eventually, an American producer named Horace Liveright approached Mrs. Stoker about bringing the play to Broadway.

Liveright originally offered the lead in the Broadway production to Raymond Huntley, the actor who played the count in London, but Huntley's salary demands forced Liveright to find a new count. He quickly settled on a relatively unknown Hungarian actor named Béla Blasko, who went under the stage name Bela Lugosi.

While Lugosi's bio materials stated he had been a huge star back in his native Hungary, his verifiable accomplishments were significantly less grand. After finding himself on the wrong side of the political fence in the Hungarian revolution of 1918, he worked his way across Europe and eventually to the United States. Despite the fact that he spoke practically no English, he was still able to land roles in New York by learning his lines phonetically. Even five years after his arrival, Lugosi still knew little English when cast in *Dracula*. He, again, delivered his lines phonetically and was directed in French. The play opened at the Fulton Theater on October 5, 1927. The American critics were far less caustic toward the Broadway production and the play quickly grew to be a huge hit. It wasn't long before Universal Pictures came calling, inquiring about turning *Dracula* into a motion picture.

Because of Mrs. Stoker's various rights schemes, acquiring the movie rights was complicated. By the time Universal had everything straight, they had struck deals with four different rights holders. By this time, Lugosi had wrapped up the Broadway production and was starring in the touring company. He was eager to hold on to the film version of the role and started lobbying aggressively—perhaps too aggressively.

Universal had other plans. They'd considered several actors for the part (including John Griffith Wray, Ian Keith, and Conrad Veidt), and had secured Tod Browning as the film's director with hopes they could lure Lon Chaney to the role. Universal executive Carl Laemmle, Jr., had gone as far as sending a telegram to Lugosi's agent saying they weren't interested. Yet Bela persisted, suggesting that his association with the role would be a big selling point for the film. Lugosi was doing everything he could to endear himself to Universal. He repeatedly interceded on behalf of Universal during their negotiations with Florence Stoker, trying to persuade her to grant them rights for a film version. Further, Lugosi donated his services to Universal by dubbing male voices for Hungarian versions of their films. However, to Universal, all these gestures came off as desperation. When their other choices for Count Dracula didn't pan out, they realized that they could get Lugosi for just about anything they offered him. And they did.

Just before filming began in September 1930, Universal gave the part to Lugosi with a salary of five hundred dollars a week. This rate was less than a quarter of the salary given to any of the other marquee actors. In fact, Lugosi was offered less than several of the minor players received. Regardless, he took it. All told, Lugosi's entire compensation for appearing as the eponymous count in *Dracula* amounted to about three thousand and five hundred dollars.

In viewing *Dracula*, there are several things that immediately surprise you. First off, for as groundbreaking a visual film that *Dracula* was—arguably setting many standards in the budding horror genre—it isn't a very visually interesting film to watch. Many of the film's scenes were filmed with long, wide shots, almost as if the filmmakers were trying to capture action in a stage play rather than create a film. One camera shot in the finished film runs almost three continuous minutes without a single cutaway, camera pan, or reaction shot. That aside, some eventual staples of the horror film genre made their first appearances in *Dracula*, such as the dank and spooky castle, copious cobwebs, the sinister winding staircase, and fog to indicate the nearby presence of evil.

Second, it's obvious that *Dracula* was still part of the first wave of talkies. Many viewers today are struck by the sparse dialogue in *Dracula*—there are long silent passages in the film. For a talkie, there sure isn't a lot of talking going on.[*]

Also, for being a supernatural horror film, the filmmakers dodged a lot of the potential for special effects. This is especially

---

[*] In partial justification for this, when *Dracula* was released it was still common to find theaters throughout the country that couldn't play sound. As a result, there was a silent version of the film that was created and shown.

odd because they were written into the script (including more of Lucy's vampire transformation and undead antics with Count Dracula, as well as an extended staking scene), but for some reason Browning altered the structure of the film to avoid producing them.

Most people are unaware that a second version of *Dracula* was shot at the same time as the Browning-Lugosi film—a Spanish-language version. It used the same sets, scenery, and props, but a different cast and crew. They would come onto the set during the evenings and film through the night. Filming simultaneous versions of movies was a budding practice at Universal during the time. Making multiple language versions of a film during the silent era was easy—just replace the dialogue cards. The invention of sound created many expensive problems. At the time, Universal received half its revenue from foreign markets and several foreign governments were threatening heavy tariffs on imported English-language films. Dubbing movies into foreign languages was expensive and very difficult, so producers began creating shadow productions like the Spanish version of *Dracula*. It was a wise tactic. While Universal spent close to four hundred and fifty thousand dollars to produce *Dracula*, the addition of the Spanish version only added sixty-six thousand dollars to the original production costs.

The Spanish *Dracula,* staring Carlos Villarias as the count and Lupita Tovar as the Mina character, is actually a far more interesting film to watch than the original—revealing all the missed opportunities in the American version. Though some of the characters were renamed (such as Juan Harker), the Spanish *Dracula* sticks to the same basic plot outline as the American version. However, the Spanish version made use of all the camera angles, lighting, and visual effects missing from the "daytime" *Dracula*. The Spanish crew would rearrange the scenery, props, and furniture to create more depth and visual tension. While the count's basic outfit is the same in both films, many of the Spanish version's actresses (especially Dracula's vampire wives) had much more sensuous, low-cut clothing and fleshed out the sexual elements of the story (pardon the pun) instead of suppressing them.

Browning and Lugosi's *Dracula* debuted at New York's Roxy Theatre on Friday the thirteenth, in February 1931. Again, the press reviews were mixed, and again, *Dracula* quickly became a runaway hit. To a degree that exceeded the novel and play before it, the movie version of *Dracula* struck a nerve with the public. It was more than a scary movie; its themes resonated with what frightened people outside the theater as well. At the time, the United States was just coming to grips with the extent and profound depth of its economic problems. There was a distrust of anyone associated with the three Bs: bankers, brokers, and businessmen. In the decades that preceded the Great Depression, foreign immigration and the rise of Communism had created a general suspicion of Eastern Europe. Count Dracula, the wealthy aristocrat from the East, invaded their lives, violated young women, and overturned their worlds.

Dracula became a popular culture juggernaut—making a deeper, more ubiquitous impression on our cultural history than any previous film. Yet despite this and the assumed advantages of its fame, *Dracula* would directly and indirectly destroy the life of the man most associated with its legacy.

Before *Dracula* even opened, Lugosi was already complaining about being typecast in the role and the pittance it had brought him. While filming, Lugosi received an offer to portray Dracula on stage . . . again. "No! Not at any price," he proclaimed. "When I'm through with this picture I hope never to hear of Dracula again. I cannot stand it . . . I do not intend that it shall possess me."

A COUPLE WEEKS after I'd finished watching all the *Buffy* episodes, I was sitting on the subway reading, when I noticed that the woman next to me was trying to check out my book. I'm fairly used to this. Over the past year and a half I've brought along quite an interesting collection of reading material on my commute—books about vampires, witchcraft, ritual killings, blood fetish, and so on. While my fellow commuters busy themselves with sudoku puzzles and James Patterson novels, I'm delighting in tales of crazed teens murdering their grandparents in order to drink their blood. Occasionally, I get looks.

Then I felt her tap my shoulder.

"Excuse me," she said. "Can I ask what book you're reading?"

It was a book about *Buffy*.

"It looks so interesting," she said.

"Are you a *Buffy* fan?" I ask.

"Oh, yeah," she replied. "I used to watch it every once in a while, but about a year ago I got interested in watching it all the way through and have been watching all the DVDs."

"Really," I replied. "I just did the same thing. . . . Are you finished yet?"

"No, I'm in the next to last season."

"Oh, that's a terribly dark one," I said.

"I know."

"Wait though, it gets even crazier at the end," I said, realizing that I was just about to spoil it for her.

If you were to ask me about the deep meanings contained in *Buffy the Vampire Slayer*, I'd probably report that it was a great chronicle of all the female clothing and accessory fads that came and went between 1997 and 2003, such as wearing muscle T-shirts with skirts, cowboy hats, impossibly short miniskirts, colorful thick belts, and pucca shell necklaces. I might further speculate that as the series went on, viewers were led to sympathize with the secondary characters more than with Buffy herself. I'd also tell examples of funny lines and scenarios. But while I had a great time watching those episodes—far better than I expected—I really didn't pick up much more from the experience than that. However, other fans of *Buffy the Vampire Slayer* have spent a considerably larger amount of time thinking about the series. And still do.

Even now, years after the show has ended, cyberspace is filled with thousands of *Buffy* fan sites, many still being filled with intense introspection, fights, and banter about the series. Many fans also write "fan fiction"—short stories meant to continue the series' story lines off into various tangential journeys.

Academics have been having a field day with *Buffy* as well. For pop culture academics looking to waste embarrassing amounts of time thinking about the nuances of things that no one really cares about, *Buffy* is a wet dream. There have been several academic conferences based on the show and their resulting papers and articles suggest barrelfuls of illusive meanings, metaphors, and subtexts. At a recent conference, a sample of presentations included, "Russian Existentialism and Vampire Slayage: A Shestovian Key to the Power and Popularity of *Buffy the Vampire Slayer*"; "Renegotiating Identity: Viewing the Post 9/11 Buffyverse in a Post 9/11 World"; "Greening the Buffyverse: Raising Environmental Awareness in the Fourth Season of *Buffy the Vampire Slayer*"; and "Postmodern Reflections on the Culture of the Consumption of Culture of Consumption: Multilayered Meanings of *Buffy the Vampire Slayer* in the U.K."*

While all this seems like overkill, it isn't that off base. The show's producers did build a lot into the show that would escape most (okay, almost *all*) viewers. For example, all the artwork hanging along the stairway in Buffy's home are pictures of doorways, arches, and other thresholds, which the creators have acknowledged were meant to symbolize Buffy's transitions documented in the series.

By the time I'd finished viewing all the *Buffy* episodes, the number of fans who'd been outed at work had grown to nine. Several of them had been regularly checking in on my progress, so I thought one way to keep them from dropping constant spoilers would be to say that once I'd finished, we'd all get together for lunch. Four of them showed up.

Once we sat down, we had surprisingly little to talk about. We all watched a lot of this show, we all work here . . . now what?

---

* In fact no less than five of the presentations at the conference had the word *postmodern* in their title.

Again, I had naïve expectations for this lunch. I assumed that anyone who was still an ardent fan of a television show almost a decade after it debuted would have a lot to say about it. With one exception,* there was not a lot of deep talk about the show. While they all liked talking about favorite episodes, dialogue, and characters, it didn't seem like something that required a lot of deep thought. They just liked it.

When I pressed them to tell me why, I heard back many of the same things I'd heard from others, and felt myself—the writing, the humor, the approachability on multiple levels.

One thing I did learn is that among *Buffy* fans, there is no "type." Looking around the table, the only things we all had in common were that we all worked at the same place and we'd all watched this show—a lot. Among my coworkers, they felt the thing that really attracted them was how much they empathized with Buffy and her friends.

"The real monsters in *Buffy* weren't the vampires and demons," said my coworker Emily. "The monsters were the bullies and the teachers and everyone else she has to battle just to get by. Who can't relate to that?"

Unlike the *Dark Shadows* fans, however, the show didn't define them. There seemed to be two reasons why. One, *Buffy* was actually a good show—or at least it *seems* good now. That also hints at the second reason—time. Buffy ended a few years ago; *Dark Shadows* ended a few decades ago. Perhaps I'm being overly optimistic, but the *Buffy* fans I meet still have a chance to move on—and I bet that 99.9 percent of them will move on. They'll find other movies, television shows, or other things to be excited about. *Buffy* is just one of several things that they'll be enchanted by in their lives.

---

* At one point Harold, a programmer in our Online department, threw down this crazy wicked dissection of the dialogue in a dream sequence that, as Harold pointed out, foreshadowed the plot outline for the next two seasons. We all paused at that one. It was pretty impressive.

Those who don't move on? I've seen their future and it involves a lot of sitting in darkened hotel ballrooms.

THINK WHAT YOU like of Bela Lugosi's acting, but it's hard to look at his decision making post-*Dracula* and not conclude that he was his career's own worst enemy. Painting himself into a corner for his *Dracula* salary was just the beginning. Shortly on the heels of *Dracula*'s success, Universal offered Lugosi the role of the monster in their upcoming adaptation of *Frankenstein*. He turned them down, thinking the heavy makeup and prosthetics would render him unrecognizable. Universal ended up offering the role to Boris Karloff instead, transforming the actor into a horror icon (and spawning Lugosi's near obsession with Karloff's successes).

One of Lugosi's first post-*Dracula* films was *White Zombie*, a bizarre story of Haitian zombies and magic potions that was shot in eleven days for less than fifty thousand dollars (even making use of some of the *Dracula* and *Frankenstein* sets and props). Even though Lugosi was a superstar who arguably was the film's only box-office appeal, he was paid only a few hundred dollars more per week than for *Dracula*.

There was something else soon complicating Lugosi's life. *Dracula* hadn't only given Bela a career-defining role, it had also given him a morphine addiction. Lugosi had recurring back trouble and was prescribed painkillers so that he could work. Soon, he was hooked, an addiction that would plague him for most of the rest of his life.*

---

* Lugosi wasn't the only *Dracula* cast member to experience tragedy after the film. Director Tod Browning created the disturbing film *Freaks* in 1932, which pretty much ended his serious film career. Helen Chandler, the actress who portrayed Mina, grew dependant on alcohol and pills and was unemployable by the mid-1930s. Dwight Frye, who played Renfield, was unfortunately typecast (despite a wide range as an actor) and died twelve years later from a heart attack.

As the years passed, Lugosi found himself cast in progressively worse films, eventually sinking to such dogs as *The Devil Bat, Ghosts on the Loose, Zombies on Broadway,* and *Return of the Ape Man* (a film that contained no Ape Man—returned or otherwise). Though he portrayed other vampire characters in film throughout his career, Lugosi portrayed Count Dracula in only one other film, *Abbott and Costello Meet Frankenstein* in 1948. The film would also be the last time Lugosi would be employed by a major studio. Though he repeatedly swore he had no interest in performing *Dracula* on stage, he'd often reluctantly accept offers just for the desperately needed cash. In the middle of one such tour, in the United Kingdom, the production went belly-up, stranding Lugosi overseas with no money to get home. In order to get back to the United States, he agreed to star in the über-clunker *Mother Riley Meets the Vampire*—later retitled and released as *My Son, the Vampire*, one of the first films I watched when I began all this vampire malarkey.

A few years later, the seventy-two-year-old Lugosi checked himself into a state hospital for his morphine addiction. At the time, Hollywood was still decades away from lionizing freshly sober celebrities and Lugosi was viewed as a pariah. The only person to hire Lugosi after his stint in rehab was director Ed Wood, Jr., who cast Lugosi in several of his films. One week into filming Wood's *Plan 9 from Outer Space,* Lugosi died of heart failure. (Wood later finished the film by using his wife's chiropractor as a stand-in, covering his face with a cape.)

"I was with him two weeks before he died—at the premiere of his final film *The Black Sleep*," Forrest Ackerman had told me during our visit. "We sat together up in the balcony and afterward we were coming downstairs. I could see that they were set up with a big TV camera to interview him. He was very vain and wouldn't be seen in public wearing glasses. So everything down there in the lobby was just a big blur to him. So we got to the bottom of the stairs and I said, 'Bela, they want to interview you' and he said,

'Just point me in the right direction.' I said take about six steps forward and you'll be there. He straightened up and filled out and all of a sudden became the tall, proud figure of Count Dracula."

According to his wishes, before burial Lugosi's family dyed his hair and eyebrows jet-black, had theatrical makeup applied, and dressed him in his *Dracula* costume and cape. As much as he tried to escape the count's shadow during his lifetime, it was a fitting tribute. During his life, he had portrayed *Dracula* more than 1,300 times.

"During the last three years of his life we went out of our way to have him in our home at parties and I took him to get groceries, have his shoes resoled, and such," Forry had told me. "One time he got out of the car, put his hand on my shoulder and said, 'I don't understand why you young people are so good to me.' And I said, 'Well, Bela, you were good to us, you know. You entertained us and we're happy to help you.' I don't think he really understood what he meant to us. Not at all."

BEFORE HEADING HOME from Los Angeles after the *Dark Shadows* convention, I took a side trip to Holy Cross Cemetery in Culver City. Most of the graves are simple slabs flush with the ground, so it's hard to locate anything or have any idea if you're even close until you step right up to the grave you're looking for. After about an hour of searching, I came upon:

BELA LUGOSI

BELOVED FATHER

1882–1956

Bela is surrounded by several generations of the McNeil, Dyke, and McKay families in a quite beautiful setting near the top of the hill and an outdoor chapel. As I looked at the marker, I was struck by the phrase "beloved father." While it is an obvious reference to his son, Bela Lugosi, Jr.,* it—like everything about vampires—has some metaphorical meanings as well.

When we think about the iconic vision of the vampire, we think of Lugosi. He held such sway over the image that it would take decades before anyone would even attempt to update it. During Lugosi's lifetime, only one other actor attempted to portray Count Dracula in a film (John Carradine in 1945's *House of Dracula*). Lugosi was not only the father of our image of the vampire, he was our vampire.

The same year that Lugosi died, the British company Hammer Film Productions started production on what it originally intended to be a seven-part *Dracula*-themed television series. By the time they had untwisted the rights, they'd committed to a series of films instead. The fifteen Hammer vampire films, starting with 1958's *Horror of Dracula*† are some of the best and worst adaptations of *Dracula* and vampire movies ever made. The Hammer films opened the floodgate of *Dracula*-inspired films, sometimes more than two dozen a year, that continues even today.

On the plane ride home that afternoon, I was lamenting the *Dark Shadows* festival and how little I'd thought I'd learned there. I really figured that people who had spent decades of time, as well as piles of cash, idolizing a vampire soap opera would have something interesting and insightful to say about vampires. I was mistaken.

---

* In addition to being a regular guest at horror conventions and frequent speaker about his father's role in pop history (let alone bearing a striking similarity to his father), Bela, Jr., is a lawyer, specializing in corporate law (a decision he once explained by saying, "Having Bela Lugosi as a criminal lawyer would be a little too much, wouldn't it?"). He made a name for himself in a groundbreaking case trying to gain control over his father's image rights. In 1963, Lugosi saw a toy model kit bearing his father's image and decided to review his dad's original contract. While Universal had rights to use Lugosi's image, it was restricted to promoting the film—no merchandising rights were given. Lugosi felt the hundreds of products bearing his father's likeness fell far outside the contract's terms and sued Universal. He won the initial suit, *Lugosi vs. Universal Pictures*, in 1974. However, it was overturned on appeal a few years later. While it could be considered a loss, Lugosi's case led to the creation of legislation that protected the rights of heirs to celebrity likenesses.
† Which starred Christopher Lee as Dracula, the first of his seven appearances as the evil count in Hammer films.

To kill time, I was going through some stuff Jeanne had recently sent me. I noticed a small, twelve-page pamphlet with a yellow cover entitled: "How to Become a VAMPIRE in 6 Easy Lessons." It was written by a vampire named Madeline X and published by Jeanne in 1985. As I thumbed through it, I got an idea. If the vampires I found were going to be so nonrevelatory, there was an alternative.

I could *make* a vampire.

Me.

VIII

WELCOME TO DARKWING MANOR

*In which the author concludes his journey celebrating Halloween in Oregon,
choking on PoliGrip, and trying not to contract salmonella.*

So, you got big plans for Halloween?" asked the hotel shuttle
driver.

"Yes, actually," I reply. "I'm visiting some friends who—"

"Here you go," the driver interrupted.

"We're here?" I asked.

"Yup."

I looked over my shoulder, the hotel I'm staying in is *maybe* 150
yards from the front entrance to the airport.

"I could have walked here just as easily," I replied. "Why do you
folks even run a shuttle?"

"Well, you know, at night, people don't want to have to walk
over in the dark."

I couldn't help but wonder what people could possibly be afraid
of. The Rogue Valley International-Medford Airport is in the
midst of a lot of nothing. I couldn't see a *tree* within sight of the
airport. Even at night, you could see someone coming so far off
that you could run to the hotel and take the stairs to the roof before they'd get to the front door.

The airport itself was tiny—a handful of gates, a gift shop, and
one baggage carousel. And I don't mean to be a stickler, but a look
at its flight schedule brought its "international" status into serious

question as well. As the title would indicate, the airport is in Medford, Oregon, a small town about twenty-five miles north of the California border. From the looks of the town, I'm surprised it can support its own Kmart, let alone an airport.

My eventual destination is about forty-five minutes down the highway—Phoenix, Oregon (population 4,400). That's where Tim and Tina Reuwsaat* live, the couple from my Romania Dracula tour who convert their home into a vampire-themed haunted house every October. I'd flown out to help out with this year's haunt.

Coming to rural southern Oregon for Halloween wasn't my original plan. I'd wanted to spend the most spooky time of the year in New Orleans, home to some of the country's best-known vampires.

Louisiana's rich history and culture includes a lot of freaky death stuff, a lot of it left over from Victorian traditions, mixed with some voodoo, and topped with a fear of the undead returning to haunt, feed from, kill, and/or otherwise bother the living. Many still exist today. These charming practices include the practice of burying bodies upside down, driving stakes through the heart before burial, weighing the eyes with coins, tying the dead's mouth shut, and "sitting up with the dead"—where families stand constant vigil over the deceased until they are buried. Some local plantations were built with the keyholes upside down to keep out vampires. Eighteenth- and nineteenth-century outbreaks of yellow fever and tuberculosis in Louisiana were blamed on vampirism.

Probably the most obvious connection between vampires and New Orleans is vampire fiction queen Anne Rice, who has somehow managed to convince millions of book purchasers to forgo other readable options and throw down for some of her New Orleanscentric tomes. In addition to crazy annual Halloween balls and parties, New Orleans has several vampire-themed attractions

---

* Pronounced "rue saht"—kinda like "blue snot."

ranging from the kitschy to the disturbing. White Wolf, makers of *Vampire: The Masquerade,* have created an entire spin-off vampire-themed game set in New Orleans. Plus, New Orleans has always had a high murder rate and number of missing persons cases. All in all—it's the perfect playground for the undead!

Unfortunately, two months earlier, Hurricane Katrina had erased my plans. In the wake of that storm, even the undead had been washed away. Like many things in New Orleans, the vampire tours, shops, and clubs eventually came back. But that Halloween, dealing with the actual dead was still a full-time, door-to-door, very real pursuit.

So Medford, Oregon, there I was.

On the plane ride out from Washington I watched what would be my last vampire film, *Legend of the Seven Golden Vampires.* It's one of the final Hammer vampire films, taking the franchise to China to battle a group of seven evil kung fu–wielding vampires. This wasn't my first kung fu vampire film, it was my third. In a thinly veiled attempt to tie this movie's plot (and marketing) to other vampire films, the movie opens in Transylvania, where a servant of the Chinese vampires calls on Count Dracula to help reawaken the dormant Chinese bloodsuckers. Dracula decides to take over the man's body, travel to China, and make the seven golden vampires his servants. Then, Dracula is pretty much out of the picture until the very end of the movie. It just so happens that Dr. Van Helsing (played by Peter Cushing) is in China giving a lecture when he hears about a village being terrorized by a group of recently reinvigorated undead. He and his companions enlist a few locals (who happen to be martial arts experts) and dust the golden vampires one by one. In the movie's final minutes, Count Dracula reveals himself again and is quickly dispensed with by Van Helsing.

While kung fu fighting does add an interesting spin on your standard vampire tale, the movie was obviously made by filmmakers who didn't have a lot of experience with marital arts movies. Watching the movie, you definitely feel like you are meant to sit back and watch from a distance, rather than get up close. The camerawork is static, not allowing the camera to become part of the action. If you are looking for a good vampire flick from the East (okay, a *better* vampire flick from the East), I'd suggest *Dragon Against Vampire*—once you get past the bad dialogue dubbing and impenetrable plot, it's a lot of fun to watch.

All told, I made it through 216 films—389 films short of my goal. At first it may seem like a failure or cop-out, but 216 films is probably about 200 more than should be humanly permissible. After the first few dozen flicks, it became quite apparent that there are only so many twists you can put on vampire lore, and I'd seen them all. By the time I finished, I had gained the uncanny ability to predict most of the action of a film just from reading the promotional description. Case in point: *Zoltan, Hound of Dracula*. As soon as the movie arrived, I wrote the probable plot outline in my notes. Knowing that Zoltan was a dog, I guessed that it would become a vampire dog and go about attacking dogs and humans until someone shoved a stake through its heart and killed it. When I watched the movie—that's exactly what happened. The only part I missed was the subplot where Zoltan sought out the modern-day descendant of Count Dracula in order to bite him, thus creating a new vampire master.

My ability to predict vampire plots continued through *Club Vampire* (a group of stripper vampires who attack horny patrons for blood), *Atom Age Vampire* (where atomic power turns a normal, nice woman into a life-sucking undead), and *Taste the Blood of Dracula* (where four guys drink Dracula's blood to gain superpowers). By the time I got to *Legend of the Seven Golden Vampires*, I could barely pay attention to vampire movies anymore. It was long past time to quit.

However, the true reason I sat through this movie on the plane was to avoid the work I'd really intended to do during the ride—reading Anne Rice's *The Tale of the Body Thief*. I'd been trying to avoid Anne Rice throughout this project, but I eventually had to come to terms with her unavoidability when exploring the subject of vampires.

Anne Rice and her husband were both professional writers in the late 1960s when she wrote a short story called "Interview with the Vampire." She fussed with it for a while but put it away after finishing and let it sit for several years. When her five-year-old daughter Michelle died of leukemia in 1972, Rice stopped writing entirely. The following year, she dug up "Interview with the Vampire" and began to flesh it out into a novel. The end result was an epic tale that provided Rice with a cathartic outlet for her own yearning, confusion, and rage over her daughter's death and internal conflicts with her own religious upbringing.

As a novel, *Interview with the Vampire* unfolds as a confession/interview between a vampire named Louis and a young reporter in San Francisco. The story follows Louis as he describes being made into a vampire in 1791 by a crude, flamboyant vampire named Lestat. Louis had been mourning the death of his brother and felt a tremendous amount of revulsion and guilt at being a vampire. To keep Louis from leaving him, Lestat turns a dying young girl named Claudia into a vampire (acknowledged by Rice to her biographer to represent her daughter Michelle), and the three of them live together for sixty years. Eventually, things fall apart, as Claudia resents being trapped in a young girl's body and decides to kill Lestat (she's not entirely successful). Claudia and Louis travel the world looking for other vampires and eventually land in Paris. Louis falls in love with an older vampire named Armand, Claudia has Louis create a vampire playmate for her, Lestat shows up and turns the Paris vampires against Claudia (they then kill her), and then Louis flees back to the United States. The novel ends with the young reporter publishing the story under the pseudonym "Anne Rice."

Interview with the Vampire was published in 1976 and became an unexpected sensation. The book itself is long, slow-paced, and just dripping with affected verbiage. However, the story was original and fairly engaging. On its own, its sins are forgivable. It's not a great read, but it's an okay-to-good read. The problem was that Rice decided to write a number of sequels, known collectively as the Vampire Chronicles, which follow the adventures of Lestat and several other minor characters. As she continued, it seemed like Rice's writing became progressively less interesting and more onerous. In a moment of inspiration, I decided to buy the mass-market versions of each of the four sequels. Reading them was about as much fun as a lower GI scan.

Yet it seems that as Rice's writing became more dense, leaden, and showy, her ardent legion of fans continued to grow exponentially. Since *Interview with the Vampire* was first published, Rice has sold a staggering seventy-five million books to fans of thinly veiled erotic tales of submission and dominance among a group of long-winded and fairly boring vampires.

If Rice is an icon of anything, it's the depths that vampire fiction has fallen in the 110 years since Bram Stoker turned in his manuscript for *Dracula* (a position, of course, that wasn't that high to start with). Over the course of more than a thousand novels since, vampire fiction has become a joke—inaccessible, pretentious, and packed with clichéd stories, language, and characters. While bad vampire movies can be enjoyable for their badness, bad vampire fiction is just . . . bad.

Rice herself has divorced herself from this body of work. Periodically throughout her career, she's played love/hate with her work, its legacy, and her fans. At one time she held massive vampire-themed parties at her home, but later she moved to La Jolla, California, and sold her New Orleans properties. She famously had a few rounds over the film adaptation of *Interview with the Vampire* (starring Tom Cruise as Lestat and Brad Pitt as Louis, which wasn't that bad of an adaptation, save for the fact that they completely removed the not-too-subtle homosexuality in the novel). Later, she claimed to love the movie and Cruise's portrayal of her franchise vampire. She's gone similarly hot and cold over the recent Elton John–penned musical *Lestat,* which suffered only a short run before it tanked and closed on Broadway. Over the past few years, Rice has said that she's done with vampires entirely, having rediscovered Jesus through the renewal of her Catholic faith. Now, Anne Rice serves the Lord. Her latest book is a novel exploring the missing teen years of Jesus.

Reading through *The Tale of the Body Thief*, I have trouble believing that *anyone*, including Rice herself, has made it all the way through this book without fighting a gag reflex. By this time (it's the fourth book in the series) Lestat has become nostalgic for life as a mortal and comes up with a scheme to temporarily trade bodies with a human. Of course, once the human test-drives all of Lestat's vampire powers, he tells Lestat that he plans to make the switch permanent. The book follows Lestat's attempts to get his own body back—or at least that's what I assumed. I was stuck on page sixty (with almost four hundred left to go) and to avoid continuing, I'd watched the kung fu vampire movie, read the SkyMall catalog *twice*, and spent thirty minutes fiddling with the latch on my tray table to see if I could get it to point upright without falling over. Fortunately, after only two hours of picking the inside of my fingernails, we landed in Medford and I was on my way without having read the book.

Tim and Tina have been morphing their house into a Halloween attraction every October for the past twenty-five years. They are part of a growing trend called "home haunts." As the technology involved in Halloween effects becomes ever cheaper and readily available, more and more people are setting up elaborate displays that rival commercial haunted houses. It works for the visitor as well—why wait in line for hours when your neighbor down the street has a fog machine and is perfectly willing to chase you around with a chain saw? Home haunt enthusiasts even have their own conventions, Web sites, and magazines. Most home haunts don't charge admission (though the costs for staging one can easily run into the thousands), though some take donations for local charities. It isn't unusual to see home haunts in almost every town, some on the same scale as Tim and Tina's. The previous year, the Reuwsaats had their largest crowds ever—1,400 people, equivalent to one-third of the population of their town.

The next morning, Halloween itself, I pulled up to Tim and Tina's dark gray, turn-of-the-century, Victorian home that sits on top of a hill and looks like it's a tad creepy all year round. There's a sign along the road with a dancing skeleton on it, welcoming visitors to Darkwing Manor—the moniker of Tim and Tina's house. The house is actually listed on the National Register of Historic Places—albeit for being the first prune farm in the Rogue Valley (which, I guess, must be known for its prune industry). Their black mailbox also featured the Darkwing moniker, wrapped underneath the talons of a black dragon.

I'd volunteered to come early to help set up. After helping Tim carry a few things, check some lights, and fill lamps with oil, I hung around with Tina in the kitchen while she prepared snacks for the evening.

Tina told me that home haunt enthusiasts even have their own lingo.

"Well, we refer to our visitors as Muggles for one, just like the name for humans in *Harry Potter*," she offered. "Halloween enthusiasts are called Weeners. There's also peetalities, which is what we call it when people get so scared they wet themselves. Most haunts keep a running tally of those."

After helping Tina slice vegetables, there really wasn't anything left for me to do, so I decided to head back over to my hotel to try on my costume and makeup.

What I was really worried about was my fangs. The only request I had for Tim and Tina was that, whatever I was assigned to do that evening, that I got to play a vampire. They happily agreed; their only concession was that I dress in a Victorian costume to match the others. I'd come to Oregon with a black cloaklike thing and two sets of fangs. The first set were caps, held over your incisors with adhesive. They presented two problems, (a.) they were bone-white and my teeth . . . aren't, and (b.) everything I'd read online suggested that the powdered adhesive they give you is garbage. The second set was a complete set of upper teeth. There were two large fangs on the sides, but all the middle teeth were twisted and plaque-covered. They looked like those Billy Joe Jim Bob teeth you buy at the convenience store counter for a dollar ninety-nine to "impress and humor your friends" and "be the life of the party." They came with no adhesive, but suggested using denture cream.

On my way back to the hotel, I bought some PoliGrip at a drugstore and decided to give it a try with the Billy Bob uppers first. I've never had any experiences with dentures or dental adhesive. In fact, the only thing I know about how it's used is from the commercials. You may remember them: A spokesman squeezes a line of PoliGrip on his finger, presses his finger against a block of pink plastic, and then wiggles his adhered finger up and down, apparently to demonstrate the resilient grip created by the dental adhesive cream.

I picked up the Billy Joe Jim Bob fangs and squeezed out a healthy smear of PoliGrip inside like I'd seen on TV, then pressed them up against my teeth. I could feel the PoliGrip ooze out everywhere. No problem, I figured, that will just help it stay in place.

Now if you ever find yourself in need of some denture adhesive cream, please allow me to endorse PoliGrip. The stuff really, really works. After holding the teeth in place for about a minute, I let go and was happy that the teeth seemed pretty firmly in place. About ten seconds later, however, I realized that I had also managed to glue my upper lip to my new fake fangs and teeth.

After a brief pang of panic, I started to slowly peel my lip away from the PoliGrip-coated teeth. This wasn't painful at all, just incredibly annoying—for every time I let go of my lip, it would slap back against the teeth and stick again. Eventually, with the aid of a washcloth soaked in hot water, I managed to get the fake teeth out and keep my lip and actual teeth from sticking together. After scrubbing the inside of my mouth to the point that it started bleeding, I finally was able to swallow and not be overwhelmed by the "flavorless" taste of PoliGrip.

Then, obviously having learned nothing from my previous experiment, I decided to try again with the fang caps. Same results, same glued lip, same scrubbing until my gums were raw in order to get all the adhesive cream out of my mouth. I decided that I'd lighten up on the PoliGrip and go with the Billy Jim Bob fangs.

Only a few weeks ago I'd hoped none of this would be necessary. Before heading to Oregon I'd tried to turn myself into a vampire—in six easy steps. Please allow me to spoil any semblance of dramatic tension: It didn't work.

According to what Jeanne told me, a woman came to her attention in the late 1970s who claimed to be a former vampire named Madeline X. She claimed to have been undead for several hundred years before falling in love with a mortal and becoming human again. As part of getting to know Jeanne, Madeline X gave her the instructions laid out in the twelve-page pamphlet in front of me, entitled "How To Become a Vampire in 6 Easy Lessons." Jeanne published the booklet in 1985 with the blessings of Madeline. Soon after, Jeanne said, Madeline disappeared and has never contacted Jeanne again.

The booklet spells out six lessons, each on different days, which need to be conducted exactly as she describes them. Madeline does note that for "convenience and accuracy" all the ancient phrases, in a language called Estralese, are spelled out in phonetic English.*

The list of items needed for the various mini-rituals included a few eggs, string, an empty bottle, twelve grains of rice, and a black human hair. There were also two items that I had no idea how to get. First was an owl figurine. This may not seem so difficult, but think about it: If you had to get a figurine of an owl *right now,* where would you go to buy one? Second was a raw chicken liver. Again, not something that strikes you as hard until you realize that all the nasty liver dishes you grew up with were all made with *beef*

---

* Estralese sounds more like an artificial fat substitute than a language. Wherever Estralese was spoken, it's been well hidden since. Googling and searching Lexis-Nexis for "Estralese" returns exactly zero hits.

liver. Chicken liver is not the part of the chicken that most people are interested in finding at the bottom of their KFC bucket.

I figured that since the liver would be the most difficult item to get, I'd have to hold off on the whole thing until I located some. I figured my best bet would be a butcher's shop, which, on request, will sell you just about any nasty animal body part you can think of. Problem is, find a butcher. Your grocery store probably doesn't have one (most have all their meat cut at a centralized facility). In my neighborhood, the only butcher was a kosher butcher.

"Is liver kosher?" I asked Katherine.

"Why wouldn't it be kosher?" she asked.

"Why isn't anything kosher—there are rules about this stuff."

"Well, can't you call and ask?"

"But what if chicken liver is really *super* un-Kosher and walking into a kosher butcher shop and asking for liver is like asking to fondle the butcher's kids."

"Why do you need kosher chicken liver, again?"

"I don't need kosher liver—any chicken liver will do. I need to chant over it to become a vampire."

"Do me a favor," Katherine asked. "Don't tell that tidbit to the butcher, either."

I'd found some chicken liver recipes online, so I knew it wasn't unreasonable to expect to find it somewhere.

Katherine and I eventually decided that the best thing to do to find chicken liver was to ask at the grocery store.

"Sure, we have some right over here," responded the clerk, before guiding me over to a dozen small tubs in the midst of fryer parts and skinless breasts. There they were—a small stack of tubs similar to those used for spread margarine, each packed full of raw chicken livers. I didn't know what to find more disturbing—that there was enough of a market among my neighbors that our grocery had about thirty-six pounds of chicken liver on hand, or that this packaged meat product was selling for less than a dollar a pound.

With most of my ingredients in hand, I was ready to roll. The booklet said that in advance of the first day I was to make small holes in three eggs, drain their contents, and draw lightning bolts on them. Afterward I was to hide them to make sure (a.) that they were the first thing I saw when I woke up and (b.) that no one else saw them. As I was cleaning out the eggs, I wondered to myself why becoming a vampire required handling so much raw food? Who knew how many little salmonella were swimming around in all this splattered and dripping raw egg, just waiting to crawl into my intestine and give me a case of life-ending diarrhea.

The next day's directions told me to wake up (making sure the first thing I saw were the hollow eggs with the lightning bolts drawn on them) and to hold each egg individually and concentrate on it for three minutes. The instructions were a little vague about what I should be concentrating about. I started off trying to think, "Boy, I'd really like to become a vampire," but my thoughts kept wandering to the microscopic salmonella calling out to each other, "Hey, this way guys—let's crawl under his fingernails—he never remembers to scrub there!" After three long minutes of concentrating on my slow and painful demise from food poisoning, I switched eggs and continued.

Day two was chicken liver day. The instructions for that day's "lesson" called for me to place the raw chicken liver in a jar with half a cup of vinegar at exactly 10:00 A.M., then store it in a dark place until exactly 11:30 A.M., when I was to pull it out, sprinkle salt on the chicken liver, then chant over it. Everything seemed to go fine until I opened the tub of chicken liver. It seems that most meat you purchase is cleaned, cut, and packaged in a way that makes it less than obvious that this substance was previously part of an animal's body. Not so with my chicken livers—they still had attached tubelike things and veins that gave you the impression that they were yanked out of a chicken carcass and dropped into this tub pretty much as they were. I prissily picked one up and put it in the container with the vinegar. After putting it in a file drawer I thought to myself—what will the vinegar do to the liver? Will it smell? Start to foam? Grow to ten times its normal size and explode out of the container?

I had a meeting in my office soon afterward and kept worrying that some embarrassing chicken liver accident was about to occur. I kept an eye on that drawer. Later on I looked at the clock—it was 11:27. The meeting was still going on.

"I'm sorry," I interrupted. "We're going to have to break this up—I have something I need to do right away."

"Is everything okay?" asked my colleague Robert. "You seem a little frazzled."

"I'm fine. I just need to chant over some raw chicken liver at exactly 11:30 and I've just got a few minutes left to go."

"You're chanting? Over raw liver?"

"Yes," I replied. "Chicken liver. I'm trying to turn myself into a vampire."

"What happened to getting bit on the neck to become a vampire?"

"This is the short, easy version . . . chicken liver."

Robert nodded.

"I'm sure you'd like the door closed," he said as he walked out of my office.

After removing the chicken liver from the drawer (it was the same size and smell as when I'd put it in there), I chanted the following, clapping my hands above the liver once for each syllable: "Pen-an-galan. Fen-an-galan. For-or-galan. Bead-a-*lee*."

So far, so good.

Day three required the owl figurine and despite looking in every bric-a-brac and gift shop I could find, no owl. With my back against the wall, I decided to improvise. I found a picture of an owl online and taped it to the front of a plaster Vlad the Impaler figurine I'd bought in Romania for fifty cents. More chanting over the "owl figurine": "Pont-ten-ask-oh. Pont-ten-ack. Listen to this plea. Rise from soil and grave mold *now*. Harken well to me." Afterward, I was supposed to put the figurine on the highest shelf in the tallest closet in my house. Check.

Lessons four and five were no problem—chanting and shaking a jar of rice grains and a black human hair (stolen from Katherine's hairbrush). Waving a gold ring around while declaring my oath to serve as a vampire for eternity. Simple.

Lesson six, on the final day, required assembling a bunch of left-over stuff from the previous five lessons, including the nasty germy eggshells (which had been sitting in my underwear drawer all week—if someone else saw them, they'd lose their power), but thankfully letting the chicken liver stay in the trash. After grinding it all together, I had to find some naked soil. Now, we live in a large apartment complex. There really wasn't a lot of "naked soil" around. There were a few trees in front of the building with some exposed dirt where the tree trunk met the ground. That would have to do.

As instructed I snuck outside at exactly 11:00 P.M. and chanted the following while spreading the mixture around the ground:* "From my grave I will wander. I will not grieve the severed links. I will love the groom I have chosen and will drink his lifeblood forever. If my race is won, young and old 'neath my vengeance will sink. I will fear naught but the cross. I will heed none but the master. I will live forever in his shadow. Oh, Master, I am yours."

According to the booklet, "If these instructions are followed TO THE LETTER—and to the master's satisfaction—you will awaken . . . AS A VAMPIRE!"

Awesome.

The next morning I woke Katherine up.

"Bad news . . . I'm not a vampire."

"You're sure?"

"Yes, I'm pretty sure. I feel no different at all."

"You really expected to become one?"

"Well, I guess not. But I did put in a lot of effort."

I called Jeanne.

"Oh, I could have told you it doesn't work."

---

* Since this was also the area where most residents walked their dogs, I hoped that adding dog urine to the mixture wouldn't turn me into a giant badger or something.

"Well, why didn't you?" I asked.

"Well, you never asked, for one," she said. "And if you read the instructions, it says you can't do any of it on a Saturday—but in order to follow the instructions exactly, you need to do things on seven consecutive days. If you can figure out how to do things on seven days in a row without doing anything on Saturday, then I guess you deserve to become a vampire."

She had me there.

"Now THIS IS a classic," Tim said as we walked out on their second-floor balcony. "Every good haunt has at least one crank ghost."

After a quick nap and grabbing something to eat, I had piled all my supplies into the car and headed back to Tim and Tina's. Once I arrived, the sun was starting to set and I went around the property helping Tim turn on lights, start CDs of spooky sounds, and crank up the various effects. There were a few last-minute snags: the bleeding headstone was clogged, there was a loose hose on the air cannon, and the electric eye controlling a vampire mannequin that jumped out of the mausoleum (a converted toolshed) kept misfiring because of the sunlight. Otherwise, everything was good to go.

The crank ghost is an exercise in engineering simplicity. With one small electric motor attached to a series of fishing lines and pulleys, a ghost could seem to float up and down in the air and also slowly raise and lower its arms. Add a black light and you have a spooky floating glowing purple ghost. Tim built this crank ghost and, with his sons, had also created just about every special effect they use. Home haunters—sorry, Weeners—tend to pride themselves on having simple home-engineered devices for scaring their neighbors.

Once everything was basically functional and running, we ran up to the house to get into costume and makeup. Costume, no problem. Hair and makeup (with Tim's assistance), no problem.

Fangs . . . well, I decided to go with the caps but use just a dab of PoliGrip. It didn't make a difference, within two minutes, my lip was glued again. I decided to just leave it that way and be a vampire with a bad case of Bell's palsy.

By the time I was ready, about two dozen of Tim and Tina's friends and coworkers had shown up to help with everything from directing people in the parking area to jumping out of bushes. Even though the haunt didn't open until 5:00 P.M., people started showing up as early as 3:30. There was a line in the parking area by 4:30.

The routine was this: Muggles would be greeted as they walked up from the parking area to the house. Having a strong theme and backstory is very important to Weeners—the Reuwsaats are no different. As visitors approach, the Darkwing Manor greeter says, "Welcome to Darkwing Manor and Morguetorium Museum, the home of the Baron and Baroness Reuwsaat, Vlad and Morticia, natives of Wallachia. The baroness is the second cousin of Vlad Țepeș, of the family Dracul. . . . Perhaps you have heard of him? Fleeing persecution in the old country, they arrived on this continent in the early 1800s. They vowed to make their new home a sanctuary for other lost and persecuted souls—the undead, the possessed, and those wrongfully executed. These poor creatures wander about searching for the way to transcend to the other side; but alas, they are trapped between the world of the living and the truly dead."

The story continues on about how all the Baron and Baroness Reuwsaats' assorted houseguests were visible to humans on All Hallow's Eve.

"Now, quickly, follow the marked path up to the Morguetorium where Morticia, Baroness Reuwsaat, awaits to guide you through the world of the past. Remember, touch nothing and nothing will touch you!"

At the house, the Muggles put on some hospital booties ("So not to track dirt onto the Baroness's carpet") and wait for Tina on the front porch. Then Tina emerges, wearing the same getup that she'd brought to Romania—black Victorian dress, white makeup, custom-made fangs, and black contacts that covered her entire eye. She escorts the Muggles into the front room of the house to show her collection of Victorian funeral items. She has several mourning dresses, death portraits, and even an authentic baby-sized coffin. Next, the Muggles are escorted into the front parlor, which is set up like a traditional Victorian wake, complete with an authentic antique casket containing an unauthentic body of a departed relative. Even though the house is obviously set up for Halloween, you get the impression that Tim and Tina's house is unusual all year long. All their furniture and decoration (down to the wallpaper in the kitchen) is either vintage Victorian or a meticulous re-creation. This, combined with macabre touches throughout (such as dried black roses, photos and portraits of black cats and skulls, and whiffs of incense), gives the whole place a period creepiness.

After looking at the décor, including several cabinets packed full of Halloween, vampire, and ghoulish bric-a-brac in the dining room, Muggles are taken out the side door into the yard. There they pass a small boat next to the pond and several mannequins dressed as pirates (and one human dressed as a mannequin dressed as a pirate—who stands among his plastic brethren, then jumps out to scare the passersby).

From there they circle back in front of the house and pass through a gate into a field between the house and street. This is where the real scary stuff happens, so there is a kid's area to deposit the young ones. There, they are given glow-in-the-dark bracelets (guaranteed to ward off all vampires, ghosts, and monsters). The kids also get some juice and someone is there reading spooky stories.

Kids and horror have always been an interesting juxtaposition for me. Kids love scary things—but not things that are too scary. I've never been able to understand where the line between them is (which is why I often end up terrorizing children I'm around). Someone once explained to me that kids love this stuff so much because it provides them with a bit of emotional exercise that they don't normally get from the happy face and fun fur world of children's entertainment. In other words, having to confront monsters teaches them coping skills for dealing with the real world.

The ultimate test if something has deeply embedded itself in our collective pop conscious is when kids and old people are aware of it. Vampires are no exception.

In the kid's world, vampires have shown up in a surprising number of books. As with any subject in kid's literature, there are dozens, if not hundreds, of them, including *Vampire Baby* (she's a bundle of monster joy!), *Hank the Cowdog in the Case of the Vampire Vacuum Sweeper, The Night of the Vampire Kitty* (where the members of the Creepy Creatures Club discover Count Catula—the scariest cat of all!), *Vampires Don't Wear Polka Dots* (about the new third-grade teacher—she's from the Transylvanian Alps!), and the granddaddy of them all—*Bunnicula*.

James Howe and his wife Deborah wrote *Bunnicula* after seeing a bunch of vampire movies on late-night television. They had no experience with writing children's books and just did it for fun. The story follows a young rabbit that comes to live with the Monroes, who name him Bunnicula because they'd just returned from seeing a vampire movie. All of a sudden, vegetables start mysteriously turning white. Bunnicula sleeps all day and has a black patch on his back that looks like a cape. Chester, the household cat, becomes convinced that Bunnicula is a vampire, and enlists the family dog in a plot to catch Bunnicula in the act and destroy him with a steak (yes, not a stake—apparently cats and dogs don't have very high reading skills). Since it was first published, the book has sold more than eight million copies and spawned a series of sequels, a stage musical, and a movie.

However, the two most notorious and well-known vampire icons for kids are Count von Count (a.k.a. the Count) from *Sesame Street* and Count Chocula.

Count von Count is basically a purple obsessive-compulsive molded in Lugosi's image. You've got to commend the researchers at *Sesame Street* for saddling their vampire with an ancient vampire trait so obscure that Stoker even passed it over for his count (though he did consider it)—arithmomania (a mental disorder compelling one to count things in their surroundings). Eastern European vampire lore suggested that one way to distract a vampire from attacking you was to scatter seeds or grains of salt along his path, since vampires cannot help themselves—they have to stop and count them. The Count doesn't (seem to) drink blood or have an aversion to sunlight, but he does live in a creepy castle filled with cobwebs and bats (which he loves to count).

Count Chocula seems molded after Lugosi as well, except that he has Nosferatu-style rat fangs. He was one of two original monster-themed cereal mascots created by General Mills in 1971.* Thought it's primarily seen around Halloween, Count Chocula is the only one of the five General Mills monsters to have remained in production since his debut.

In 1987, Chocula got himself into some deep cocoa when General Mills created a box front featuring a pencil drawing of a Lugosi lookalike standing behind Count Chocula and a bowl of cereal. People complained that the medallion pictured in the Lugosi drawing looked like a Star of David and was therefore anti-Semitic. Considering this, it's somewhat ironic that Count Chocula was developed by a Jewish copywriter. That box is now a serious collector's item.

Over the years, Count Chocula has become a true pop culture staple. In the past several years alone, shout-outs to the Count's chocolatey crunch bits and "spooky fun marshmallow shapes" have shown up in episodes of *The Simpsons, Family Guy, The Office,* and in the movies *Wedding Crashers* and *Blade: Trinity.* There is even a Count Chocula reference in the John Mayer song "Always Her That Ends Up Getting Wet."

---

* The other was Franken Berry, soon to be joined by Boo Berry, Fruit Brute, and Yummy Mummy over the next two years.

THE GLOW BRACELETS seem to do the trick for the kids at Darkwing Manor, who are running around the play area jumping on bales of hay while the adults are making their way through the yard. Along the way, they pass a bunch of skeletons holding a wedding, then past a graveyard (complete with a fog machine, the now-working bleeding headstone, and the mausoleum with the ejecting vampire lady), a witch trial (with a twitching witch hanging from a noose in a tree), a scarecrow (really a motionless actor waiting to pounce) guarding over some wilted crops (which also hid another worker), underneath a massive spider with a skull head, and, finally, the Muggles accidentally trigger the air cannon before passing the Red Cross donation box and back out to the parking area. Along the way and as part of every scene, Tim and Tina's family and friends are hiding in bushes and behind scenery and props.

Hundreds and hundreds of people came through that evening. Tim felt like there weren't as many as last year, but with the constant streams of people I couldn't imagine how anyone could keep track. I was pleasantly surprised that despite marching many hundreds of people through their house, past valuable collectibles and antiques, as well as through all the props and gear around the property, nothing was stolen or damaged. The worst tragedy of the evening was that a spring in one of the pop-up mannequins gave out about 9:30.

During one of my breaks I was hanging out along the path when I saw a family walking toward me, the father with a costumed (and obviously tired) monster in his arms. As you can imagine in such a small town, they knew some people waiting in line and stopped for a conversation. Eventually the father put the boy on the ground so the assembled adults could admire his costume.

He was dressed in a white shirt buttoned to the collar and a black cape. His hair was slicked back and his parents had drawn a black widow's peak onto his white forehead. Inspired by the sudden attention, he grabbed the corners of his cape, raised his arms above his head, and made a scary face, revealing a set of plastic fangs wedged into his tiny mouth.

The adults squealed with glee and applauded.

This kid couldn't have been any older than four. He probably couldn't even spell his own name, yet he knew the routine. He was a vampire. This is what vampires look like. This is what vampires do.

When people hear that I am writing a book about vampires, they all have the same first question: "So, are they real? Is there any such thing as vampires?"

That amazes me, because by asking it's apparent that these people are still holding on to a thread of possibility that dead people return from the grave, hunt humans, drink blood, and have superpowers. Anyone who thinks that faith and optimism are dead in our modern world need only look into the eyes of a grown, rational adult asking me that question.

I always offer the same explanation. Are there such things as literal vampires? No. In fact, absolutely and unconditionally, no. However, figuratively speaking, it's a whole different story.

I've come to a conclusion about vampires that's similar to my thoughts on Satan. I'm always taken aback when I encounter those who truly believe in Beelzebub's literal existence. That's because there is no real need for the devil. There is plenty of evil in the world; plenty of inducement for people to make wrong, bad, selfish, evil, and hurtful choices on their own. While I still hold on to the optimistic belief that people are inherently good, everyone—including you and I—does bad things. There is no need for a red-skinned fallen angel with a pitchfork, wings, and a long, pointy tail to try to influence us. We do fine on our own.

The same is true with vampires. Even if vampires had existed at some point in the past,* they would have been shown the Darwinian door long ago. Why? Because our metaphorical vampire

---

* And no, they didn't exist then, either. Sorry.

has evolved into a perfect being, well beyond the need to physically exist.

The four-year-old in the vampire getup could have performed his routine in front of people in Rome, Stockholm, Kinshasa, Moscow, or Tokyo—and he would have gotten the same reaction. Some minor details might change, but everyone would recognize the vampire. That's because everyone has their own fear, longing, desire, and darkness to deal with. Some of their vampires wear capes and have fangs, others are far more subtle. Some are so obvious that we don't even notice they are there.

I'm haunted by my own vampires, too. Take, for example, the vampire that has controlled my life for the last two years—it's sitting in front of you now. This book.

Writing a book is something I generally don't recommend to people. It seems like fun until you actually sit down and try to do it. Many people inflict pain on themselves for various stupid reasons. Some are masochists, others are religious freaks—I write books.

Not to get all melodramatic about it, but I've poured every part of myself into what you are about to finish reading. It has permeated itself into every area of my life. It has strained every relationship I have, left me exhausted, burnt-out, and fifteen pounds heavier than when I started.

The real darkness in my life? Worrying what happens to me in two pages, when this book ends. My biggest fear? That when the vampire loosens its grip on me, it will have sucked out so much of my life that there will be nothing left.

All the vampire folks I met—Anthony from *Bite,* my Romania tourmates, Nefarious Wrath and the Court of Lazarus folks, CrimSol and her friends at Jillian's—even Jeanne—they are all at least marginally aware of the darkness in their own lives. The only difference between them and us is that they've styled their physical world to match their inner one. I'm sure there is darkness in your life too. Among your own shadows lurks the vampire. All we hope for is to hold on until morning, when light comes. As the sun rises, the vampires are gone.

After the last of the Muggles had left for the evening, there were just a few of the Darkwing crew left, gathered around the kitchen door munching on some leftover snacks.

Tired and exhausted, I found myself sitting down next to an eleven-year-old girl who was "helping out" that evening. Her father was one of the greeters and her "help" amounted to hiding behind trees and running around screaming most of the evening. She was outfitted in a long black cloak and a skull mask, which was now positioned on top of her head while she ate some chicken wings.

"Those wings any good?" I asked.

She half-shrugged her shoulders, giving me the vibe that nothing I was about to say could be more interesting to her than that chicken wing.

"You know, I once knew this guy who loved fried chicken," I said. "He was a soldier in Iraq, and all he wanted was some fried chicken. Then one day . . ."

I noticed that she looked up from her wing long enough to slowly roll her eyes, as if mustering the strength to endure a lame story from some boring adult.

"Oh, never mind," I said, grabbing a wing for myself off the table.

Teriyaki. Yum.

Acknowledgments

In which the author shouts out to his peeps, yo.

NOTHING PROVES FRIENDSHIP like reading early drafts of book chapters and giving thoughtful feedback, like David Giffels, Chuck Klosterman, Patricia Cervini, Jeanne Keyes Youngson, Michelle Chyatte, and my mom did.

To my Dractour tourmates: Kitty, Sandy, Huge, Jeanette, Brad, Elaina, Natalie, Shannon, Tim, Tina, Greta, Caroline, Craig, Marge, Mark, Phyllis, Wayne, Ralph, Julian, Antonio, Tricia, Alan, Samantha, Butch, and Radu. (Info on the tour we took is available at www.dractour.com.)

To everyone I interviewed, hung out with, and pestered about information for this book.

To Stacey Foxwell, Jay Kernis, and Margaret Low Smith for being so understanding, supportive, and great to work with while I was writing this (and for suffering through more than your fair share of vampire anecdotes).

To my eighth-grade English teacher, Mr. K–, who told me I had no talent or skill as a writer and would never end up being anything other than a smart-ass. You were half right, but go fuck yourself anyhow.

To everyone I spoke with from February 2004 to March 2006 for letting me "test-drive" some of these stories on them.

To Peter Joseph, for being an editor I could drink beer with and for giving this book a good home at Thomas Dunne. To Peter Karanjia for his mighty fine lawyerin'. And to Jane Dystel, for encouraging me to do it in the first place.

To Dixie Evans, Tempest Storm, Cynthiana, Pillow, and all the beautiful and talented women of Exotic World—I'm sorry this book isn't about you. However, if it wasn't for you, I couldn't have done this.

To my parents, family, and friends, for being so understanding about the demands of this and for being so cool about my sudden interest in death, blood, and putting myself in slightly dangerous situations.

To anyone who will be even slightly pissed that I didn't include their name in this list.

And to Katherine, I know I promised that it would take months less to finish than it did. I know I promised it wouldn't be so difficult. I know I promised *I* wouldn't be so difficult. Thank you for seeing me for who I am and still agreeing to let me hang around you every day.

To all of you, thank you.